the attire of taqwa

Omar Yassin

PARTRIDGE

To order additional copies of this book, contact
Toll Free 800 101 2657 (Singapore)
Toll Free 1 800 81 7340 (Malaysia)
orders.singapore@partridgepublishing.com

www.partridgepublishing.com/singapore

DEDICATION

---— — ---—

This book is dedicated to those who have devoted all or part of their
lives to the service of the Holy Qur'an, Allah's final
message to humankind.

CONTENTS

CHAPTER 4

CHAPTER 5

CHAPTER 6

CHAPTER 7

CHAPTER 8

CHAPTER 9

CHAPTER 10

PREFACE

The idea of writing this book started when I became interested in the exploration of the Qur'anic speech that addresses different human emotions. Initially, I identified the ayahs (Qur'anic verses) that excite these emotions; then I classified them into different categories, based on the emotions they address. Having accomplished this, I noticed a strong relationship between specific types of the Qur'anic speech, human emotions, and the issue of religiosity. As a result, I decided to write an Arabic book on the relationship between the Qur'anic speech that elicits different psychological feelings and the phenomenon of religiosity, which I called "Emotions and Religiosity in the Holy Qur'an."[1]

In preparation for this book, nevertheless, I discovered it would be better to change the previous topic of the book to "The Attire of Taqwa," which required me to change most of the plan I had already made. Also because Muslims who can read in English outnumber those who can read in Arabic, I decided to write this book in English. However, I realized that—with the exception of the translations of the Holy Qur'an and another couple of books—all my references were written in Arabic. So I had to translate into English all the Arabic material I have cited.

Due to the genre of this book, I have used the APA[2] style in writing it. However, I have occasionally deviated a little from this style in order to treat Islamic holy texts more sensitively and more appropriately. For instance, APA requires that a quotation of forty words or more be treated as a block, and thus it shouldn't be enclosed in quotation marks. Applying this rule to the Qur'an, the Holy Book of Islam, is

---

¹ العاطفة والتديُّن في القرآن

[2] APA refers to the American Psychological Association, which has developed a set of rules and guidelines for scholarly writing in social sciences.

both inappropriate and unacceptable because in the Islamic culture the traditional way to quote a text from the actual Holy Qur'an, not from its translated versions, is to enclose it in parentheses. Accordingly, I have used parentheses in quoting the original Qur'anic texts and double quotation marks in quoting their English-translated versions.

Similarly, the application of the above APA rule to the Holy Prophet's *hadiths*[3] may not be acceptable to the vast majority of Muslims, who are not used to seeing these hadiths written without quotation marks. Some of these "hadiths," in addition, consist of quotations within other quotations because they include dialogues. Hence, they must be enclosed in double quotation marks that contain single ones to avoid confusion. Also APA doesn't require the provision of page numbers for paraphrased material, but I have indicated the page numbers of almost all the written texts I have fully translated or paraphrased to help my potential Arabic readers who might be interested in accessing—for more information—specific sources I have cited in this book. Further, I have provided the original texts of the Holy Qur'an and hadith in this book to aid this specific audience in reading them in Arabic, instead of reading their English translations.

Some Arabic words express profound religious concepts that are not clearly suggested by their English equivalents; therefore, I have transliterated and explained them in the text or in the Glossary or in both. Examples of such words are *laghw, israf,* and *taqwa*—the topic of this book. I have also transliterated other Arabic words due to the nature or the objective of the issues under discussion. Examples of these words are the ones that Allah employs to refer to the human heart as well as others that He uses in reference to the heart's good and evil work. Furthermore, I have retained some more Arabic words because they refer to particular types of Islamic worship—such as *salah* and *tahajjud*—or because they signify a specific level of servitude that Muslims are encouraged to reach in their honourable journey to Allah, for instance, *inabah* and *ihsan*. In their first appearance in this book, these transliterated words are italicized; in their subsequent occurrences, however, they aren't.

Besides, I have provided the English meaning of each *surah's* name only the first time the surah is mentioned in the text. I have also

---

[3] The singular form of this word is *hadith;* it refers to whatever the Holy Prophet Mohammad said, did, or approved.

provided a table, at the end of this book, in which I have written the names of all the surahs I have mentioned as well as their numbers and their English meanings. Moreover, since this book includes the original ayahs of the Holy Qur'an and their English interpretations, I've provided the surahs' and the ayahs' numbers after the translated versions of the ayahs. An example of this is (Qur'an 18:57), where the first number indicates the surah's, and the second represents the ayah's.

The translations of the Holy Qur'an I have quoted in this book are from the works of A. Y. Ali's, Abdel Haleem's, A. Ahmed's, Al-Hilali and Khan's, Asad's, Khalidi's, and Pickthall's. In addition, I have quoted some translations of the Holy Qur'an from two popular and credible Qur'anic websites, namely The Holy Qur'an and Tafsir Ibn Kathir. The objective of this is to provide the most accurate interpretations available, a goal that—I admit—I haven't been able to accomplish. I've also modernized the old English style in A. Y. Ali's and Pickthall's to facilitate understanding. And because these different translations of the Holy Qur'an have adopted the British spelling system, I have—for consistency—done the same in writing this book.

Here it is imperative to advise my readers who are not familiar with the Arabic language that the different translations of the Holy Qur'an do not always communicate the Qur'anic message accurately. This, of course, isn't due to the translators' lack of competence or expertise, but it is owing to the nature of the extremely difficult—yet honourable—mission they undertook. In other words, the accomplishment of an accurate translation of the Holy Qur'an is impossible—no matter how profoundly translators understand it, or how versed in both languages they are, or how diligently they may try.

This challenge, in fact, stems from the nature of the Qur'anic style of expression and from the nature of the Arabic language itself. For example, a word or an expression in the Holy Qur'an may suggest more than one meaning. Addressing His Holy Messenger, for instance, Allah says, (وَثِيَابَكَ فَطَهِّرْ). The literal meaning of the word *thiyab*[4] in this

---

[4] In different translations of the Holy Qur'an, this word was treated as follows: One group—A. Y. Ali, Khalidi, and Pickthall—rendered it as "garments" or "raiment," and another group—Asad and Abdel Haleem—translated it as "self." Maybe one solution to such a problem is to choose the literal meaning and provide a footnote that explains all the other suggested meanings so that the audience will have

ayah is clothes. Some scholars of the Qur'anic exegesis took it literally, whereas others argued it refers to other more important issues. Al-Shawkani (2012), for example, reported that this word refers to "clothes, deeds, the heart, the soul, the body, faith, and morals" (p. 403).

In a situation like this, translators of the Holy Qur'an are faced with a real dilemma: Should they communicate the literal meaning of such a word or expression, or should they provide its figurative meaning? And if they decide to communicate the figurative meaning, then which one should they choose if the word or expression has more than one? The Holy Qur'an, in addition, has words that can be read (pronounced) differently, and thus they offer different meanings. [5] With respect to this issue, Ali ibn Abi Talib—the Holy Prophet's outstanding companion and distinguished scholar—was quoted to have said, "The Qur'an is a bearer of multiple meanings."

Concerning this extremely challenging nature of the translation of the Holy Qur'an, Asad (2003), a prominent translator of this Holy book, stated the following:

> The position of individual words in a sentence, the rhythm and sound of its phrases and their syntactic construction, the manner in which a metaphor flows almost imperceptibly into a pragmatic statement, the use of acoustic stress not merely in the service of

---

a better idea. Unfortunately, with the exception of A. Y. Ali and Asad, none of the other—above-mentioned—translators provided a footnote of explanation.

[5] One example of this can be found in the following ayah from surah Al-A'raf. In reference to disbelievers, Allah says:

(إِنَّ الَّذِينَ كَذَّبُوا بِآيَاتِنَا وَاسْتَكْبَرُوا عَنْهَا لَا تُفَتَّحُ لَهُمْ أَبْوَابُ السَّمَاءِ وَلَا يَدْخُلُونَ الْجَنَّةَ حَتَّى يَلِجَ الْجَمَلُ فِي سَمِّ الْخِيَاطِ وَكَذَلِكَ نَجْزِي الْمُجْرِمِينَ).

"Those who reject Our signs and treat them with arrogance, opening will there be of the gates of heaven, nor will they enter the Garden, until the camel can pass through the eye of the needle: such is Our reward for those in sin."   *(Qur'an 7:40)*

According to Al-Shawkani, the word (الجمل) in this ayah can be read in two different ways: *aljamal*, meaning the camel, and *aljummal*, which means a thick rope (2012, p. 257).

rhetoric but as a means of alluding to unspoken but clearly implied ideas: all this makes the Qur'an, in the last resort, unique and untranslatable—a fact that has been pointed out by many earlier translators and by all Arab scholars. (p. x)

Moreover, Abdel Haleem (2008), who also had the honour of translating the Holy Qur'an into English, said, "The present translator fully recognizes how very difficult the task is of translating the Qur'an" (p. xxix). Also speaking about the same issue, Khalidi, who, according to him, endeavoured to produce a more meaningful translation of the Holy Qur'an, stated:

> Where it is in any sense 'dramatic', I have arranged the lines in a vertical 'poetic' fashion. But here too I cannot claim to have done anything other than to highlight a problem of translation and offer a tentative solution to it. (2008, p. xxi)

Another problem with the translations of the Holy Qur'an is that the addressee of many messages is, unfortunately, the male gender, whereas—with the exception of specific situations in which the addressee is either the male or the female gender—the Holy Qur'an addresses men and women equally. One example of bias against females reflects on—ironically—the interpretation of the first ayah in *surah* Al-Nisa' (Women). Allah opens this surah with a vocative case saying, (يَا أَيُّهَا النَّاس), which means "O people" or "O humankind." With the exception of Abdel Haleem, who translated this expression as "People," the rest of the translators I referred to preferred an expression that ignores the female gender, though, again, the surah's title is "Women." More specifically, A., Ali, A. Y. Ali, Asad, Hilali and Khan, Khalidi, as well as Pickthall rendered it as "O mankind."

Also the Arabic word *insan*, which means human, recurs often in the Holy Qur'an, and it is frequently translated as man, such as in the translation of the first ayah in surah 76, provided by all of the above-mentioned translators. Besides, the name of this surah is *alinsan*, but it is translated as "Man," as opposed to "The Human" or "The Human Being."

Sometimes, however, the translations of the Holy Qur'an put the males, not the females, in trouble. An example of this can be found in the following ayah's translation in which the male gender is expressed by the possessive pronoun "his," which occurs twice:

(وَمَنْ أَظْلَمُ مِمَّنْ ذُكِّرَ بِآيَاتِ رَبِّهِ فَأَعْرَضَ عَنْهَا وَنَسِيَ مَا قَدَّمَتْ يَدَاهُ، إِنَّا جَعَلْنَا عَلَىٰ قُلُوبِهِمْ أَكِنَّةً أَنْ يَفْقَهُوهُ وَفِي آذَانِهِمْ وَقْرًا ، وَإِنْ تَدْعُهُمْ إِلَى الْهُدَىٰ فَلَنْ يَهْتَدُوا إِذًا أَبَدًا).

"And who does more wrong than one who is reminded of the signs of his Lord, but turns away from them, forgetting the (deeds) which his hands have sent forth? Verily, We have set veils over their hearts lest they should understand this, and over their ears, deafness, if you call them to guidance, even then will they never accept guidance." (Qur'an 18: 57)

Also in Arabic, when the message concerns a group of males and females, the male gender takes over. Another situation in which the male gender dominates occurs when the message concerns an indefinite reference, such as in the previous ayah. Being an Arabic text, the Holy Qur'an is, therefore, full of messages expressed in this manner, but Arabic native speakers do not construe this phenomenon as bias against females.

Again, the bottom line is that the different English translations of the Holy Qur'an are not perfect representations of the actual Qur'anic message, and the Holy Qur'an addresses both genders without any bias. This is, in fact, an extremely important issue that should be explained, especially to non-Muslims who may read the translated Qur'anic texts in this book or elsewhere and mistakenly arrive at a conclusion that the Holy Qur'an addresses only men or that it is biased against females.

ACKNOWLEDGMENTS

I am indebted to my wife, Bakhita Salman, for her continuous support in writing this book. In fact, regardless of her painstaking and extremely demanding Ph.D. program, she insisted on having a specific, tangible contribution to this book—she repeatedly reviewed all the ayahs in it and corrected the errors she found. Countless thanks to Eithar, my elder son, who—though just came home from a long, tiring medical school year—scrupulously read the entire final manuscript of this book and provided me with invaluable feedback and suggestions, in addition to his endless technical support. Many thanks to my middle son, Awwab, for his psychological support, and I should mention that, because of his involvement in major college courses last summer, I wasn't lucky to benefit from his intellectual and critical thinking skills by reading this book's final manuscript. Special thanks to my youngest son, Muneeb, for the different types of assistance he provided, especially his help in matters that required investigations of linguistic issues and his assistance in checking format consistency throughout this text.

I am also grateful to my colleagues and friends Dr. Rafik Al-Samarraei, Hilmi Abu Hamad, Jermaine Francis, and Sheikh Abdul Qader Aldaqadosy for providing me with books and other sources of information indispensable for the accomplishment of this work. My prayers go out to Sheikh Mahmoud Khaleel Al-Hussary, whose beautiful, solemn recitations have always been the Qur'an's smooth gateway to my heart. Special prayers for scholar Mohammad Mutwali Al-Sha'rawi, whose rich TV lessons on the exegesis of the Qur'an have ignited my love for this Qur'anic discipline. I also pray Allah to bestow His Mercy on Sheikh Abd Al-Hameed Kishk, whose zealous cassette-recorded speeches have lit candles of guidance in millions of hearts—mine is one. Finally, I am grateful to all the scholars, thinkers, and *imams* (community religious leaders) whose books, articles, and/or speeches have illuminated our path to Allah, especially the ones whose works have aided me in writing this book.

Omar Yassin
Prince Mohammad Bin Fahd University
Al Khobar, Kingdom of Saudi Arabia
March 31, 2017

INTRODUCTION

Early in the surah of Al-Baqarah (The Cow), Allah declares that the guidance in His final Book to humanity, the Holy Qur'an, is confined to those who have taqwa. He says:

$$ذَٰلِكَ الْكِتَابُ لَا رَيْبَ فِيهِ هُدًى لِّلْمُتَّقِينَ.$$

"This is the Scripture in which there is no doubt, containing guidance for those who are mindful of God."
(Qur'an 2:2)

In reference to this ayah, Al-Qurtubi (2014) argued, "Though the Qur'an's guidance is for all humanity, Allah has confined its actual guidance to those who have taqwa, as an honour to them because they believe in it" (p. 133). Similarly, Al-Saadi claimed, "The people of taqwa are the ones who benefit from the signs in the Qur'an and the signs in the universe" (2011, p. 21).

Also in the surah of Al-Imran (The Family of Imran), which comes next to the previous one, Allah emphasizes the confinement of His book's guidance to the people of taqwa. He, again, states:

$$هَٰذَا بَيَانٌ لِّلنَّاسِ وَهُدًى وَمَوْعِظَةٌ لِّلْمُتَّقِينَ.$$

"This is a clear statement for men, and a guidance and an admonition to those who guard (against evil)."
(Qur'an 3:138)

So—just like underground water, which requires power to bring it out—the guidance of the Holy Qur'an needs the authority of taqwa to make it dynamic and effective in believers' lives. Also as a blind man cannot benefit from a lamp he carries, a believer without taqwa will not enjoy the guidance in the Holy Qur'an, even if he or she has perfectly memorized it.

Thus, as a book, the Holy Qur'an is available to everyone; as guidance, however, it isn't, until believers exert a substantial effort into the observance of Allah and obedience to Him—that is, until they develop a significantly high level of taqwa. In this case, taqwa transforms into a bright light that sheds on their hearts in a form of wisdom that enables them to distinguish between right and wrong and assist them to observe Allah closely and consistently.

In a strongly inviting message, in fact, Allah calls believers' attention to this unique role of taqwa in the enjoyment of His guidance. He says:

(... يَا أَيُّهَا الَّذِينَ ءَامَنُواْ إِن تَتَّقُواْ اللَّهَ يَجْعَل لَّكُمْ فُرْقَانًا)

"O you who believe! If you obey and fear Allah, He will endow you with a standard by which to discern the true from the false..."   *(Qur'an 8:29)*

Explaining the meaning of this part of this ayah, A-Tabari (2010) argued that if a person has taqwa, such a person will be given *"furqan* in his [her] heart with which he [or she] distinguishes between right and wrong" (p. 695). Likewise, Ibn Kathir (2014) claimed that if a person "has taqwa, such a person will be successful in distinguishing between right and wrong" (p. 78).

Allah could have created humans like angels, without the ability to disobey Him, but He has, in fact, created them with this special human nature—which can be attracted to good and evil—and He has granted them a free will in order to test them and see whether they will obey or disobey Him. So people are put to the test, and the qualification they need in order to pass it is taqwa, which is not a gift or a genetically inherited trait. Rather, it is a special power that they are responsible for its development.

Because of its prominent presence in the Holy Qur'an and due to the significant role it plays in both believers' relationship with Allah and their destiny in the Hereafter, the issue of taqwa generated many questions among the first generation to receive the Holy Qur'an—the Holy Messenger's companions. Omar ibn Al-Khattab, for instance, was narrated to have asked Ubai ibn Kaab, a prominent companion of the Holy Prophet's and a distinguished scholar, about the meaning of taqwa. The latter answered him saying:

> "Have you ever walked on a thorny road?" "Yes," answered Omar. Then Ubai asked him another question: "What did you do?" Omar replied, "I picked up my clothes and did my best [to avoid the thorns]." Then Ubai responded, "That is taqwa." (Al-Qurtubi, 2014, p 134)

Al-Shawkani (2012) narrated a similar hadith about a man who asked Abu Hurairah the same question, and Abu Hurairah provided him with an answer similar to the previous one (p. 43). It is also reported that when Imam Ali ibn Abi Talib was asked about the meaning of taqwa, he answered,

> "It is fear of Al-Jaleel [Allah], living according to Al-Tanzeel [the Holy Qur'an and the Holy Prophet's Sunnah], and getting ready for the departure from this world [preparing oneself for the Day of Judgment]."

Thus, this book attempts to understand the issue of taqwa through the exploration of different aspects of the Qur'anic speech that ignite its fire deep in the heart. To achieve this, the book explores and discusses different topics of taqwa, based on the context in which they occur in the Holy Qur'an. One of the different issues it examines and discusses in this respect is the high frequency of the element of taqwa in the Holy Qur'an and the underlying reasons for it. In this context, the book discusses the "Treaty of Al-Hudaibiyah," and it casts light on the surah of Al-Talaq (Divorce), as a model in which the subject of taqwa has the highest rate of occurrence in the entire Holy Qur'an.

It also discusses the psychology of taqwa based on different aspects of the Qur'anic speech that excite particular psychological feelings conducive to the ignition of the flames of taqwa in believers' hearts. Moreover, this work highlights the different Arabic words that Allah uses in reference to the human heart; it also identifies and explains the heart's positive and negative influence on people's lives today and on their destinies in the Hereafter. Further, it discusses the element of reflection as a fundamental factor in the growth and the flourish of taqwa; besides, it highlights the heart's crucial role in this matter.

Furthermore, this book investigates and explains the dynamic nature of taqwa. It also sheds light on the element of the Qur'anic question, as a powerful linguistic tool that Allah recurrently employs to deliver Qur'anic messages. In other words, this work attempts to examine the role of the Qur'anic question in critical thinking and in the creation of special effects essential for the generation of taqwa. In addition, it analyses and discusses both Luqman's advice for his son and Ibad Al-Rahman's attributes in relation to the question of taqwa.

Also The Attire of Taqwa casts light on the explicit Qur'anic analogies—one of the three types of analogies in the Holy Qur'an—that Allah uses to teach humankind the essence of this life and to warn them against its false, misleading charm. Concerning this issue, the book analyses three Qur'anic analogies in connection with the issue of taqwa. Finally, this work throws a little light on the Qur'anic stories as a predominant genre in the Holy Qur'an that Allah employs to teach invaluable lessons of taqwa. With respect to this, it discusses the story of Adam and Eve, the story of Prophet Yusuf, and the horrible eradication of disbelievers, represented by three major communities: the people of Prophet Noah, the people of Prophet Hud, and those of Prophet Salih.

CHAPTER 1

—— — ——

Taqwa in the Holy Qur'an:
Perspectives and Frequency

Taqwa from a Morphological Perspective

Morphologically, taqwa is derived from the Arabic root *w-q-i*[6] (Ibn Manthoor, 2008, pp. 266–267). One of the different present forms derived from this root and helpful in understanding the lexical meaning of taqwa is *yaqi*,[7] meaning to protect. Two more present forms derived from the same root are *yattaqi*[8], meaning to avoid something harmful, and *yatawaqqa*,[9] which denotes seeking protection. Generally speaking, therefore, taqwa refers to avoidance of harm—any harm, whether it is physical, psychological, social, economic, or other.

Taqwa from a Grammatical Perspective

The element of taqwa in the Holy Qur'an comes in different parts of speech. Specifically, Allah uses its root—again, w-q-i—as a verb, as a noun, and as an adjective. But what does this suggest? Languages help speakers express different issues in their lives; thus, when a root provides different words that belong to different parts of speech, this indicates two things: the dynamic nature of the root itself and the importance of the concepts that these derivatives represents in the

---

[6] وَقِي

[7] يَقِي

[8] يَتَّقِي

[9] يَتَوَقَّى

1

speakers' lives. Similarly, the occurrence of different derivatives of the root w-q-i in the Holy Qur'an suggests the significance of the concepts they represent and their roles in believers' lives. As an adjective, for example, taqwa describes believers' righteous characters and creates a positive image of them in other people's minds. As a verb, nevertheless, taqwa seems to determine all believers' actions. When making choices, handling issues, and accepting or rejecting things, for instance, true believers are inspired, motivated, and governed by taqwa.

Taqwa from a Diagnostic Perspective

Taqwa is the underlying power that motivates believers to persistently and consistently observe Allah's rules, carry out His commands, and stay away from whatever He forbids and whatever exists in the grey area. It is the believers' blueprint that controls their thinking and determines the different reaction they make in response to various stimuli and situations, throughout their lives. When it reaches a considerably high level, taqwa represents a harmonious blend of the believer's mental state and psychological condition that leads to the development of an ideal Islamic attitude that expresses itself in ideal Islamic behaviour and way of life. The following provides a brief explanation of these four aspects of taqwa: the believer's mentality, psychology, attitude, and behaviour.

First, broadly speaking, the mental state of taqwa represents the believer's good understanding of Islam. It also suggests his or her strong determination to continuously and consistently observe Allah and live according to the Holy Qur'an's teachings and the Holy Prophet's Sunnah so that he or she may avoid Allah's wrath and win His approval. Allah points to this fact in the surah of Fatir (The Originator) saying:

$$ (...إِنَّمَا يَخْشَى اللَّهَ مِنْ عِبَادِهِ الْعُلَمَاءُ...) $$

"...it is only those who have knowledge among His slaves that fear Allah..."   *(Qur'an 35:28)*

Second, the psychological state of taqwa occurs as a result of the effect of the mental status on the believer's heart,[10] and it consists of two major groups of feelings: pleasurable and distressing. The pleasurable feelings of taqwa consist of love for Allah, longing for Him,[11] longing for His Gardens of bliss, hope, and happiness. All of these feelings, in fact, occur as a result of specific Qur'anic messages that are meant to address and trigger them in the heart. They also develop as a result of an excellent quality of recurrent reflection on the creation of Allah and on events of special nature.

The distressing feelings of taqwa, nevertheless, consist of four major elements: fear of Allah's wrath, fear of His punishment, sadness, sorrow, and anxiety (worry). Like the pleasurable feelings, these ones develop in reaction to particular types of the Qur'anic speech that address and excite them in the believer's heart. They also develop as a result of a good quality of reflection on specific kinds of negative events, such as natural disasters and bad ends of people who are known for their cruelty and evilness. The emotion of fear, in fact, constitutes the main ingredient in this group of feelings. The other ones—sadness, sorrow, and anxiety—are inter-related, and they overlap to a degree that different fear-provoking messages in the Holy Qur'an may excite all of them simultaneously. In other words, the threatening Qur'anic speech elicits fear, which, in turn, triggers sadness, anxiety, and sorrow.

Both the pleasurable and the distressing groups of psychological feelings represent a major factor in the growth, development, and blossom of the precious plant of taqwa in believers' hearts.

Third, the attitude aspect of taqwa is an inevitable product of the interplay between the believer's mental and psychological states, and it reflects his or her positive position on the Islamic teachings. In surah Al-Ahzab (The Confederates), for instance, Allah demonstrates the believers' ideal attitude towards both His teachings and His Holy Prophet's. He says:

---

[10] The relationship between the brain and the heart in connection with the question of taqwa is discussed in "The Heart's Role in Reflection."

[11] Love for Allah and longing for Him, for example, can develop as a result of frequent, thoughtful reflection on His amazing, endless creation.

(وَمَا كَانَ لِمُؤْمِنٍ وَلَا مُؤْمِنَةٍ إِذَا قَضَى اللَّهُ وَرَسُولُهُ أَمْرًا أَن يَكُونَ لَهُمُ الْخِيَرَةُ مِنْ
أَمْرِهِمْ...)

"It is not for a believer, man or woman, when Allah and His Messenger have decreed a matter that they should have any option in their decision..."

(Qur'an 33:36)

Commenting on the message in this ayah A. Y. Ali (2008) said:

> We must not put our own wisdom in competition with God's wisdom. God's decree is often known to us by the logic of facts. We must accept it loyally, and do the best we can to help in our own way to carry it out. We must make our will consonant [agreeing with] . . . the God's will. (1117)

Addressing His Holy Messenger, in the surah of Al-Nisa', Allah highlights—emphatically—the same previous issue of believers' ideal attitude towards His commands and His Holy Messenger's. He states:

(فَلَا وَرَبِّكَ لَا يُؤْمِنُونَ حَتَّى يُحَكِّمُوكَ فِيمَا شَجَرَ بَيْنَهُمْ ثُمَّ لَا يَجِدُوا فِي أَنفُسِهِمْ
حَرَجًا مِّمَّا قَضَيْتَ وَيُسَلِّمُوا تَسْلِيمًا).

"But no, by your Lord, they can have no faith, until they make you (O Mohammad) judge in all disputes between them, and find in themselves no resistance against your decisions, and accept (them) with full submission."

(Qur'an 4:65)

Inspired by the message in this ayah, A. Y. Ali explained the significance of believers' ideal attitude in the issue of taqwa. He said:

> The test of true faith is not mere lip profession, but bringing all our doubts and disputes to the one in whom we profess faith. Further, when a decision is given we are not only to accept it, but find in our inmost souls no difficulty and no resistance, but on the contrary a joyful acceptance springing from the conviction of our own faith. (2008, p. 199)

Finally, the action aspect of taqwa represents the actual reflection of the believer's mentality, psychology, and attitude on his or her behaviour and speech, for—most of the times—human behaviour and speech constitute a good reflection of whatever occupies these three human aspects: thinking, feelings, and attitude.

The Frequency of Taqwa in the Holy Qur'an

The issue of taqwa has a prominent presence in the Holy Qur'an, and it sometimes occurs repeatedly in the same surah. In surah Al-Baqarah alone, for example, it recurs 37 times, scoring its highest number of occurrence on the surah's level. In surah Al-Talaq, on the other hand, the issue of taqwa has a considerably high rate of existence. In only twelve *ayahs*, it occurs five times, scoring its highest rate of frequency on the level of the surah in the entire Holy Qur'an. That is, almost 42% of the ayahs in this surah highlight the issue of taqwa.

On the level of the ayah, the issue of taqwa usually occurs once, such as in this ayah from surah Taha:

(وَأْمُرْ أَهْلَكَ بِالصَّلَاةِ وَاصْطَبِرْ عَلَيْهَا ، لَا نَسْأَلُكَ رِزْقًا ، نَحْنُ نَرْزُقُكَ ، وَالْعَاقِبَةُ لِلتَّقْوَى).

"And command your family to pray and be constant in performing it. We seek no sustenance from you: it is We Who sustain you. Piety shall ultimately prevail."
(Qur'an 20:132)

Occasionally, however, the issue of taqwa may occur twice in the same ayah. Consider the following example from surah Al-Baqarah:

(يَسْأَلُونَكَ عَنِ الأَهِلَّةِ ، قُلْ هِيَ مَوَاقِيتُ لِلنَّاسِ وَالْحَجِّ ، وَلَيْسَ الْبِرُّ بِأَن تَأْتُواْ الْبُيُوتَ مِن ظُهُورِهَا وَلَكِنَّ الْبِرَّ مَنِ اتَّقَى ، وَأْتُواْ الْبُيُوتَ مِنْ أَبْوَابِهَا، وَاتَّقُوا اللَّهَ لَعَلَّكُمْ تُفْلِحُونَ).

"They ask you about the new moons. Say: 'These are signs to mark fixed periods of time for mankind and for the pilgrimage.' It is not Al-Birr (piety, righteousness) that

you enter the houses from the back but Al-Birr (is the quality of the one) who fears Allah. So enter houses through their proper doors, and fear Allah that you may be successful." (Qur'an 2:189)

Interestingly, in only one ayah, Allah highlights the issue of taqwa three times. This happens only once in the entire Holy Qur'an, precisely in surah Al-Ma'idah (The Feast), in which He states:

(لَيْسَ عَلَى الَّذِينَ ءَامَنُواْ وَعَمِلُواْ الصَّالِحَاتِ جُنَاحٌ فِيمَا طَعِمُواْ إِذَا مَا اتَّقَواْ وَءَامَنُواْ وَعَمِلُواْ الصَّالِحَاتِ ثُمَّ اتَّقَواْ وَءَامَنُوا ثُمَّ اتَّقَواْ وَّأَحْسَنُواْ ، وَاللّهُ يُحِبُّ الْمُحْسِنِينَ).

"Those who believe and do righteous good deeds, there is no sin on them for what they ate (in the past), if they fear Allah (by keeping away from His forbidden things), and believe and do righteous good deeds, and again fear Allah and believe, and once again fear Allah and do good deeds with ihsan (perfection). And Allah loves the good-doers.)" (Qur'an 5:93)

Sometimes the issue of taqwa comes in the first ayah of the surah. This occurs six times in the Holy Qur'an, particularly in the surahs of Al-Nisa', Al-Anfal (The Spoils of War), Al-Hajj (The Pilgrimage), Al-Ahzab, Al-Hujurat (The Chambers), and Al-Talaq.

In the first surah mentioned above, for instance, Allah advises the entire human society to observe taqwa. He says:

(يَا أَيُّهَا النَّاسُ اتَّقُواْ رَبَّكُمُ الَّذِي خَلَقَكُم مِّن نَّفْسٍ وَاحِدَةٍ وَخَلَقَ مِنْهَا زَوْجَهَا وَبَثَّ مِنْهُمَا رِجَالاً كَثِيرًا وَنِسَاءً وَاتَّقُواْ اللّهَ الَّذِي تَسَاءَلُونَ بِهِ وَالأَرْحَامَ ، إِنَّ اللّهَ كَانَ عَلَيْكُمْ رَقِيبًا).

"O humankind! Be dutiful to your Lord, Who created you from a single person (Adam), and from him (Adam) He created his wife (Eve), and from them both He created many men and women; and fear Allah through Whom you demand (your mutual rights), and (do not cut the relations

of) the wombs (kinship). Surely, Allah is Ever an All-Watcher over you." (Qur'an 4:1)

In the third surah, He warns the same previous audience saying:

(يَا أَيُّهَا النَّاسُ اتَّقُوا رَبَّكُمْ إِنَّ زَلْزَلَةَ السَّاعَةِ شَيْءٌ عَظِيمٌ)!

"People, be mindful of your Lord, for the earthquake of the Last Hour will be a mighty thing!" (Qur'an 22:1)

In the fourth, nevertheless, He addressed the Holy Prophet himself to observe taqwa. He said to him:

(يَا أَيُّهَا النَّبِيُّ اتَّقِ اللَّهَ وَلَا تُطِعِ الْكَافِرِينَ وَالْمُنَافِقِينَ إِنَّ اللَّهَ كَانَ عَلِيماً حَكِيماً).

"O Prophet! Keep your duty to Allah, and obey not the disbelievers and the hypocrites. Verily, Allah is Ever All-Knower, All-Wise." (Qur'an 33:1)

In addition to its occurrence in the first ayah of the previous surahs, the issue of taqwa comes in the last ayahs of some other surahs. For example, both the surahs of Al-Imran and Al-Nahl (The Bees) conclude with a reminder of this issue.

In the former, Allah commands:

(يَا أَيُّهَا الَّذِينَ آمَنُوا اصْبِرُوا وَصَابِرُوا وَرَابِطُوا وَاتَّقُوا اللَّهَ لَعَلَّكُمْ تُفْلِحُونَ).[12]

"O you who believe! Endure and be more patient (than your enemy), and guard your territory by stationing army units permanently at the places from where the enemy can attack you, and fear Allah so that you may be successful." (Qur'an 3:200)

---

[12] Interestingly, whereas surah Al-Imran ends with advice for believers to adhere to taqwa, surah Al-Nisa', which comes immediately after it, begins with the same advice.

In the latter, He declares:

(إِنَّ اللَّهَ مَعَ الَّذِينَ اتَّقَواْ وَّالَّذِينَ هُم مُّحْسِنُونَ).

*"Verily, Allah is with those who are conscious of Him
and are doers of good withal!"*   *(Qur'an 16:128)*

But why does the issue of taqwa have this high frequency of
occurrence in the Holy Qur'an? Of course, there must be a strong
reason for this Qur'anic phenomenon, for the speaker is Allah Himself.
To answer this question, we should consider, at least, three issues: the
human nature, the presence of different negative factors and stimuli in
human life, and the nature of some Qur'anic commands.

First, since humans are the audience of the Qur'anic message, part of
the answer to our question requires a close look at human nature that
necessitates this frequent reminder of taqwa in the Holy Qur'an.
Specifically, human nature has many shortcomings that hinder people
from observing Allah's teachings. Humans, for example, have a
natural tendency to forget, neglect, reject, disobey, and even rebel.
Second, the presence of so many negative factors and stimuli in
people's lives, such as the Satan and daily challenges, exacerbates their
inclination to forget, neglect, reject, disobey, and rebel.

Third, sometimes the Qur'anic commands themselves can be
significantly challenging to human nature; consequently, they require a
considerably high level of taqwa to carry them out. This is obvious in
different commands that Allah has issued to believers, such as this
one, from the surah of Al-Ma'idah, in which His command to observe
taqwa occurs twice. He says:

(... وَلَا يَجْرِمَنَّكُمْ شَنَآنُ قَوْمٍ أَنْ صَدُّوكُمْ عَنِ الْمَسْجِدِ الْحَرَامِ أَنْ تَعْتَدُوا
وَتَعَاوَنُوا عَلَى الْبِرِّ وَالتَّقْوَىٰ ، وَلَا تَعَاوَنُوا عَلَى الْإِثْمِ وَالْعُدْوَانِ ، وَاتَّقُوا اللَّهَ ، إِنَّ
اللَّهَ شَدِيدُ الْعِقَابِ).

*"...do not let your hatred for the people who barred you
from the Sacred Mosque induce you to break the law:
help one another to do what is right and good; do not*

help one another towards sin and hostility. Be mindful of God, for His punishment is severe."

(Qur'an 5:2)

According to Ibn Kathir (2014), this command was revealed in the year of *Al-Hudaibiyah* (p. 383). Specifically, the Holy Prophet and his companions left Al-Madinah for Makkah to perform *umrah*,[13] but as a gesture of hostility, the disbelievers in Makkah decided not to let them enter the city. The Holy Prophet, as a result, started a dialogue with Quraysh's leaders, hoping they would let him and his companions enter Makkah to perform their intended umrah. Finally, the Holy Prophet arrived at an agreement with Quraysh called *Sulh Al-Hudaibiyah* (Treaty of Al-Hudaibiyah).

Part of this treaty was that the Holy Prophet and his companions had to return back to Al-Madinah, without entering Makkah, but they could come back for umrah in the following year. Because of this, the Holy Prophet's companions became extremely angry. To realize the level of their resentment, consider their reaction in the following two examples.

Omar ibn Al-Khattab, who was overwhelmed with bitterness as a result of this treaty, went to Allah's Holy Messenger and said:

> "O Messenger of Allah! Are you not surely the Messenger of Allah?" "Yes," the Holy Prophet answered him. Then Omar asked him again saying, "Are we not the people of guidance, and aren't our enemies the misguided?" The Holy Messenger of Allah replied, "Yes." So Omar said, "Then why did we agree to be in the position of the weak?" The Prophet said, "I am the Messenger of Allah. He will, certainly, grant me victory, and I am not disobeying Him." Then Omar asked him, "Didn't you promise us to perform umrah?" The Holy Prophet said, "Yes, but did I say it would happen this year?"

> "After that, Omar went to Abu Bakr Al-Siddiq and asked him the same questions, but the latter gave him an answer similar to the Holy Prophet's. He also

---

[13] It is also called the "lesser *hajj* (lesser pilgrimage)."

advised him to hold fast to the Holy Prophet's way
until his [Omar's] death." (Al-Mubarakpuri, 2007, pp.
316–317)

Obviously, Omar's position reflects a very high level of resentment, as
a result of Quraysh's nasty attitude at Al-Hudaibiyah.

In addition, it is narrated that after this treaty, the Holy Prophet
commanded his companions to sacrifice their sacrifices and shave
their heads; surprisingly—due to their extreme bitterness—none of
them responded. The Holy Prophet repeated this command three
times, yet none of his companions obeyed him. Then, feeling afraid
that Allah might punish them as a result of this, the Holy Prophet
entered his tent and told his wife Um Salamah about this incident. She
suggested that he go out, sacrifice his own sacrifice, and ask one of his
companions to shave his head for him. As she had expected, all the
Holy Prophet's companions sacrificed their sacrifices; then some of
them shaved their heads and others cut their hair immediately after he
did (Al-Jaza'iri, 2004, p. 274).

Further, concerning this ayah, Ibn Kathir (2014) narrated that after the
incident of Al-Hudaibiyah and while the Holy Prophet and his
companions were still camping outside Makkah, a group of
disbelievers (from the east) came in the latter's direction heading to
Makkah for umrah. So the Holy Prophet's companions determined to
stop them from entering that city. They said, "We will stop these
people from entering Makkah, the same way their friends [in Makkah]
treated us" (p. 383). As a result, Allah revealed the previous ayah to
forbid these believers from letting their hatred for others treat them
unfairly.

So the people who had to carry out this command when it was freshly
revealed were the same ones who were treated that unfairly and, as a
result, had experienced that extremely high level of frustration and
bitterness at Al-Hudaibiyah. To them, the event was an opportunity to
retaliate and appease their badly wounded egos. To Allah,
nevertheless, it was the right time for believers to learn a unique
Islamic value and achieve a high level of self-restraint, based on taqwa.

The context in which the above ayah was revealed helps realize the
difficult nature of its command and the extremely high level of

challenge it faced the Holy Prophet's companions with at that moment. It also manifests the significant role of taqwa in the obedience to such a challenging command of Allah.[14] Now in the light of this explanation, examine the ayah's message once again and notice the repetition of Allah's command to believers to observe taqwa. Also notice the emphatic tone He has clothed this message in. He says:

(...وَلَا يَجْرِمَنَّكُمْ شَنَآنُ قَوْمٍ أَنْ صَدُّوكُمْ عَنِ الْمَسْجِدِ الْحَرَامِ أَنْ تَعْتَدُوا وَتَعَاوَنُوا عَلَى الْبِرِّ وَالتَّقْوَىٰ ، وَلَا تَعَاوَنُوا عَلَى الْإِثْمِ وَالْعُدْوَانِ ، وَاتَّقُوا اللَّهَ ، إِنَّ اللَّهَ شَدِيدُ الْعِقَابِ).

"...Do not let your hatred for the people who barred you from the Sacred Mosque induce you to break the law: help one another to do what is right and good; do not help one another towards sin and hostility. Be mindful of God, for His punishment is severe."

(Qur'an 5:2)

Of course, this command was not confined to the Holy Prophet's companions at Al-Hudaibiyah. It also addresses all Muslims at all times.

The Role of Taqwa in Divorce

In addition to the Treaty of Al-Hudaibiyah, the topic of divorce in Islam represents another good example that explains the underlying

---

[14] This command occurs again in this surah—after only five ayahs—and because it is difficult to carry out, the issue of taqwa recurs twice in it, too. Allah says:

(يَا أَيُّهَا الَّذِينَ آمَنُوا كُونُوا قَوَّامِينَ لِلَّهِ شُهَدَاءَ بِالْقِسْطِ ، وَلَا يَجْرِمَنَّكُمْ شَنَآنُ قَوْمٍ عَلَى أَلَّا تَعْدِلُوا ، اعْدِلُوا هُوَ أَقْرَبُ لِلتَّقْوَى ، وَاتَّقُوا اللَّهَ ، إِنَّ اللَّهَ خَبِيرٌ بِمَا تَعْمَلُونَ).

"O you who believe! Stand out firmly for Allah as just witnesses; and let not the enmity and hatred of others make you avoid justice. Be just: that is nearer to piety; and fear Allah. Verily, Allah is Well-Acquainted with all that you do." *(Qur'an 5:8)*

reason for the frequent recurrence of the issue of taqwa in the Holy Qur'an. As mentioned earlier, in the entire Holy Qur'an, surah Al-Talaq has the highest rate of this issue—again, almost 42% of the ayahs in this surah command and motivate Muslims to firmly adhere to taqwa. This is due to, at least, four major factors: human nature, the nature of divorce and the circumstances in which it occurs, the nature of the Qur'anic firm rules governing it, and the Satan's continuous, relentless effort to ruin the Muslim family.

In the Muslim world, divorce mostly takes place as a result of lack of objectivity and lack of common sense—when both spouses are extremely defensive, angry, hostile, and threatening. In such a bad atmosphere of interaction, the brain's chemistry becomes poisoned, the emotions inflamed, the tongue loose, and the reactions extreme and out of control. Even worse, the Satan becomes in charge of the spouses' feelings, thinking, speech, decisions, and behaviour. Because of these and because of many bad consequences of divorce that are harmful to Muslim spouses, their children, their families, and their community at large, Allah, in this surah, has prescribed specific, firm rules to govern the issue of divorce.

With the exception of the one who has received her third divorce, the divorced wife has to stay in her husband's house for a specific period. Allah calls this period and the situation in which divorce should take place *iddah*, and He prescribes three types of it. The first one is that the wife to be divorced shouldn't have the menstruation, and the husband shouldn't have had sex with her in this period of time (Al-Shawkani, 2012, p. 298). The period that the divorced wife has to spend in her husband's house in this case can be three successive periods of purification (from menstruation), according to some scholars, or three successive menstruations, according to another group of scholars (Al-Saadi, 2011, p. 77 & p. 813).

With respect to this, Allah says:

$$\text{(يَا أَيُّهَا النَّبِيُّ إِذَا طَلَّقْتُمُ النِّسَاءَ فَطَلِّقُوهُنَّ لِعِدَّتِهِنَّ...)}$$

"O Prophet! When you divorce women, divorce them at their iddah and count their iddah..."

(Qur'an 65:1)

The second type of iddah, however, concerns the wife who hasn't experienced the menstruation yet, due to her young age or due to any other reason. Also this second type of iddah concerns the wife whose menstruation has been an issue of doubt; that is, it isn't known for sure whether she has reached her menopause yet.[15] The iddah in both of these two cases is three months.

In this regard, Allah says:

$$(وَاللَّائِى يَئِسْنَ مِنَ الْمَحِيضِ مِن نِّسَآئِكُمْ إِنِ ارْتَبْتُمْ فَعِدَّتُهُنَّ ثَلَاثَةُ أَشْهُرٍ وَاللَّائِى لَمْ يَحِضْنَ...)$$

"Those in menopause among your women, for them the iddah, if you have doubt, is three months; and for those who have not yet menstruated..." (Qur'an 65: 4)

The third type of iddah involves the pregnant, and her iddah, according to Al-Tabari (2010), is to stay in her home (her husband's) until she gives birth to her child (pp. 854–855).

Concerning this, Allah states:

$$(...وَأُوْلَاتُ الْأَحْمَالِ أَجَلُهُنَّ أَن يَضَعْنَ حَمْلَهُنَّ...)$$

"...and for those who are pregnant, their iddah is until they lay down their burden..." (Qur'an 65:4)

According to scholars of the Qur'anic exegesis, such as Al-Shawkani (2012), the iddah has two goals to achieve. First, it helps verify whether the divorcee is pregnant or not. Second, it keeps the divorced spouses together, in one place, in the hope that their physical proximity will help them reconcile (p. 299).

---

[15] Scholars have different opinions on this part of the ayah. For example, Al-Shawkani (2012) reported Al-Zajjaj to have argued that this rule concerns the wife who doesn't menstruate anymore, though other women of her age still do. In this case, according to him, her iddah is three months. Al-Shawkani, in addition, reported that some scholars claimed that this part of the ayah refers to the woman who experiences the blood, but it is not clear whether it is menstruation or not. In this case, her iddah is three months (p. 301).

If taqwa isn't closely observed, the amount of time that the divorced wife is required to spend in her husband's house after her divorce may lead to many wrong doings, especially from the husband's side toward his divorcee. Therefore, Allah has prescribed further firm rules to govern this time of iddah.

First, the period of iddah has to be counted accurately until it reaches its end (Al-Shawkani, 2012, p. 298). In this regard, Allah says:

(...وَأَحْصُواْ الْعِدَّةَ...)

"...and count the iddah..."   *(Qur'an 65:1)*

Besides the verification of whether the divorcee is pregnant or not, this accurate counting of iddah protects the divorced wife from her husband's potential unfairness and abuse of authority. Precisely, some husbands may reinstate their divorcees' marital status—just before the end of their iddah—with the intention to divorce them again and again (Al-Shawkani, 2012, p. 304). Their purpose, in this case, is, unfortunately, to humiliate their divorcees and torture them psychologically by prolonging their period of iddah.[16]

Second, during the period of iddah, the husband should not ill-treat his divorced wife, but he should treat her kindly and with dignity until

---

[16] In surah Al-Baqarah, Allah strongly warns against this unethical practice. He also commands Muslims to observe taqwa so that they may obey His rules. He says:

(وَإِذَا طَلَّقْتُمُ النِّسَاء فَبَلَغْنَ أَجَلَهُنَّ فَأَمْسِكُوهُنَّ بِمَعْرُوفٍ أَوْ سَرِّحُوهُنَّ بِمَعْرُوفٍ ، وَلاَ تُمْسِكُوهُنَّ ضِرَارًا لَّتَعْتَدُواْ ، وَمَن يَفْعَلْ ذَلِكَ فَقَدْ ظَلَمَ نَفْسَهُ ، وَلاَ تَتَّخِذُواْ آيَاتِ اللّهِ هُزُوًا ، وَاذْكُرُواْ نِعْمَتَ اللّهِ عَلَيْكُمْ وَمَا أَنزَلَ عَلَيْكُمْ مِّنَ الْكِتَابِ وَالْحِكْمَةِ يَعِظُكُم بِهِ ، وَاتَّقُواْ اللّهَ وَاعْلَمُواْ أَنَّ اللّهَ بِكُلِّ شَيْءٍ عَلِيمٌ).

"And when you have divorced women and they have fulfilled the term of their prescribed period, either take them back on reasonable basis or set them free on reasonable basis. But do not take them back to hurt them, and whoever does that, then he has wronged himself. And treat not the Verses (Laws) of Allah as a jest, but remember Allah's favours on you, and that which He has sent down to you of the Book and Al-Hikmah (the Prophet's Sunnah, legal ways, Islamic jurisprudence) whereby He instructs you. And fear Allah, and know that Allah is All-Aware of everything."   *(Qur'an 2:231)*

she leaves his home. Third, the husband has to furnish her with a quality of housing equal to that of his own, and he has to provide her with a living that matches his economic status, not lower than that by any means. Fourth, if the divorcee is pregnant, her husband should take care of her until she delivers her baby, and if she chooses to breastfeed the baby, he should pay her for this. Fifth, during this period, the divorced spouses are commanded to deal with each other in good manners (Al-Shawkani, 2012, pp. 304–305).

With respect to all of this, Allah states:

(أَسْكِنُوهُنَّ مِنْ حَيْثُ سَكَنتُم مِّن وُجْدِكُمْ وَلاَ تُضَآرُّوهُنَّ لِتُضَيِّقُواْ عَلَيْهِنَّ
وَإِن كُنَّ أُوْلَاتِ حَمْلٍ فَأَنِفِقُواْ عَلَيْهِنَّ حَتَّى يَضَعْنَ حَمْلَهُنَّ ، فَإِنْ أَرْضَعْنَ لَكُمْ
فَئَاتُوهُنَّ أُجُورَهُنَّ وَأْتَمِرُواْ بَيْنَكُمْ بِمَعْرُوفٍ ، وَإِن تَعَاسَرْتُمْ فَسَتُرْضِعُ
لَهُ أُخْرَى . لِيُنِفِقْ ذُو سَعَةٍ مِّن سَعَتِهِ ، وَمَن قُدِرَ عَلَيْهِ رِزْقُهُ فَلْيُنفِقْ مِمَّا
ءَاتَاهُ اللَّهُ ، لاَ يُكَلِّفُ اللَّهُ نَفْساً إِلاَّ مَا ءَاتَاهَا سَيَجْعَلُ اللَّهُ بَعْدَ عُسْرٍ يُسْراً).

"House the (divorced) women where you live, according to your means; but do not harass them so as to reduce them to straitened circumstances. And if they are pregnant, then spend on them until they give birth to the child. And if they suckle the child for you, then make the due payment to them, and consult each other appropriately. But if you find this difficult, let some other woman suckle (the child) for him. Let the man of means spend according to his means, and he whose means are limited, should spend of what Allah has given him. Allah does not burden a soul beyond what He has given it. God will bring ease after hardship."

(Qur'an 65:6–7)

If the husband decides to get his divorced wife back before the end of the iddah, he may do so, but with due respect and in full regard to her. However, if the time that the divorcee has to stay in her husband's house is over, and she is about to leave, the husband should let her do so with dignity. With respect to the restoration or the termination of the marital status, scholars have three different viewpoints. One group argues that two impartial witnesses must be present in both cases—the restoration and the separation. Another group claims that these witnesses are supposed to witness only the separation of the spouses. A third group, on the other hand, argues that these witnesses are required for the restoration of the marital status (Al-Qurtubi, 2014, p. 298).

In reference to this, Allah says:

(فَإِذَا بَلَغْنَ أَجَلَهُنَّ فَأَمْسِكُوهُنَّ بِمَعْرُوفٍ أَوْ فَارِقُوهُنَّ بِمَعْرُوفٍ وَأَشْهِدُواْ ذَوَيْ عَدْلٍ مِّنكُمْ وَأَقِيمُواْ الشَّهَادَةَ لِلَّهِ ، ذَلِكُمْ يُوعَظُ بِهِ مَن كَانَ يُؤْمِنُ بِاللَّهِ وَالْيَوْمِ الآخِرِ...)

"Then when they are about to attain their term appointed, either take them back in a good manner or part with them in a good manner. And take as witness two just persons from among you. And establish the testimony for Allah. That will be an admonition given to him who believes in Allah and the last Day..."
(Qur'an 65:2)

Obviously, these commands are difficult to observe without a significantly high level of taqwa. Allah, as a result, associates this frequent recurrence of the issue of taqwa in this surah with extremely attractive incentives to help believers observe His commands. Explicitly, He frequently promises those who adhere to taqwa—in handling divorce and all other affairs—desirable rewards, soon in this life and later in the Hereafter.

First, He guarantees such people a way out of hardship and a provision from unexpected avenues. He promises:

(...وَمَن يَتَّقِ اللَّهَ يَجْعَل لَّهُ مَخْرَجاً . وَيَرْزُقْهُ مِنْ حَيْثُ لاَ يَحْتَسِبُ...)

"...and whosoever fears Allah and keeps his duty to Him, He will make a way for him to get out (from every difficulty). And He will provide him from where he never could imagine..." *(Qur'an 65:2–3)*

Commenting on these two ayahs, Ibn Taymiyyah (2006) said that Allah protects those who have taqwa from harm and makes their provision easy (p. 37).

Second, Allah promises to make the affairs of the divorced couple easy—again, if they observe taqwa. With respect to this, He declares:

$$(...وَمَن يَتَّقِ اللَّهَ يَجْعَل لَّهُ مِنْ أَمْرِهِ يُسْراً).$$

"...and whosoever fears Allah and keeps his duty to Him, He will make his matter easy for him."
(Qur'an 65:4)

Third, He promises these people forgiveness, along with bountiful and grand rewards—still, on condition that they observe taqwa. He says:

$$(...وَمَن يَتَّقِ اللَّهَ يُكَفِّرْ عَنْهُ سَيِّئَاتِهِ وَيُعْظِمْ لَهُ أَجْراً).$$

"...and whosoever fears Allah and keeps his duty to Him, He will expiate from him his sins, and will increase his reward."
(Qur'an 65:5)

A believer's dreams can't be better than these enormous and generous rewards that Allah promises in these ayahs: removal of hardship, a provision from unexpected sources, ease in life affairs, forgiveness, and an enlarged reward in the Hereafter. According to different scholars of the Qur'anic exegesis, such as Al-Tabari and Al-Shawkani, all believers who observe taqwa in handling other life affairs also qualify for these rewards, yet it is important to remember that Allah has mentioned them in the context of how Muslims should handle the issue of divorce.

As mentioned earlier, today Muslims badly abuse the issue of divorce and fail dramatically in observing its rules. Men, for example, divorce their wives any time they want, and the divorcees leave their homes immediately after their divorce. Allah knows this will happen. As a result, He has almost ended this surah with an extremely threatening warning to help believers subdue the negative side in their human nature, observe the Qur'anic challenging rules of divorce, and overcome the Satan's continuous plotting to ruin the Muslim society through the destruction of the Muslim family. He has also accompanied this strong warning with a final reminder of the issue of taqwa. He states:

(وَكَأَيِّن مِّن قَرْيَةٍ عَتَتْ عَنْ أَمْرِ رَبِّهَا وَرُسُلِهِ فَحَاسَبْنَاهَا حِسَابًا شَدِيدًا وَعَذَّبْنَاهَا عَذَابًا نُكْرًا . فَذَاقَتْ وَبَالَ أَمْرِهَا وَكَانَ عَاقِبَةُ أَمْرِهَا خُسْرًا . أَعَدَّ اللَّهُ لَهُمْ عَذَابًا شَدِيدًا ، فَاتَّقُوا اللَّهَ يَا أُولِي الْأَلْبَابِ الَّذِينَ آمَنُوا ، قَدْ أَنزَلَ اللَّهُ إِلَيْكُمْ ذِكْرًا).

"And how many populations that insolently opposed the command of their Lord and of His apostle, did We not then call to account?—And We imposed on them an exemplary punishment. Then did they taste the evil result of their conduct, and the end of their conduct was perdition. Allah has prepared for them a severe punishment (in the hereafter). Therefore, fear Allah, O you men of understanding who have believed, for Allah has indeed sent down to you a Reminder."
(Qur'an 65:8—10)

That is an attempt to shed some light on some of the reasons underlying the frequent occurrence of the issue of taqwa in the Qur'an. The experience of the Holy Prophet's companions at Al-Hudaibiyah and the issue of divorce in surah Al-Talaq are mentioned and explained to exemplify real-life circumstances that require a high level of taqwa and a frequent Qur'anic reminder to observe it.

CHAPTER 2

Spiritual Reflection

Reflection on Allah's creation plays a fundamental role in eiman and taqwa. In fact, the presence of these two issues (eiman and taqwa) in our lives, their influence on our relationship with Allah, their effect on our perception of this life, and their impact on our attitude towards the next one depend considerably on the quality of our spiritual reflection and its frequency in our lives. Perhaps this is why the issue of reflection has a prominent presence in the Holy Qur'an. In reference to it, Allah employs the Arabic root *f-k-r*. One of the different present forms derived from this root, for example, is *yatafakkar,*[17] which means to reflect or contemplate on issues, events, or things for better understanding, better decisions, and better results. Further, the issue of reflection in the Holy Qur'an always takes the verb form. Thus, one may ask, "Why?" One possible answer to this important question is that since verbs, in general, express actions, and since actions require effort, the occurrence of the issue of reflection in the verb form in the Holy Qur'an may suggest the effort that reflection requires before it offers its excellent fruits.

Spiritual reflection or the lack of it is, actually, a learned human behaviour—we learn to spiritually reflect, and we learn not to. Hence, with regard to this type of reflection, people are two categories: those who are involved in it and those who aren't. The latter group of people frequently run into different situations that invite spiritual reflection, but they fail to reflect. When they enter a fruit-and-

---

[17] All the other present forms derived from this root give the same meaning, which is, again, "to reflect" or "to contemplate." Also most of these forms are gender-and-number specific—that is, they indicate whether they refer to a male, female, singular, dual, or plural.

vegetable market, for example, they see a wide spectrum of wonderful products, in different shapes and amazing colours and with pleasant fragrances. They buy what they need and leave, but without a moment of spiritual reflection on that marvellous display of nature, represented by those various, colourful products they see in that place. Accordingly, they miss a good opportunity to connect with their Lord and appreciate Him.

The recurrence of such a negative experience in reaction to other similar situations, unfortunately, reinforces this negative attitude. As a result, it gradually becomes dominant in these people's lives—they see, hear, earn, own, and experience different things, yet they fail to reflect and, thus, fail to connect!

When those who reflect enter that place or another similar one, however, they immediately think of the Creator Who has created all those blessings and gave them those amazing colours, beautiful shapes, pleasant smells, and enjoyable tastes. They, consequently, recognize and thank Him for creating and making these products available to them. And when they leave the place, they are, actually, happier with the feeling of gratitude overwhelming their reflecting hearts than they are with the vegetables and fruits overflowing their shopping bags!

These two examples, in fact, apply to countless things and situations in human life. Thus, people—especially believers—should never fail to reflect, for every moment of a good quality of spiritual reflection strengthens and sweetens their relationship with the Creator and plants more seeds of love and longing for Him in their heart.

The following sheds some light on five issues that the Qur'an invites people to reflect on: Allah's creation, the Holy Qur'an, the Holy Prophet's character, the Qur'anic stories, and the essence of this life, along with the humans' destinies in the Hereafter.

Reflection on Allah's Creation

Reflection on Allah's creation is one of the most spiritually rewarding and pleasurable experiences in believers' lives. Those who know its value in Allah's sight and have enjoyed its unparalleled mental, psychological, and spiritual effects wouldn't exchange a moment of it with—hypothetically speaking—the entire wealth in the world! Ibn Al-

Qayyim narrated that Ibn Taymiyyah said, "This life has a garden. Those who haven't entered it won't enter the Garden in the Hereafter!" Obviously, a major element in the garden that Ibn Taymiyyah refers to in this statement is reflection, for it overflows the reflecting heart with the love for Allah, the overwhelming experience of His Majesty, and the indescribable pleasure of His glorification.

In many ayahs, Allah points to different universal phenomena—as indications of His existence, His oneness, and His incredible power—and He invites people to reflect on them. In the following two ayahs from surah Al-Nahl, for example, Allah invites people to reflect on His amazing ability to create countless plants, fruits, and crops as a result of the union of rainwater and soil. These ayahs, in fact, come in a context that highlights different blessings that Allah bestows on humankind. Most importantly, in the second ayah, Allah declares that only those who reflect will they realize the greatness of the power behind the creation of all these blessings that the ayah highlights. He declares:

$$\text{(هُوَ الَّذِي أَنزَلَ مِنَ السَّمَاءِ مَاءً ، لَّكُم مِّنْهُ شَرَابٌ وَمِنْهُ شَجَرٌ فِيهِ تُسِيمُونَ . يُنبِتُ لَكُم بِهِ الزَّرْعَ وَالزَّيْتُونَ وَالنَّخِيلَ وَالْأَعْنَابَ وَمِن كُلِّ الثَّمَرَاتِ ، إِنَّ فِي ذَلِكَ لَآيَةً لِّقَوْمٍ يَتَفَكَّرُونَ).}$$

"He it is Who sends down water from the sky; from it you drink and from it (grows) the vegetation on which you send your cattle to pasture. With it He causes to grow for you the herbage, and the olives, and the palm trees, and the grapes, and of all the fruit. Verily, in this is indeed an evident proof and a manifest sign for a people who reflect."   *(Qur'an 16:10–11)*

Another couple of ayahs from the same surah, Al-Nahl, call people's attention to another aspect of Allah's creation. In particular, in these ayahs, Allah invites people to reflect on the bees and their amazing ability to make honey of different colours and tastes that people use for many purposes. He says:

$$\text{(وَأَوْحَى رَبُّكَ إِلَى النَّحْلِ أَنِ اتَّخِذِي مِنَ الْجِبَالِ بُيُوتًا وَمِنَ الشَّجَرِ وَمِمَّا يَعْرِشُونَ .}$$

ثُمَّ كُلِي مِن كُلِّ الثَّمَرَاتِ فَاسْلُكِي سُبُلَ رَبِّكِ ذُلُلاً ، يَخْرُجُ مِن بُطُونِهَا شَرَابٌ
مُّخْتَلِفٌ أَلْوَانُهُ فِيهِ شِفَاء لِلنَّاسِ إِنَّ فِي ذَلِكَ لآيَةً لِّقَوْمٍ يَتَفَكَّرُونَ) .

"And your Lord inspired the bees, saying: 'Take your habitations in the mountains and in the trees and in what they build. Then eat of all the fruits and walk in the ways of your Lord submissively.' There comes forth from within it a beverage of many colours, in which there is healing for people; most surely there is a sign in this for a people who reflect." (Qur'an 16:68–69)

In reference to the second ayah, A. Y. Ali (2008) said:

The bee assimilates the juice of various kinds of flowers and fruit, and forms within its body the honey, which it stores in its cells of wax. The different kinds of food from which it makes its honey give different colours to the honey, e.g., it is dark-brown, light-brown, yellow, white, and so on. The taste and flavour also vary, as in the case of heather honey, the honey formed from scented flowers, and so on. As food it is sweet and wholesome, and it is used in medicine. (p. 674)

The flowers and fruits from which the bees get their food, the sweet honey of different tastes and various colours they produce, as well as people's different needs for it invite reflection on the overwhelmingly amazing power behind them. The result of such reflection must lead to one significant fact. Precisely, the creator of all these—the bees, their source of food, the honey, and the people who need it—must be one: Allah.

Another ayah that invites reflection on Allah's creation is this one from surah Al-Zumar (The Groups). It invites humans to reflect on the issues of sleep and death. Here, in fact, sleep represents a simple form of death:

(اللَّهُ يَتَوَفَّى الأَنفُسَ حِينَ مَوْتِهَا وَالَّتِي لَمْ تَمُتْ فِي مَنَامِهَا ، فَيُمْسِكُ الَّتِي قَضَى
عَلَيْهَا الْمَوْتَ وَيُرْسِلُ الأُخْرَى إِلَى أَجَلٍ مُسَمًّى ، إِنَّ فِي ذَلِكَ لآيَاتٍ لِّقَوْمٍ
يَتَفَكَّرُونَ).

"Allah takes the souls at the time of their death and those that die not during their sleep; then He withholds those on whom He has passed the decree of death and sends the others back till an appointed term; most surely there are signs in this for a people who reflect." (Qur'an 39:42)

Scholars of the exegesis of the Holy Qur'an argued that the underlying message in this ayah is that only Allah is in command over the human soul. He sends it to sleep, brings it back to life, or ceases it forever! Al-Qurtubi (2014) narrated that Jabir ibn Abd Allah had reported that the Holy Prophet was asked:

"O Messenger of Allah! Do the people of the Garden sleep?" He answered, 'No, . . . sleep is death, and there is no death in the Garden.'" (p. 171)

Also according to Imam Al-Bukhari, whenever Allah's Holy Messenger woke up from his sleep, he would say:

"Praise be to Allah Who has brought us back to life after death, and onto Him is resurrection."

"الحمد لله الذي أحيانا بعدما أماتنا وإليه النشور."

In addition, because Allah loves the worship of reflection, He praises believers who recurrently reflect on His creation. In surah Al-Imran, for example, He emphatically states:

(إِنَّ فِي خَلْقِ السَّمَاوَاتِ وَالْأَرْضِ وَاخْتِلَافِ اللَّيْلِ وَالنَّهَارِ لَآيَاتٍ لِأُولِي الْأَلْبَابِ. الَّذِينَ يَذْكُرُونَ اللَّهَ قِيَامًا وَقُعُودًا وَعَلَىٰ جُنُوبِهِمْ وَيَتَفَكَّرُونَ فِي خَلْقِ السَّمَاوَاتِ وَالْأَرْضِ رَبَّنَا مَا خَلَقْتَ هَٰذَا بَاطِلًا سُبْحَانَكَ فَقِنَا عَذَابَ النَّارِ).

"Most surely in the creation of the heavens and the earth and the alternation of the night and the day there are signs for people who understand. Those who remember Allah standing and sitting and lying on their sides and reflect on the creation of the heavens and the earth: 'Our Lord! You have not created this in vain! Glory be to You; save us then from the chastisement of the Fire.'"

(Qur'an 3:190–191)

These two ayahs imply the vital role that reflection plays in believers' mentality, psychology, attitude, and behaviour. Allah calls those who are involved in it *"ulu al-albab,"*[18] meaning people who have wisdom and thus are able to understand the essence and objective of this life. According to Isma'il, ulu al-albab are believers who "have reached an excellent level of reflection and remembrance [of Allah]." She also cited Al-Nisaburi (1978) to have said that the brain reaches its perfect stage [full intellectual and spiritual development] when it becomes *lub*, [which is the singular form of *albab*] (1993, p. 73).

The second ayah highlights these people's two unique characteristics that make them stand out. First, they remember Allah in all situations: when they are standing, when they are sitting, and when they are laying down. In other words, ulu al-albab's wisdom has led them to establish a strong bond with Allah that reflects on continuous observance, remembrance, glorification, and appreciation of Him—with their brains, with their tongues, and most importantly, with their hearts.

Second, ulu al-albab's continuous remembrance and glorification of Allah, as this ayah indicates, is accompanied with reflection on His marvellous creation on the earth and that in the heavens. Obviously, this message demonstrates the significant position of reflection in Allah's sight.

Al-Shawkani (2012) reported that Ayishah, the Holy Prophet's wife, narrated that when this ayah was revealed to him, he said:

"Woe to whoever reads it and fails to reflect" (p. 518).

"ويل لمن قرأ هذه الآية ولم يتفكَّر فيها ".

Reflection on the Holy Qur'an

The understanding of the Holy Qur'an and a positive reaction to its message require an excellent quality of reflection. With regard to this, Allah addressed His Holy Messenger saying:

(...وَأَنزَلْنَا إِلَيْكَ الذِّكْرَ لِتُبَيِّنَ لِلنَّاسِ مَا نُزِّلَ إِلَيْهِمْ وَلَعَلَّهُمْ يَتَفَكَّرُونَ).

"...and We have also sent down to you the Reminder that you may explain clearly to people what has been sent down to them, and that they may reflect."

(Qur'an 16:44)

Generally, those who fail to believe in the Qur'an and thus deprive themselves of the enjoyment of its light, wisdom, and guidance have a problem with their brains and hearts. In reference to this type of people, Allah—in a disapproving tone—says:

(أَفَلَا يَتَدَبَّرُونَ الْقُرْآنَ أَمْ عَلَى قُلُوبٍ أَقْفَالُهَا)؟

"Do they not ponder on what the Qur'an says? Or have their hearts been sealed with locks?"

(Qur'an 47:24)

The disapproving, exclamatory question in this ayah indicates that the Holy Qur'an should make sense to everyone who reflects on it. Explaining the message in this ayah, Al-Saadi (2011) said that if these people had reflected on the Holy Qur'an, it would have certainly filled their hearts with the light of eiman, guided them to righteousness, distanced them from all kinds of evil, and led them to the Gardens of bliss (pp. 731–732). Al-Shawkani (2012), in addition, mentioned that these people failed to reflect on the Holy Qur'an and to believe in it because their hearts were—figuratively speaking— shielded and thus its light wasn't able to enter them (p. 48).

People in general have, unfortunately, failed to reflect on the Qur'an; thus, they have failed to make the ideal response to it. Allah strongly condemns this negative human attitude saying:

(لَوْ أَنزَلْنَا هَذَا الْقُرْآنَ عَلَى جَبَلٍ لَّرَأَيْتَهُ خَاشِعًا مُّتَصَدِّعًا مِّنْ خَشْيَةِ اللَّهِ ، وَتِلْكَ الْأَمْثَالُ نَضْرِبُهَا لِلنَّاسِ لَعَلَّهُمْ يَتَفَكَّرُونَ).

"Had We sent down this Qur'an on a mountain, you would certainly have seen it humbling itself and splitting asunder because of the fear of Allah. Such are the parables which We put forward to people that they may reflect."

(Qur'an 59:21)

This ayah demonstrates, to humankind, the ideal reaction to the Holy Qur'an, represented by that of a mountain's had Allah revealed His Book to it! The message is, certainly, humiliating to everyone who rejects the Holy Qur'an or fails to react positively to it. Such humiliation stems from the underlying comparison that Allah establishes between the humans' negative attitude towards the Holy Qur'an and the ideal response of a mountain's—any mountain—if, again, Allah had revealed the Qur'an to it. The message, in addition, suggests the amazing power that Allah has favoured the Holy Qur'an with.

Further, because reflection is the gate to the belief in Allah, the realization of His infinite power, and the experience of His Majesty, this ayah ends with an open invitation to all humankind to reflect on it. It says:

$$ \text{(...وَتِلْكَ الْأَمْثَالُ نَضْرِبُهَا لِلنَّاسِ لَعَلَّهُمْ يَتَفَكَّرُونَ).} $$

"...and We set forth these parables to men that they may reflect."

Commenting on this part of the ayah, Al-Saadi (2011) said:

> Then Allah states that He provides people with parables and shows them the lawful and the unlawful issues so that they may reflect on his ayahs, for reflection opens the treasures of knowledge and helps people distinguish between the path of righteousness and that of wickedness; it also motivates them to adopt good morals. (p. 797)

When Europe was extremely prejudiced against Islam and its Holy Prophet, Bonaparte was able to see the guidance and happiness that the Holy Qur'an has for all humans, regardless of their times and environments. Dreaming of creating a happy, united world, he explained the crucial role that the Holy Qur'an would play in the achievement of his dream. He said:

> I hope the time is not far off when I shall be able to unite all the wise and educated men of all the countries and establish a uniform regime based on the principles of the Qur'an which

alone are true and which alone can lead men to happiness. (What-Muslim, n.d.)

Reflection on the Holy Prophet's Character

In the early days of dawah, Quraysh tried to stigmatize the Holy Prophet with insanity. Their objective was, of course, to distract the public from listening to the Holy Qur'an and embracing Islam. In a question form, therefore, Allah reprimanded Quraysh's failure to reflect on the Holy Prophet's excellent character saying:

(أَوَلَمْ يَتَفَكَّرُواْ ، مَا بِصَاحِبِهِم مِّن جِنَّةٍ ، إِنْ هُوَ إِلاَّ نَذِيرٌ مُّبِينٌ).

"Do they not reflect? Their companion is not seized with madness: he is but a plain warner."

(Qur'an 7:184)

Once again—in surah Saba' (Sheba)—Allah called upon Quraysh to reflect on the Holy Prophet's ideal character and to reconsider their negative attitude towards him and the message he was sent with. He says:

(قُلْ إِنَّمَا أَعِظُكُم بِوَاحِدَةٍ ، أَن تَقُومُوا لِلَّهِ مَثْنَى وَفُرَادَى ثُمَّ تَتَفَكَّرُوا ، مَا بِصَاحِبِكُم مِّن جِنَّةٍ إِنْ هُوَ إِلَّا نَذِيرٌ لَّكُم بَيْنَ يَدَيْ عَذَابٍ شَدِيدٍ) .

"Say: 'I do admonish you on one point: that you do stand up before Allah, (It may be) in pairs, or (it may be) singly, and reflect (within yourselves): your Companion is not possessed: he is no less than a warner to you, in face of a severe torment.'"
(Qur'an 34:46)

The above ayah shows that Allah did not coerce the disbelievers of Makkah to believe in Mohammad as a messenger to them. Instead, He invited them to reflect on his excellent character and judge for themselves. Had they seriously done so, they would have certainly realized that he was truly Allah's Messenger. The Makkan disbelievers, in fact, knew—for sure—Mohammad was a perfectly ethical man who never lied, drank alcohol, involved himself in any immoral issue, or participated in any belittling activity—even when he was a child. They also knew he was a wise man, and they acknowledged his unparalleled credibility and unmatched moral character before and after he received Allah's message to him.

When Quraysh was reconstructing Al Kabah, for example, and the building reached a stage at which the Black Stone was supposed to be laid in its proper spot, each tribe in Quraysh wanted to have the honour of doing this. As a result, the men who were involved in that honourable work almost started a bloody fight, but they finally decided to accept whoever would come from the way of Al-Safa to be the judge who would decide on this difficult issue. Luckily, it was Mohammad who came from that direction. When they saw him, they became happy and started to shout joyfully: "There comes the Trustworthy; we accept him to be our judge."

He told them to spread a piece of cloth on the ground; then he picked up the Black Stone, put it in the middle of that piece of cloth, and told each tribe's representative to lift the stone using a certain side of the cloth. When they did and the stone reached a specific spot on the wall, he picked it up and placed it in its proper position. So "this is how a very tense situation was eased and grave danger averted by the wisdom of the Prophet [on whose character, Allah invited the disbelievers of Quraysh to reflect]" (Al-Mubarakpuri 1979/2008, p. 80).

In addition, until the Holy Prophet secretly left Makkah for Al-Madinah, different men from Quraysh were still keeping their valuables with him because he was honest. So before he immigrated, he delegated Ali ibn Abi Talib to return those valuables back to their owners. Also in surah Al-An'am, Allah states that Quraysh had no doubt about the Holy Prophet's outstanding credibility. In reference to this matter, He addressed him saying:

(قَدْ نَعْلَمُ إِنَّهُ لَيَحْزُنُكَ الَّذِي يَقُولُونَ فَإِنَّهُمْ لَا يُكَذِّبُونَكَ وَلَٰكِنَّ الظَّالِمِينَ بِآيَاتِ اللَّهِ يَجْحَدُونَ).

"We know indeed the grief which their words cause you:
It is not you that they disbelieve, but it is the signs of
Allah that the wicked deny."   *(Qur'an 6:33)*

In his explanation of this ayah, Al-Qurtubi (2014) stated:

Abu Maisarah said that when the Holy Prophet came across Abu Jahl and his companions, they said to him, "O Mohammad! By the name of Allah, we do not disbelieve you, but we disbelieve what you came with." Accordingly, Allah revealed the above ayah from surah Al-An'am. (p.552)

In the world of Monotheism, spirituality, morality, purity, virtue, self-restraint, and beauty—to mention only a few—Prophet Mohammad remains more prominent than the sun on a sunny day and brighter than the moon on a full-moon night. After his physical departure from our world, there always came people of different origins, cultures, and linguistic backgrounds who learned about him, and—though they didn't embrace Islam—they were able to see his unprecedented righteousness, purity, credibility, and absolute greatness reflecting on everything he represented, did, and said. The following are only a few examples of some famous, non-Muslims' impressions of him.

First, Lamartine,[19] who was obviously—but unsurprisingly—fascinated by the Holy Prophet, said:

If greatness of purpose, smallness of means, and astounding results are the three criteria of human genius, who could dare to compare any great man in modern history with Muhammad? The most famous men created arms, laws and empires only. They founded, if anything at all, no more than material powers which often crumbled away before their eyes. This man moved not only armies, legislations, empires, peoples and dynasties, but millions of men in one-third of the then inhabited world; and more than that, he moved the altars, the gods, the religions, the ideas, the beliefs and souls... the forbearance in victory, his ambition, which was entirely devoted to one idea and in no manner striving for an empire; his endless prayers, his mystic conversations with God, his death and his triumph after death; all these attest not to an imposture but to a firm conviction which gave him the power to restore a dogma. This dogma was twofold, the unity [oneness] of God and the immateriality of God; the former telling what God is, the latter telling what God is not; the one overthrowing false gods with the sword, the other starting an idea with words.

---

[19] Lamartine, 1790–1869, was a French writer, poet, and politician.

> As regards all standards by which human greatness may be measured, we may well ask, is there any man greater than he? (What Non-Muslim, n.d.)

Second, Besant[20] had greatly admired the Holy Prophet—which isn't a surprise—and had expressed her strong admiration for him in the following sincere, reverential words:

> It is impossible for anyone who studies the life and character of the great Prophet of Arabia, who knows how he taught and how he lived, to feel anything but reverence for that mighty Prophet, one of the great messengers of the Supreme. And although in what I put to you I shall say many things which may be familiar to many, yet I myself feel whenever I re-read them, a new way of admiration, a new sense of reverence for that mighty Arabian teacher. (What Non-Muslim, n.d.)

Third, speaking about the way the Holy Prophet and his companions related to each other and explaining the Holy Prophet's unique and unprecedentedly effective communication style, Lane-Poole[21] stated:

> He was the most faithful protector of those he protected, the sweetest and most agreeable in conversation. Those who saw him were suddenly filled with reverence; those who came near him loved him; those who described him would say, "I have never seen his like either before or after." He was of great taciturnity, but when he spoke it was with emphasis and deliberation, and no one could forget what he said. (What Non-Muslim, n.d.)

Fourth, Shaw[22] spoke with intense passion about the Holy Prophet and described him as the "Saviour of Humanity," solver of the world's problems, and bringer of happiness and peace. He also spelled out his positive vision of Islam in Europe saying:

---

[20] Annie Besant, 1847–1933, was a prominent British socialist, theosophist, women's rights activist, writer, and orator.

[21] Stanley Lane-Poole, 1854–1931, was a British orientalist and archaeologist.

[22] George Bernard Shaw, 1856–1950, was a prominent Irish playwright and critic.

I have always held the religion of Mohammad in high estimation because of its wonderful vitality. It is the only religion which appears to me possesses that assimilating capacity to the changing phase of existence which can make itself appeal to every age. I have studied him—the wonderful man and in my opinion is far from being an anti-Christ. He must be called the Saviour of Humanity. I believe that if a man like him were to assume the dictatorship of the modern world, he would succeed in solving its problems in a way that would bring much needed peace and happiness: I have prophesied about the faith of Mohammad that it would be acceptable to the Europe of tomorrow as it is beginning to be acceptable to Europe today. (Being an Unforgivably, n.d.)

Fifth, Gandhi[23] shed light on some of the Prophet's excellent qualities that made him capture billions of people's hearts and enabled Islam to easily and quickly pervade across the globe. He said:

I wanted to know the best of the life of one (Muhammad) who holds today an undisputed sway over the hearts of millions of mankind. I became more than ever convinced that it was not the sword that won a place for Islam in those days in the scheme of life. It was the rigid simplicity, the utter self-effacement of the Prophet the scrupulous regard for pledges, his intense devotion to his friends and followers, his intrepidity, his fearlessness, his absolute trust in God and in his own mission. These and not the sword carried everything before them and surmounted every obstacle. (What Non-Muslim, n.d.)

Finally, reflecting on the Holy Prophet Mohammad, Hart (1992) wrote the following:

My choice of Muhammad to lead the list of the world's most influential persons may surprise some readers and may be questioned by others, but he was the only man in history who was supremely successful on both the religious and secular levels.

---

[23] M. K. Gandhi, 1869 –1948, was the leader of the Indian Independence Movement.

Of humble origins, Muhammad founded and promulgated one of the world's great religions, and became an immensely effective political leader. Today, thirteen centuries after his death, his influence is still powerful and pervasive.

The majority of the persons in this book had the advantage of being born and raised in centers of civilization, highly cultured or politically pivotal nations. Muhammad, however, was born in the year 570, in the city of Mecca, in southern Arabia, at that time a backward area of the world, far from the centers of trade, art, and learning. Orphaned at age six, he was reared in modest surroundings. Islamic tradition tells us that he was illiterate. His economic position improved when, at age twenty-five, he married a wealthy widow. Nevertheless, as he approached forty, there was little outward indication that he was a remarkable person.

How, then, is one to assess the overall impact of Muhammad on human history? Like all religions, Islam exerts an enormous influence upon the lives of its followers. It is for this reason that the founders of the world's great religions all figure prominently in this book. Since there are roughly twice as many Christians as Moslems [Muslims] in the world, it may initially seem strange that Muhammad has been ranked higher than Jesus. There are two principal reasons for that decision. First, Muhammad played a far more important role in the development of Islam than Jesus did in the development of Christianity. Although Jesus was responsible for the main ethical and moral precepts of Christianity (insofar as these differed from Judaism), St. Paul was the main developer of Christian theology, its principal proselytizer, and the author of a large portion of the New Testament.

Muhammad, however, was responsible for both the theology of Islam and its main ethical and moral principles. In addition, he played the key role in proselytizing the new faith, and in establishing the religious practices of Islam . . . Since the Koran [Qur'an] is at least as important to

Moslems [Muslims] as the Bible is to Christians, the influence of Muhammed through the medium of the Koran [Qur'an] has been enormous. It is probable that the relative influence of Muhammad on Islam has been larger than the combined influence of Jesus Christ and St. Paul on Christianity. On the purely religious level, then, it seems likely that Muhammad has been as influential in human history as Jesus. (pp. 3–10)

Indeed, the Holy Prophet's life and character represent a perfect reflection of the Holy Qur'an's teachings. Today, reflection on his character and on his life is possible through a careful study of his biography. Ambitious Muslims are, therefore, expected to be regularly involved in it—at least once a year—so that they can be in touch with his Qur'anic morals, which perfectly reflect on the way he reacted to and dealt with countless stimuli and situations throughout his life.

Reflection on this Life and on the Hereafter

Allah recommends that people reflect on the essence of this life so that they may prepare themselves for the Day of Judgment. Consider the following couple of ayahs from surah Al-Baqarah:

(أَيَوَدُّ أَحَدُكُمْ أَن تَكُونَ لَهُ جَنَّةٌ مِّن نَّخِيلٍ وَأَعْنَابٍ تَجْرِي مِن تَحْتِهَا الْأَنْهَارُ لَهُ فِيهَا مِن كُلِّ الثَّمَرَاتِ وَأَصَابَهُ الْكِبَرُ وَلَهُ ذُرِّيَّةٌ ضُعَفَاءُ فَأَصَابَهَا إِعْصَارٌ فِيهِ نَارٌ فَاحْتَرَقَتْ، كَذَلِكَ يُبَيِّنُ اللَّهُ لَكُمُ الْآيَاتِ لَعَلَّكُمْ تَتَفَكَّرُونَ).

"Does one of you like that he should have a garden of palms and vines with streams flowing beneath it; he has in it all kinds of fruits; and old age has overtaken him and he has weak offspring, then a whirlwind with fire in it smites it, so it becomes blasted. Thus Allah makes His signs clear to you that you may reflect."

(Qur'an 2:266)

Scholars of the exegesis of the Qur'an, such as Ibn Kathir (2014), argued that this ayah warns humankind about being losers on the Day of Judgment. According to them, some people may spend most of their lives doing righteousness; later, however, they decline and start to follow the Satan's footprints until they find themselves in Hellfire (p. 192).

Ibn Al-Qayyim (1988) sheds light on another side of this ayah. He cited Al-Hasan to have said that this example refers to an old man who has many kids; at this stage of his life, his need for his garden multiplies, of course. Similarly, on the Day of Judgment, a servant of Allah will be in a desperate need for good deeds (p.162). People should, therefore, take this short life as an opportunity to prepare diligently for the next permanent one; otherwise, they will reap nothing, but sorrow, despair, and misery.

Reflection on the Qur'anic Stories

Finally, in the Holy Qur'an, the issue of reflection comes in connection with the Qur'anic stories, which will be discussed later in a separate chapter, namely "The Qur'anic Stories."

CHAPTER 3

— — —

The Heart's Role in Taqwa

The heart is the human's centre; it is, therefore, the audience of the Qur'anic speech. It is the first that Allah honours and the first He blames, [24] for it is responsible for people's belief, disbelief, and their outcomes. A careful survey of the Holy Qur'an shows the significant position that the heart occupies in it and the dynamic role it plays in people's lives today and in their destiny on the Day of Judgment. Of all human organs, it is the heart that develops and enjoys love and longing for Allah. It is also the only one that develops fear of Him, and with the heat of this fear, it glitters and shines! Perhaps this is why the heart is the only human organ that Allah has honoured with the experience and the enjoyment of the unparalleled taste of the realization of His Majesty.

Based on different Qur'anic messages, one can easily infer that the heart can develop and adopt numerous positive and negative attributes.

---

[24] The heart's central role in humans' lives today and in their destiny in the Hereafter is demonstrated in the following ayahs from the surahs of Al-Hajj and Qaf:

(فَإِنَّهَا لاَ تَعْمَى الأَّبْصَارُ وَلَكِن تَعْمَى الْقُلُوبُ الَّتِي فِي الصُّدُورِ).

"It is not the eyes that grow blind, but it is the hearts which are in the breasts that grow blind."　　　　*(Qur'an 22:46)*

(من خَشِيَ الرَّحْمَنَ بِالْغَيْبِ وَجَاءَ بِقَلْب منيب).

"Who feared the Most Gracious in the unseen and brought a heart turned in repentance."　　　　*(Qur'an 50:33)*

This, of course, implies the necessity of constant, wise cultivation of this human organ, in a way that increases and nourishes its positive attributes and—at the same time—eliminates its negative ones. Believers, in other words, should continuously and earnestly sharpen their hearts by thoughtful recitation of the Holy Qur'an, remembrance of Allah, His glorification, and fruitful reflection on His infinite, miraculous creation.

Allah's Holy Messenger has emphasized the fundamental role that the heart plays in human life, especially in the issues of belief and taqwa. According to Al-Samarraei (2011), Imam Ahmed reported Abu Saeed Al-Khudri to have narrated the following hadith about the Holy Prophet:

> "Hearts are four: a polished heart that shines as a radiating lamp, a sealed one with a knot tied around its seal, an upside-down heart; and wrapped up one. The polished heart is the believer's; the lamp in it is the light of faith. The sealed heart is the disbeliever's, and the one that is turned upside down is the heart of a complete hypocrite, who knows the truth but denies it. The wrapped up heart is the one that has belief and hypocrisy. The issue of faith in this heart is like a herb sustained by pure water, and the hypocrisy in it is like an ulcer that thrives on puss and blood, so whichever of these substances becomes dominant will have more influence on this heart." (p. 73)

"القلوب أربعة : قلب أجرد فيه مثل السراج يزهر ، وقلب أغلف مربوط على غلافه ، وقلب منكوس ، وقلب مصفّح . فأما القلب الأجرد فقلب المؤمن فسراجه فيه نوره . وأما القلب الأغلف فقلب الكافر . وأما القلب المنكوس فقلب المنافق [الخالص] ، عرف ثم أنكر ، وأما القلب المصفح فقلب فيه إيمان ونفاق. ومثَل الإيمان فيه كمثَل البقلة يمدها الماء الطيب. ومثل النفاق فيه كمثل القرحة يمدها القيح والدم ، فأي المادتين غلبت على الأخرى ، غلبت عليه ." [25]

The Ways the Holy Qur'an Refers to the Heart

The Arabic language enables its speakers to use many words in reference to the heart. Each of these words, in fact, denotes and

---

[25] This hadith was narrated by Imam Ahmed and Imam Al-Tabari.

connotes specific aspects of the heart's intricate types of work and issues in which it is involved. Some of the Arabic words that refer to it are, for example, *qalb, fu'ad, rawa,*[26] *jinan, sadr, wijdan,* and *bal.* In the Holy Qur'an, Allah refers to it using different words, depending on the nature of the message He is communicating

First, He refers to it using the word fu'ad.[27] This word comes in both the singular and the plural forms. In the singular form, it recurs four times; half of these recurrences, interestingly, come in reference to the firming of the Holy Prophet's heart. In surah Hud and with regard to this issue, Allah addressed His Holy Messenger saying:

(وَكُلاًّ نَّقُصُّ عَلَيْكَ مِنْ أَنْبَاءِ الرُّسُلِ مَا نُثَبِّتُ بِهِ فُؤَادَكَ...)

"And all that We relate to you of the news of the Messengers is in order that We make strong and firm your heart thereby..." *(Qur'an 11:120)*

Also in surah Al-Furqan (The Differentiator), Allah reiterates the same previous issue—the strengthening of the Holy Messenger's heart with the revelation of the Holy Qur'an in parts, meaning at different times and on specific occasions. He states:

(وَقَالَ الَّذِينَ كَفَرُوا لَوْلَا نُزِّلَ عَلَيْهِ الْقُرْآنُ جُمْلَةً وَاحِدَةً ، كَذَلِكَ لِنُثَبِّتَ بِهِ فُؤَادَكَ...)

"And those who disbelieve say: 'Why is not the Qur'an revealed to him all at once?' Thus (it is sent down in parts), that We may strengthen your heart thereby..." *(Qur'an 25:32)*

In the plural form, which *is af'idah,*[28] this noun occurs in different surahs, where it refers to either the heart or the brain. The ayahs in which the word "af'idah" is used in reference to the heart exist in, for example, the surahs of Al-An'am, Ibrahim, and Al-Humazah (The

---

[26] روع

[27] فؤاد

[28] أفئدة

Slanderer). In surah Ibrahim and in reference to the disbelievers' awful situation and extreme horror they will experience on the Day of Judgment, Allah says:

(مُهْطِعِينَ مُقْنِعِي رُءُوسِهِمْ لاَ يَرْتَدُّ إِلَيْهِمْ طَرْفُهُمْ وَأَفْئِدَتُهُمْ هَوَاءٌ)!

"They will rush forward, craning their necks, unable to divert their eyes, a gaping void in their hearts."
                                                    (Qur'an 14:43)

Also describing the ruthlessness of Hellfire, Allah explains how it deals with disbelievers' hearts—the very hearts that refused to believe in Him and in His messages. He warns and threatens:

(نَارُ اللَّهِ الْمُوقَدَةُ . الَّتِي تَطَّلِعُ عَلَى الْأَفْئِدَةِ)!

"The fire of Allah kindled, which leaps up over the heart!"   *(Qur'an 104:6–7)*

Second, Allah refers to the heart using the word *sadr*,[29] which literally means chest—the place where the heart exists. Like the word fu'ad, sadr comes in the singular and in the plural forms. In the following ayah from surah Al-Mulk (The Dominion), for example, Allah uses the plural form of this word in reference to the human heart. He says:

(وَأَسِرُّوا قَوْلَكُمْ أَوِ اجْهَرُوا بِهِ ، إِنَّهُ عَلِيمٌ بِذَاتِ الصُّدُورِ).

"And (whether) you keep your talk secret or disclose it, verily, He is All-Knower of what is in the breasts."
                                                    (Qur'an 67:13)

In his exegesis, Ibn Kathir (2014) indicated that the word *sudoor*[30]—the plural form of sadr—in this ayah refers to the heart (p. 428).

Third, Allah frequently refers to the human heart using the word

---

[29] صدر
[30] صدور

qalb.[31] This noun, in fact, comes in all forms: singular, dual, and plural. For instance, it occurs many times in the singular form, such as in the following ayah from the surah of Qaf:

$$\text{(مَنْ خَشِيَ الرَّحْمَنَ بِالْغَيْبِ وَجَاءَ بِقَلْبٍ مُّنِيبٍ)}.$$

"Who feared the Most Gracious (Allah) in the unseen, and brought a heart turned in devotion (to Him)"
(Qur'an 50:33)

The usage of the word qalb in the dual form, however, occurs only once in the entire Qur'an—specifically, in surah Al-Ahzab. With regard to this, Allah declares:

$$\text{(ما جَعَلَ اللَّهُ لِرَجُلٍ مِّن قَلْبَيْنِ فِي جَوْفِهِ...)}$$

"Allah has not assigned unto any man two hearts within his body..."
(Qur'an 33:4)

According to Al-Qurtubi (2014), since the heart is the place where *eiman* (belief in Allah) exists, in this ayah the usage of the word "heart" in the dual form indicates that the heart cannot accommodate eiman and *kufr* (disbelief) simultaneously (p. 319).

Further, the plural form of the word qalb, which is *quloob,*[32] occurs many times in the Holy Qur'an. In surah Al-Imran and in reference to His support for the believers with angels at the Battle of Badr, Allah says:

$$\text{(وَمَا جَعَلَهُ اللَّهُ إِلاَّ بُشْرَى لَكُمْ وَلِتَطْمَئِنَّ قُلُوبُكُم بِهِ ، وَمَا النَّصْرُ إِلاَّ مِنْ عِندِ}$$
$$\text{اللَّهِ الْعَزِيزِ الْحَكِيمِ)}.$$

"Allah made it not but a message of good news for you and as an assurance to your hearts. And there is no victory except from Allah, the All-Mighty, The All-Wise."
(Qur'an 3:126)

---

[31] قلب
[32] قُلُوب

The Heart's Positive Role

When they are aware of the heart's role in humans' relationship with Allah, and when they actively and seriously aspire to enter the Gardens of bliss, scrupulous believers—like diligent farmers—treat their hearts as a piece of land on which they grow many positive attributes fundamental to the development of taqwa. Based on many ayahs in the Holy Qur'an, the following sheds light on some of the heart's positive characteristics.

First, the heart is the organ that accommodates eiman. It is where eiman develops and exists, as the following ayah from surah Al-Hujurat declares:

(قَالَتِ الأَعْرَابُ ءَامَنَّا ، قُل لَّمْ تُؤْمِنُواْ وَلَكِنْ قُولُواْ أَسْلَمْنَا وَلَمَّا يَدْخُلِ الإِيمَانُ فِى قُلُوبِكُمْ) [33]

"The Bedouins say: 'We believe.' Say: 'You do not believe.' But say, 'We have submitted, for faith has not yet entered your hearts.'"   (Qur'an 49:14)

Also the surah of Al-An'am (Livestock) confirms the previous message, from surah Al-Hujurat. Again, the heart is the organ that accepts and accommodates eiman. In this regard, Allah says:

(فَمَن يُرِدِ اللَّهُ أَن يَهْدِيَهُ يَشْرَحْ صَدْرَهُ لِلإِسْلاَمِ...)

"And whomsoever Allah wills to guide, He opens his breast to Islam..."   (Qur'an 6: 125)

Here the reader might say, "In the previous ayah, from surah Al-Hujurat, Allah uses the word 'eiman,' whereas in this one, from surah

---

[33] The Holy Prophet's hadith proves that the word "quloob" in the above ayah refers to the heart, not to the brain. He says:

"Eiman resides in the chest (the heart), and it is confirmed by (reflected on) deeds."

"الإيمان ما وقر في الصدر وصدَّقه العمل."

Al-An'am, He uses the word 'Islam,' and these two words are not interchangeable." In fact, according to Bin Baz, when either of the words "eiman" or "Islam" is used in the absence of the other, it refers to the other one, too. In other words, in a specific context, if the word "eiman" is used in the absence of the word "Islam," it also refers to Islam, and vice versa. Thus, the word "Islam" in this ayah refers to "eiman," too.

In this same ayah, Allah refers to the heart using the noun "sadr," which, as mentioned earlier, is the Arabic word for chest. Ibn Kathir (2014) narrated that when the Holy Prophet's companions asked him about the meaning of *sharh alsadr* in this ayah, which literally means the "opening of the chest," he answered them, "It is a light that Allah puts in the heart." Ibn Kathir also cited Ibn Abbas to have said that this expression means "to widen the heart for *tawheed* [Allah's oneness]" (p. 496). Here the heart's widening, which is used figuratively, denotes its happiness with tawheed and its full accommodation of it.

Second, it is the heart that receives and accepts *huda*,[34] which is the Arabic word for guidance, as in the following ayah from surah Al-Taghabun (Mutual Loss and Gain):

$$(\text{...وَمَن يُؤْمِن بِاللَّهِ يَهْدِ قَلْبَهُ}).$$

"...and whosoever believes in Allah, He guides his heart."　　　　　　　　　　　　　　　　　*(Qur'an 64:11)*

Third, the heart is the organ upon which Allah revealed the Holy Qur'an to His Holy Prophet. In surah Al-Shu'ara' (The Poets) and in reference to the Holy Qur'an, Allah addressed His Holy Messenger saying:

$$(\text{نَزَل بِهِ الرُّوحُ الْأَمِين . عَلَى قَلْبِكَ لِتَكُونَ مِنَ الْمُنْذِرِين}).$$

"With it came down the Truthful Spirit. Upon your heart that you may be (one) of the warners."
　　　　　　　　　　　　　　　　　　　　(Qur'an 26:193–194)

---

[34] هدى

Fourth, the heart is responsible for the development of taqwa and its influence in the believer's life. In the surah of Al-Hajj, Allah points to the heart's role in the issue of taqwa saying:

(ذَلِكَ ، وَمَن يُعَظِّمْ شَعَائِرَ اللَّهِ فَإِنَّهَا مِن تَقْوَى الْقُلُوبِ).

"Thus it is [what has been mentioned in the above said verses (27, 28, 29, 30, 31) is an obligation that mankind owes to Allah] and whosoever honours the symbols of Allah, then it is truly from the piety of the hearts."
(Qur'an 22:32)

Fifth, the heart is the organ that develops *ikhlass,*[35] meaning purity from shirk, which leads to the dedication of believers' all worship and deeds to only Allah. The status of eiman, ikhlass, and taqwa determines the person's position on the Day of Judgment. The following ayah, from surah Al-Shu'ara', indicates this significantly important fact. It says:

(يَوْمَ لَا يَنفَعُ مَالٌ وَلَا بَنُونَ . إِلَّا مَنْ أَتَى اللَّهَ بِقَلْبٍ سَلِيمٍ).

"The Day whereon neither wealth nor sons will avail. Except him who comes to Allah with a clean heart."
(Qur'an 26:88–89)

Al-Tabari (2010) argued that the word *saleem*[36] in this ayah means "free of shirk [meaning, it doesn't associate others with Allah], and it has no doubt concerning the issue of resurrection" (p. 598). Al-Shawkani (2012), in addition, reported Saeed ibn Al-Musayib to have said that the "saleem heart is the believer's one, for the disbelievers' and the hypocrites' hearts are sick" (p. 133). Also the heart is where people's intention (*niyyah*) originates; thus, it is responsible for the purification of deeds from shirk. So one of the principal characteristics of the "saleem" heart is its freedom from "shirk of intention" and "shirk of deeds."

---

[35] إخلاص
[36] سليم

Commenting on this ayah, Qutb (1992) stated that the heart's realization of the nature of the Day of Judgment leads to its freedom from whatever that leads to misery on that day (p 2604). It is narrated that the Holy Prophet—in reaction to the message in the previous ayah—used to pray Allah to offer him a saleem heart. He said:

"Oh Allah, [please] grant me a 'saleem' heart."[37]

Also the heart that this ayah refers to is predominantly concerned with and involved in the pleasure of its Creator. Such a heart is, actually, the true believer's whose salah, sacrifice, life, and death are but for Allah, the Lord of the worlds. This is a fact that Allah early commanded His Holy Messenger to announce. He said to him:

(قُلْ إِنَّ صَلَاتِي وَنُسُكِي وَمَحْيَايَ وَمَمَاتِي لِلَّهِ رَبِّ الْعَالَمِينَ).

"Say: 'Truly, my prayer and my service of sacrifice, my life and my death, are (all) for Allah, the Cherisher of the Worlds.'"   *(Qur'an 6:162)*

Sixth, it is the heart that originates *khair*[38] (goodness), and from it, this goodness reflects on the person's entire life, for the heart influences the human's mind, attitude, intentions, concerns, longings, aspirations, speech, and actions. Allah addressed His Holy Messenger concerning the men he held captives at the Battle of Badr saying:

(يَا أَيُّهَا النَّبِيُّ قُل لِّمَن فِي أَيْدِيكُم مِّنَ الْأَسْرَى إِن يَعْلَمِ اللَّهُ فِي قُلُوبِكُمْ خَيْراً يُؤْتِكُمْ خَيْراً مِّمَّا أُخِذَ مِنكُمْ وَيَغْفِرْ لَكُمْ ، وَاللَّهُ غَفُورٌ رَّحِيمٌ).

"O Prophet! Say to the captives that are in your hands: 'If Allah knows any good in your hearts, He will give you something better than what has been taken from you, and He will forgive you, and Allah is Oft-Forgiving, Most Merciful.'"   *(Qur'an 8:70)*

---

[37] "اللهم إني أسألك قلبا سليما."

[38] خير

Seventh, the heart is the organ that develops *thabat*,[39] meaning steadfastness and firmness of belief, which positively influence the believer's character, attitude, and behaviour. The heart that enjoys "thabat" remains strong, faithful, and obedient to Allah, even at extremely difficult times in which a believer experiences high levels of adversities.

To express their negative attitude towards the Islamic message and to cast doubt on the truthfulness of the Holy Qur'an, the Makkan disbelievers suspiciously asked, "Why hasn't Allah revealed the entire Holy Qur'an altogether?" So in response to this, Allah addressed His Holy Messenger saying:

$$ (... كَذَلِكَ لِنُثَبِّتَ بِهِ فُؤَادَكَ ...) $$

"...thus, that We may strengthen your heart thereby..."
(Qur'an 25:32)

Eighth, the heart is also responsible for the development of *ikhbat*, which is humbleness and complete submission to Allah. In reference to the heart's acceptance of the Holy Qur'an and submission to it, Allah says:

$$ (وَلِيَعْلَمَ الَّذِينَ أُوتُوا الْعِلْمَ أَنَّهُ الْحَقُّ مِن رَّبِّكَ فَيُؤْمِنُوا بِهِ فَتُخْبِتَ لَهُ قُلُوبُهُمْ ...) $$

"And that those who have been given knowledge may know that it (the Qur'an) is the truth from your Lord so that they may believe therein, and their hearts may submit to it with humility..." (Qur'an 22:54)

Ninth, the heart is the place where *tuma'neenah* develops and exists. Lexically, tuma'neenah refers to a feeling of utter security and peace. It occurs as a result of perfect belief in Allah and in the wisdom of His decrees and deeds, which, in fact, leads to perfect submission to Him. In addition, the heart that enjoys tuma'neenah is free from shirk and *nifaq*—it neither associates others with Allah nor does it develop any type of hypocrisy.

---

[39] ثبات

The Holy Qur'an has, more than once, indicated that tuma'neenah is the heart's work. In surah Al-Ra'd (The Thunder), for instance, Allah says:

(الَّذِينَ ءَامَنُواْ وَتَطْمَئِنُّ قُلُوبُهُم بِذِكْرِ اللَّهِ ، أَلاَ بِذِكْرِ اللَّهِ تَطْمَئِنُّ الْقُلُوبُ).

"Those who believed and whose hearts find rest in the remembrance of Allah. Verily, in the remembrance of Allah do hearts find rest." (Qur'an 13:28)

Al-Shawkani (2012) stated that the security of the heart mentioned in this ayah is a result of *thikr*—remembrance of Allah—with the tongue, such as making *tasbeeh, tahmeed, takbeer,* and *tawheed*[40] (p. 100).

Also in surah Al-Baqarah and in reference to Prophet Ibrahim, Allah says:

(وَإِذْ قَالَ إِبْرَاهِيمُ رَبِّ أَرِنِي كَيْفَ تُحْيِ الْمَوْتَى ، قَالَ أَوَلَمْ تُؤْمِن ، قَالَ بَلَى وَلَكِن لِّيَطْمَئِنَّ قَلْبِي...)

"And (remember) when Ibrahim said, 'My Lord! Show me how You give life to the dead.' He (Allah) said: 'Do you not believe?' He (Ibrahim) said: 'Yes, but so that my heart can be at peace...'" (Qur'an 2:260)

Tenth, the heart is the place of *sakeenah*,[41] which generally refers to tranquillity, calmness, and full security due to a high level of eiman, complete submission to Allah, and a strong belief in His wisdom. It seems that the heart experiences sakeenah as a result of tuma'neenah; that is, tuma'neenah occurs first then sakeenah follows it. Sakeenah is, actually, what Allah filled His Holy Prophet's heart with in one of the most dangerous experiences in his life. He was then sheltering himself in the Cave of Thawr, for he was hiding from the Makkan disbelievers who were standing at the cave's gate looking for him. In reference to this incident, Allah says:

[40] These are prescribed rituals concerning the glorification of Allah, giving thanks to Him, and acknowledging His Oneness.

سكينة [41]

(إِلاَّ تَنصُرُوهُ فَقَدْ نَصَرَهُ اللّهُ إِذْ أَخْرَجَهُ الَّذِينَ كَفَرُواْ ثَانِيَ اثْنَيْنِ إِذْ هُمَا فِي الْغَارِ

إِذْ يَقُولُ لِصَاحِبِهِ لاَ تَحْزَنْ إِنَّ اللّهَ مَعَنَا ، فَأَنزَلَ اللّهُ سَكِينَتَهُ عَلَيْهِ وَأَيَّدَهُ بِجُنُودٍ

لَّمْ تَرَوْهَا وَجَعَلَ كَلِمَةَ الَّذِينَ كَفَرُواْ السُّفْلَى ، وَكَلِمَةُ اللّهِ هِيَ الْعُلْيَا ، وَاللّهُ

عَزِيزٌ حَكِيمٌ).

> *"If you will not aid him, Allah certainly aided him when
> those who disbelieved expelled him, the second of the
> two; when they were both in the cave, when he said to
> his companion: 'Grieve not, surely Allah is with us.' So
> Allah sent down His tranquillity upon him and
> strengthened him with hosts which you did not see, and
> made lowest the word of those who disbelieved; and the
> word of Allah, that is the highest; and Allah is Mighty,
> Wise.'"*   *(Qur'an 9:40)*

Ibn Al-Qayyim (2005), interestingly, classified sakeenah into three
categories, and he claimed that the third one was what Allah sent
down into the Holy Prophet's and the believers' hearts (p. 408). Here
Ibn Al-Qayyim is referring to the following ayah from surah Al-Fath
(The Victory):

(...فَأَنْزَلَ اللّهُ سَكِينَتَهُ عَلَى رَسُولِهِ وَعَلَى الْمُؤْمِنِينَ وَأَلْزَمَهُمْ كَلِمَةَ التَّقْوَى).

> *"...then Allah sent down His Tranquillity upon His
> Messenger and upon the believers, and made them stick
> close to the word of piety."*   *(Qur'an 48:26)*

Eleventh, the heart is responsible for the origination and growth of
inabah,[42] which generally means devotion to Allah, love for Him, and
complete submission to Him. The following ayah from surah Qaf
indicates the heart's role in the issue of inabah. It says:

(مِنْ خَشِيَ الرَّحْمَنَ بِالْغَيْبِ وَجَاءَ بِقَلْبٍ مُنِيبٍ).

إنابة [42]

*"Who feared the Most Gracious in the unseen and
came with a heart turned in repentance."*

(Qur'an 50:33)

Scholars of the exegesis of the Holy Qur'an, such as Al-Tabari (2008),
argued that inabah refers to repentance and obedience to Allah (p.
329). Ibn Al-Qayyim, in addition, claimed that when the heart reaches
the inabah stage, it becomes occupied with the love for Allah, His
service, remembrance, and glorification (2005, p. 18). He also
mentioned that "inabah includes four factors: love for Allah,
submission to Him, distancing oneself from whatever He doesn't
allow, and engagement in deeds that please Him." Moreover, he
claimed that only those who enjoy these four qualities qualify for the
attribute of inabah (1996, pp. 231–232).

Twelfth, the heart is the organ where *khushua*[43] originates; then it,
subsequently, reflects on the believer's entire life. According to Al-
Samirraei (2012), "The heart's 'khushua'[44] refers to its submission [to
Allah], fear [of Him], humbleness [before Him], and glorification [of
Him]" (p. 121). Allah has indicated the heart's role in the issue of
khushua saying:

$$\text{(أَلَمْ يَأْنِ لِلَّذِينَ ءَامَنُواْ أَن تَخْشَعَ قُلُوبُهُمْ لِذِكْرِ اللَّهِ وَمَا نَزَلَ مِنَ الْحَقِّ...)؟}$$

*"Has not the time yet come for the believers that their
hearts should be humble for the remembrance of Allah
and that which has been revealed of the truth...?"*

(Qur'an 57:16)

Thirteenth, it is the heart that originates *tuhr*,[45] the Arabic word for
purity. When tuhr occurs in the heart, it extends to the brain, the soul,
the eyes, the ears, the tongue, and the whole body, until it colours the
entire believer's life. Allah, in surah Al-Ahzab, taught the Holy
Prophet's companions the discipline of addressing the Holy Prophet's
wives and explained to them that way was purer for their own hearts

---

[43] خشوع

[44] The issue of "khushua" will be discussed in more detail in chapter nine: "Lessons
of Taqwa from Luqman's Advice."

[45] طُهْر

and purer for the Holy Prophet's wives' hearts, too. With respect to this matter, Allah says:

$$ (...وَإِذَا سَأَلْتُمُوهُنَّ مَتَاعاً فَسْأَلُوهُنَّ مِن وَرَاءِ حِجَابٍ ، ذَلِكُمْ أَطْهَرُ لِقُلُوبِكم وقُلُوبِهِنَّ...) $$

> *"...and when you ask them (the Prophet's wives) for anything you want, ask them from behind a screen: that is purer for your hearts and for their hearts..."*
>
> *(Qur'an 33:53)*

Fourteenth, it is the heart that develops love and establishes harmony between individuals and community members. The Holy Qur'an refers to this harmony using the concept of *ilf*.[46] The two ayahs below, from the surahs of Al-Imran and Al-Anfal, exemplify this clearly.

In the former surah, Allah says:

$$ (وَاعْتَصِمُوا بِحَبْلِ اللَّهِ جَمِيعاً وَلَا تَفَرَّقُوا ، وَاذْكُرُوا نِعْمَتَ اللَّهِ عَلَيْكُمْ إِذْ كُنْتُمْ أَعْدَاءً فَأَلَّفَ بَيْنَ قُلُوبِكُمْ فَأَصْبَحْتُمْ بِنِعْمَتِهِ إِخْوَانًا وَكُنْتُمْ عَلَى شَفَا حُفْرَةٍ مِنَ النَّارِ فَأَنْقَذَكُمْ مِنْهَا ، كَذَلِكَ يُبَيِّنُ اللَّهُ لَكُمْ آيَاتِهِ لَعَلَّكُمْ تَهْتَدُونَ) . $$

> *"And hold fast, all of you together, to the Rope of Allah, and be not divided among yourselves, and remember Allah's favour on you, for you were enemies of one another but He joined your hearts together, so that, by His grace, you became brethren, and you were on the brink of a pit of the Fire, and He saved you from it. Thus Allah makes His revelations clear to you, that you may be guided."*   *(Qur'an 3:103)*

In the latter, He states:

$$ (وَأَلَّفَ بَيْنَ قُلُوبِهِمْ ، لَوْ أَنْفَقْتَ مَا فِي الْأَرْضِ جَمِيعاً مَّا أَلَّفْتَ بَيْنَ قُلُوبِهِمْ وَلَكِنَّ اللَّهَ أَلَّفَ بَيْنَهُمْ ، إِنَّهُ عَزِيزٌ حَكِيمٌ) . $$

---

[46] إلْف

"And united their hearts; had you spent all that is on the earth, you could not have united their hearts, but Allah united them; surely He is Mighty, Wise."

(Qur'an 8:63)

Fifteenth, fear of Allah represents a fundamental aspect of eiman and taqwa. Allah, in fact, has revealed a huge portion of the Holy Qur'an to help the human heart develop fear of Him, for fear of Him results in a lot of good in this life and, indeed, in the Hereafter. One form of fear of Allah that the heart may develop is *wajal*,[47] which according to different Arabic dictionaries denotes fear, strong fear, and even terror. It seems that wajal is a strong wave of fear that suddenly attacks the heart in response to a frightening stimulus, for example, a Qur'anic message that refers to or describes Allah's punishment. Al-Shawkani (2012) argued that one of the situations in which the heart may experience wajal is that when a believer is about to commit a sin, he becomes afraid if someone reminds him of Allah's punishment (p. 356). Also Al-Saadi argued that this type of fear deters those who experience it from the violations of Allah's rules (2011, p. 268).

So "wajal" isn't a goal per se; rather, it's a means, and its objective is the positive effects it creates in believers' lives. Precisely, it aids them to live today in a way that helps them avoid trouble on the Day of Judgment.

In surah Al-Anfal, for instance, Allah points to the heart as the organ that experiences wajal saying:

(إِنَّمَا الْمُؤْمِنُونَ الَّذِينَ إِذَا ذُكِرَ اللَّهُ وَجِلَتْ قُلُوبُهُمْ وَإِذَا تُلِيَتْ عَلَيْهِمْ ءَايَاتُهُ

زَادَتْهُمْ إِيمَانًا وَعَلَى رَبِّهِمْ يتوكلون).

"The believers are only those who, when Allah is mentioned, feel a fear in their hearts and when His revelations are recited unto them, they increase their faith; and they put their trust in their Lord."

(Qur'an 8:2)

---

[47] وجل

Also in surah Al-Hajj and in reference to the believers and their hearts'
fear of Him, Allah says:

$$\text{(الَّذِينَ إِذَا ذُكِرَ اللَّهُ وَجِلَتْ قُلُوبُهُمْ وَالصَّابِرِينَ عَلَى مَآ أَصَابَهُمْ وَالْمُقِيمِي}$$
$$\text{الصَّلَاةِ وَمِمَّا رَزَقْنَاهُمْ يُنفِقُونَ).}$$

"Those whose hearts tremble when Allah is mentioned,
and those who are patient under that which afflicts them,
and those who keep up prayer, and spend (benevolently)
out of what We have given them."

(Qur'an 22:35)

Finally, Allah's Holy Messenger has considered the heart an advisor
that believers should consult when they are suspicious about whether
the issues they are facing are Islamically permissible or not—*halal* or
haram. Imam Ahmed narrated that Wabisa Ibn Maabad reported that
he went to Allah's Holy Messenger who asked him:

"Have you come to ask about the *birr*?" I said, "Yes."
Then he said, "Consult your heart. Birr[48] is whatever the
soul and the heart identify with and, accordingly, you feel
secure. *Ithm* [sin], however, is whatever generates a state of
uncertainty and insecurity . . . ." (Ibn Al-Uthaymeen, 1431,
p. 496)

"جئت تسأل عن البرِّ ؟ قلت: نعم . فقال : استفت قلبك . البرُّ ما اطمأنَّت إليه
النَّفس واطمأنَّ اليه القلب، والإثم ما حاك في النَّفس وتردد في الصَّدر ، وإن أفتاك
النَّاس وأفتوك . "

But the heart that one may consult when there is confusion about the
lawfulness or the lack of it concerning specific issues is a special one:
the pious. In other words, not all Muslims can depend on what their
hearts may tell them in such circumstances. Scholars argued that
Allah's Holy Messenger counselled Wabisa to consult his own heart
because he sensed that Wabisa had an intelligent brain and a good

---

[48] According to Ibn Manthoor (2008), "Birr is honesty and obedience [to Allah and
His Messenger]." He also reported that scholars have different opinions about birr:
some argued it is righteousness; others claimed it is goodness" (p. 58).

heart. Most importantly, this hadith indicates the heart's significant role in believers' lives. It also substantiates a previously mentioned point that believers are under a strong obligation to wisely and earnestly cultivate their hearts so that they may earn wisdom that enables them to distinguish between right and wrong, especially when issues are confused and tangled.

According to A. Al-Ghazali (2004), the Holy Prophet said:

> "If Allah wants to do His servant a special favour, He makes his heart his own preacher." (p.16)

"إذا أراد الله بعبده خيراً ، جعل له واعظاً من قلبه."

The Heart's Negative Role

On the other hand, the heart can afflict humans with all the evils of misguidance—by being fertile soil on which many negative and harmful attributes develop. In this case, Allah's infinite and marvellous creation as well as His powerful speech and guidance in the Holy Qur'an will, unfortunately, have no effect on it. The worst harm that the heart may afflict a human with is, of course, the rejection of eiman and denial of Allah's messages.

First, surah Al-An'am shows the heart's role in the rejection of eiman. Here, Allah refers to the heart using the word sadr, He says:

(فَمَن يُرِدِ اللَّهُ أَن يَهْدِيَهُ يَشْرَحْ صَدْرَهُ لِلْإِسْلَامِ ، وَمَن يُرِدْ أَن يُضِلَّهُ يَجْعَلْ صَدْرَهُ ضَيِّقاً حَرَجاً كَأَنَّمَا يَصَّعَّدُ فِى السَّمَآءِ ، كَذَلِكَ يَجْعَلُ اللَّهُ الرِّجْسَ عَلَى الَّذِينَ لَا يُؤْمِنُونَ).

> *"And whomsoever Allah wills to guide, He opens his breast to Islam; and whomsoever He wills to send astray, He makes his heart closed and constricted, as if he is climbing up to the sky. Thus Allah puts the wrath on those who believe not."*   *(Qur'an 6:125)*

With respect to the negative attitude that some people's hearts develop towards Islam, which is mentioned in the above ayah, Al-

Saadi (2010) said that such people are involved in evil deeds and worldly desires in a way that disables their hearts from accepting righteousness (p. 226). The surah of Al-Kahf (The Cave) highlights the same issue. Allah, in this surah, explains that due to the disbelievers' negative attitude towards His message, He shields their hearts—as a punishment—so that the light of His guidance will not enter them. He says:

(وَمَنْ أَظْلَمُ مِمَّنْ ذُكِّرَ بِآيَاتِ رَبِّهِ فَأَعْرَضَ عَنْهَا وَنَسِيَ مَا قَدَّمَتْ يَدَاهُ ، إِنَّا جَعَلْنَا عَلَىٰ قُلُوبِهِمْ أَكِنَّةً أَنْ يَفْقَهُوهُ وَفِي آذَانِهِمْ وَقْرًا ، وَإِنْ تَدْعُهُمْ إِلَى الْهُدَىٰ فَلَنْ يَهْتَدُوا إِذًا أَبَدًا).

"And who does more wrong than the one who is reminded of the Signs of his Lord, but turns away from them, forgetting the (deeds) which his hands have sent forth. Verily, We have set veils over their hearts lest they should understand this, and over their ears, deafness, if you call them to guidance, even then will they never accept guidance."   *(Qur'an 18: 57)*

Also the surah of Al-Mutaffifeen (The Dealers in Fraud) sheds light on the heart's role in the same issue, but from a different angle. It declares:

(كَلَّا ، بَلْ رَانَ عَلَى قُلُوبِهِم مَّا كَانُوا يَكْسِبُون).

"Nay! Rather, what they used to do has become like rust upon their hearts."   *(Qur'an 83:14)*

According to Ibn Al-Qayyim (1997), "*rayn*[49] refers to [figuratively speaking] a cover that prevents the heart from seeing the right things" (p. 110). Based on what exegetes of the Holy Qur'an say about this issue, it seems that disbelievers' hearts, again—figuratively speaking— are covered with a rust-like substance, which signifies the accumulation of sins around their surfaces. Thus, these poor hearts become shielded in a way that prevents the Holy Qur'an's light from entering them.

---

[49] رَيْن

Second, the heart is held responsible for people's blindness and failure to learn lessons of *ibrah* (instructive admonition) from the awful, exterminatory punishment of previous disbelieving communities. In reference to the Makkan disbelievers and their failure to learn such lessons, Allah—in a condemning tone—says:

(أَفَلَمْ يَسِيرُوا فِي الأَرْضِ فَتَكُونَ لَهُمْ قُلُوبٌ يَعْقِلُونَ بِهَا أَوْ ءَاذَانٌ يَسْمَعُونَ بِهَا، فَإِنَّهَا لاَ تَعْمَى الأَبْصَارُ وَلَكِن تَعْمَى الْقُلُوبُ الَّتِي فِي الصُّدُورِ). [50]

"Have they not travelled through the land, and have they hearts wherewith to understand and ears wherewith to hear? Verily, it is not the eyes that grow blind, but it is the hearts which are in the breasts that grow blind!"

(Qur'an 22:46)

In addition to its usage to refer to the heart, the Arabic word "qalb" can also be used to refer to the brain (Manthoor, 2008, p. 169). Accordingly, the first usage of the word "quloob"—the plural form of qalb—in the above ayah refers to the brain because it is associated with understanding and reasoning. Also according to Ibn Kathir (2014), in this ayah, Allah condemns these disbelievers' brains for failing to realize that the only reason behind the obliteration of previous communities was their disbelief (p. 438).

The second usage of the word "quloob" in this ayah, however, refers to the heart itself, for Allah provides a distinction between its meaning in this case and its meaning in the first one. More precisely, He follows its second usage with the restrictive clause *"which are in the chests"*

---

[50] Khalidi (2008) has translated the first "quloob" in this ayah as "minds." His full translation of the ayah is the following: *"Have they not journeyed in the land, and had minds to apprehend with, or ears to listen with? It is not their eyes that are blind; rather, it is the hearts in their breasts"* (p. 270). However, A. Y. Ali, Abdel Haleem, Ali, A., Asad, Hilali and Khan, as well as Pickthall have translated this word as "hearts." For example, A., Ahmed's translation of the whole ayah is this: "Have they not travelled in the land that they could have the hearts to understand, and ears to hear? It is not the eyes alone that do not see, oblivious are the hearts within their breasts" (1993, p. 287).

to indicate that He is referring to the heart, not to the brain. So here He projects the heart as guilty as nothing else could be!

In reference to the heart's negative role in human life, A. Y. Ali (2008) stated the following:

> The word for heart in Arabic speech imports both the seat of intelligent faculties and understanding as well as the seat of affections and emotions. Those who reject God's Message may have their physical eyes and ears, but their hearts are blind and deaf. If their faculties of understanding were active, would they not see the signs of God's providence and God's wrath in nature around them and in the cities and ruins if they travel intelligently? (p. 863)

Al-Qurtubi, in addition, cited Mujahid to have said:

> Every person has four eyes: two on his head to help him with his worldly affairs and two in his heart to help him with his affairs in the Hereafter. If his head's eyes are blind and his heart's eyes are able to see, he will have no problem on the Day of Judgment. However, if his head's eyes are able to see and his heart's eyes aren't, then he is in trouble. (2014, p 234)

Third, sometimes Allah mentions the heart's blindness in association with disbelievers' bad ends. In such a context, He explains that He punished them because their hearts had failed to do their work. Examine the following ayah from surah Al-Ahqaf (The Curved Sand-hills):

(وَلَقَدْ مَكَّنَّاهُمْ فِيمَا إِن مَّكَّنَّاكُمْ فِيهِ وَجَعَلْنَا لَهُمْ سَمْعاً وَأَبْصَاراً وَأَفْئِدَةً فَمَا أَغْنَى عَنْهُمْ سَمْعُهُمْ وَلاَ أَبْصَارُهُمْ وَلاَ أَفْئِدَتُهُم مِّن شَيْءٍ إِذْ كَانُواْ يَجْحَدُونَ بِآيَاتِ اللَّهِ وَحَاقَ بِهِم مَّا كَانُواْ بِهِ يَسْتَهْزِءُونَ).[51]

---

[51] Scholars of the exegesis of the Holy Qur'an interpreted the word *af'idah* in this ayah differently. Some, such as Al-Saadi and Ibn Ashoor, claimed it refers to the brain (2011, p. 726; 1994, p. 53). Al-Qurtubi, however, argued it refers to the heart (2014, p. 380). Translators of the Holy Qur'an—specifically, Abdel Haleem, A., Ahmed, Asad, Hilali and Khan, Khalidi, and Pickthall translated this word as

"And indeed We had firmly established them with that wherewith We have not established you! We also gave them hearing, vision, and hearts. But their hearing, vision, and hearts availed them nothing since they used to deny the signs of Allah, and they were completely encircled by that which they used to ridicule."

(Qur'an 46:26)

Such hearts are said to have solidified[52] because of their denial of Allah's signs. In surah Al-Baqarah, Allah harshly attacks the hearts of the Jews who were contemporary with Prophet Musa, and He stigmatizes them with the fact that their hearts became harder than stones. He declares:

$$\text{(ثُمَّ قَسَتْ قُلُوبُكُم مِّن بَعْدِ ذَلِكَ فَهِيَ كَالْحِجَارَةِ أَوْ أَشَدُّ قَسْوَةً، وَإِنَّ مِنَ الْحِجَارَةِ}$$
$$\text{لَمَا يَتَفَجَّرُ مِنْهُ الْأَنْهَارُ ، وَإِنَّ مِنْهَا لَمَا يَشَّقَّقُ فَيَخْرُجُ مِنْهُ الْمَاءُ ، وَإِنَّ مِنْهَا}$$
$$\text{لَمَا يَهْبِطُ مِنْ خَشْيَةِ اللَّهِ...)}$$

"Then after that your hearts were hardened and became as stones or even worse in hardness. And indeed, there are stones out of which rivers gush forth, and indeed, there are of them (stones) which split asunder so that water flows from them, and indeed, there are of them (stones) which fall down from fear of Allah..."

(Qur'an 2:74)

The idea of comparing a human heart to a stone is humiliating, indeed. In the above ayah, Allah begins His attack on these people by comparing their hearts to rocks. He says:

$$\text{(ثُمَّ قَسَتْ قُلُوبُكُم مِّن بَعْدِ ذَلِكَ فَهِيَ كَالْحِجَارَةِ...)}!$$

"heart." Asad added—in a footnote—that it refers to "intellect and feeling, both of which are comprised in the noun *fu'ad*" (2012, 879). And A. Y. Ali interpreted it as "heart and intellect."

[52]According to Ibn Al-Qayyim, "The furthest heart from Allah is the rigid one" (2005, p. 99).

"Then after that your hearts were hardened and became as stones...!"

Then He goes on to explain that these people's hearts were even harder than rocks! He states:

(...أَوْ أَشَدُّ قَسْوَةً...)!

"...or even worse in hardness...!"

But this comparison becomes even more humiliating when Allah declares that some rocks are, actually, softer than these people's hearts. Here He draws the addressee's attention to a natural phenomenon that reflects the potential goodness in such rocks, compared to the hardness that characterizes these people's hearts. He says:

(...وَإِنَّ مِنَ الْحِجَارَةِ لَمَا يَتَفَجَّرُ مِنْهُ الْأَنْهَارُ ، وَإِنَّ مِنْهَا لَمَا يَشَّقَّقُ فَيَخْرُجُ
مِنْهُ الْمَاءُ...)

"...and indeed, there are stones out of which rivers gush forth, and indeed, there are of them (stones) which split asunder so that water flows from them..."

The Arabic verb *yatafajjar*[53] in this context indicates that the water coming out of these rocks is plenty and considerably strong in flow. In addition to being a major support for life, water is the source of every living thing, according to the Creator Himself;[54] this, of course, emphasizes the goodness in these stones. What is more, the comparison between these stones and these people's hearts raises to another even higher level of humiliation when Allah declares—emphatically—that some stones fall down in prostration to Him due to the extreme level of fear and awe they experience as a result of their realization of His Majesty. In this regard, He states:

---

[53] يَتَفَجَّر

[54] (وَجَعَلْنَا مِنَ الْمَاءِ كُلَّ شَيْءٍ حَيٍّ).

"We made from water every living thing."   *(Qur'an 21:30)*

(...وَإِنَّ مِنْهَا لَمَا يَهْبِطُ مِنْ خَشْيَةِ اللَّهِ...)!

"...and indeed, there are of them (stones) which fall down from fear of Allah...!"

Fourth, the heart is the organ that originates or commits sins. The following ayah, from surah Al-Baqarah, demonstrates the heart's role in the origination of sins. Addressing believers of all times, Allah says:

(...وَلاَ تَكْتُمُواْ الشَّهَادَةَ ، وَمَن يَكْتُمْهَا فَإِنَّهُ آثِمٌ قَلْبُهُ ، وَاللّهُ بِمَا تَعْمَلُونَ عَلِيمٌ).

"...and do not conceal testimony, and whoever conceals it, his heart is surely sinful; and Allah knows what you do." (Qur'an 2:283)

According to Al-Shawkani (2012), in this ayah, Allah has confined the concealment of testimony to the heart—not to any other human organ—because it is the master of all the other organs. When it is righteous, the entire body becomes righteous; and when it is evil, however, the whole body shapes itself to match it (p. 384).

Fifth, it is the heart that gets afflicted with *zaygh*,[55] which is, according to Al-Qurtubi, misguidance or deviation from Allah's path (2014, p. 250). People who have hearts afflicted with zaygh become not only distracted from Allah's guidance but also indifferent to it and unaware of their loss. As a punishment for the nasty attitude of some of Prophet Musa's people, Allah diverted their hearts from His guidance.

In surah Al-Saff and with regard to this issue, He declares:

(وَإِذْ قَالَ مُوسَىٰ لِقَوْمِهِ يَا قَوْمِ لِمَ تُؤْذُونَنِي وَقَدْ تَعْلَمُونَ أَنِّي رَسُولُ اللَّهِ إِلَيْكُمْ ، فَلَمَّا زَاغُوا أَزَاغَ اللَّهُ قُلُوبَهُمْ ، وَاللَّهُ لَا يَهْدِي الْقَوْمَ الْفَاسِقِينَ).

"And when Musa said to his people: 'O my people! Why do you annoy me while you know certainly that I am the messenger of Allah to you?' So, when they turned away

(from the path of Allah), Allah turned their hearts away (from the right path). And Allah guides not the people who are rebellious."   *(Qur'an 61:5)*

According to Al-Qurtubi (2014), this ayah shows that when these people diverted from the right path, Allah diverted their hearts from His guidance (p. 250). Fearing such a reaction from Allah, the knowledgeable believers humbly and frequently pray Him not to afflict their hearts with zaygh or lead them astray. They say:

(رَبَّنَا لاَ تُزِغْ قُلُوبَنَا بَعْدَ إِذْ هَدَيْتَنَا وَهَبْ لَنَا مِن لَّدُنكَ رَحْمَةً، إِنَّكَ أَنتَ الْوَهَّابُ).

"Our Lord! Let not our hearts deviate now after You have guided us, but grant us mercy from Your own Presence; for You are the Grantor of bounties without measure."   *(Qur'an 3:8)*

Another ayah that shows the heart's association with the issue of zaygh is this one from surah Al-Tawbah:

(لَّقَد تَّابَ الله عَلَى النَّبِيِّ وَالْمُهَاجِرِينَ وَالأَنصَارِ الَّذِينَ اتَّبَعُوهُ فِي سَاعَةِ الْعُسْرَةِ مِن بَعْد مَا كَادَ يَزِيغُ قُلُوبُ فَرِيقٍ مِّنْهُمْ ثُمَّ تَابَ عَلَيْهِمْ ، إِنَّهُ بِهِمْ رَؤُوفٌ رَّحِيمٌ).

"Certainly, Allah has turned (mercifully) to the Prophet and those who fled (their homes) and the helpers who followed him in the hour of straightness after the hearts of a part of them were about to deviate, then He turned to them (mercifully); surely to them He is Compassionate, Merciful."   *(Qur'an 9:117)*

Sixth, it is the heart that develops *nifaq*,[56] which is, as previously mentioned, the Arabic word for hypocrisy. The Qur'an includes many ayahs that point to this awful disease that afflicts the human heart. In surah Al-Tawbah (The Repentance) and in reference to Al-Madinah's hypocrites, Allah says:

---

[56] نفاق

(فَأَعْقَبَهُمْ نِفَاقاً فِي قُلُوبِهِمْ إِلَى يَوْمِ يَلْقَوْنَهُ بِمَا أَخْلَفُواْ اللَّهَ مَا وَعَدُوهُ وَبِمَا كَانُواْ يَكْذِبُون).

"So He punished them by putting hypocrisy into their hearts till the Day whereon they shall meet Him, because they broke that (covenant) with Allah which they had promised to Him and because they used to tell lies."

(Qur'an 9:77)

Occasionally, however, Allah refers to nifaq using the Arabic word *maradh*,[57] which literally means disease. Examine the following ayah, from surah Al-Imran, in which He refers to the hypocrites of Al-Madinah, too:

(فِي قُلُوبِهِم مَّرَضٌ فَزَادَهُمُ اللَّهُ مَرَضًا ، وَلَهُمْ عَذَابٌ أَلِيمٌ بِمَا كَانُواْ يَكْذِبُونَ).

"In their hearts is a disease (of doubt and hypocrisy) and Allah has increased their disease. A painful torment is theirs because they used to tell lies."

(Qur'an 2:10)

Seventh, the heart is the place of *khubth*,[58] which is wickedness, internal dirtiness, and evilness; it develops as a result of disbelief and hypocrisy. Like cancer, this filthiness of the heart extends to afflict the brain, the soul, the eyes, the ears, and the tongue. In such a situation, "khubth" reflects on filthy thinking, speech, concerns, longings, dreams, and actions. Further, Allah deprives such hearts of purification, as a result of countless evil attributes they harbour. The following ayah from surah Al-Ma'idah reveals this fact. It proclaims:

(... أُوْلَئِكَ الَّذِينَ لَمْ يُرِدِ اللَّهُ أَن يُطَهِّرَ قُلُوبَهُمْ، لَهُمْ فِى الدُّنْيَا خِزْىٌ، وَلَهُمْ فِي الآخِرَةِ عَذَابٌ عَظِيمٌ).

"Those are the ones whose hearts Allah does not want to

---

[57] مرض

[58] خُبْث

purify (from disbelief and hypocrisy); for them there is a disgrace in this world, and in the Hereafter a great torment."   (Qur'an 5:41)

Eighth, it is the heart that develops an excessive aversion to the belief in Allah's oneness. According to the scholars of the exegesis of the Qur'an, when the Makkan disbelievers saw the believers worship Allah alone and when these believers advised them to believe in the oneness of Allah, their hearts became scandalized (Al-Qurtubi, 2014, p. 173; Al-Saadi, 2011, p. 668).

Allah points to this issue in the surah of Al-Zumar using the concept of *ishmi'zaz*, which literally means disgust or extreme dislike. He says:

(وَإِذَا ذُكِرَ اللَّهُ وَحْدَهُ اشْمَأَزَّتْ قُلُوبُ الَّذِينَ لَا يُؤْمِنُونَ بِالْآخِرَةِ...)

"And when Allah Alone is mentioned, the hearts of those who believe not in the Hereafter are scandalized..."   (Qur'an 39:45)

Scholars, such as Ibn Kathir, argued that this ayah demonstrates the disbelievers' strong aversion to *tawheed*[59]—belief in Allah's oneness. They abhor even thinking about it, and they hate deserting their idols and worshiping Allah only.

Ninth, it is the heart that develops doubt about the truthfulness of the Holy Qur'an and about the Holy Messenger's prophethood. Allah reveals this fact about the heart in surah Al -Tawbah. He declares:

(إِنَّمَا يَسْتَأْذِنُكَ الَّذِينَ لاَ يُؤْمِنُونَ بِاللَّهِ وَالْيَوْمِ الآخِرِ وَارْتَابَتْ قُلُوبُهُمْ فَهُمْ فِي رَيْبِهِمْ يَتَرَدَّدُونَ).

"It is only those who believe not in Allah and the Last Day and whose hearts are in doubt that ask your leave (to be exempted from jihad). So in their doubts they waver."   (Qur'an 9:45)

---

[59] See Al-Saadi (2011, p. 668) and Ibn Kathir (2014, p. 180) .

Analogically, the heart's reaction to the Holy Qur'an resembles that of the soil to the rain. Some types of soil are fertile; as a result, they grow different kinds of vegetation in response to any amount of rainfall. Other types of soil, however, are solid and infertile—they grow almost nothing, no matter how much rain falls on them! When the heart reacts to the Holy Qur'an in this negative manner, such a reaction is called *juhood*, meaning denial and ingratitude.

Allah employs the root of this word, which is *j-h-d*,[60] in association with disbelievers' negative attitude towards Him and His message. In surah Al-Ahqaf, for example, He states:

(وَلَقَدْ مَكَّنَّاهُمْ فِيمَا إِن مَّكَّنَّاكُمْ فِيهِ وَجَعَلْنَا لَهُمْ سَمْعاً وَأَبْصَاراً وَأَفْئِدَةً فَمَا أَغْنَى عَنْهُمْ سَمْعُهُمْ وَلاَ أَبْصَارُهُمْ وَلاَ أَفْئِدَتُهُم مِّن شَيْءٍ إِذْ كَانُواْ يَجْحَدُونَ بِآيَاتِ اللَّهِ وَحَاقَ بِهِم مَّا كَانُواْ بِهِ يَسْتَهْزِؤُونَ).

"And indeed We had firmly established them with that wherewith We have not established you. We also gave them hearing, vision, and hearts. But their hearing, vision, and hearts availed them nothing since they used to deny the signs of Allah, and they were completely encircled by that which they used to ridicule."

(Qur'an 46:26)

He also confirms that it is this negative attribute that has rendered these people to dwell permanently in Hellfire. In surah Fussilat (Made Distinct) and in reference to this issue, He proclaims:

(ذَلِكَ جَزَاءُ أَعْدَاءِ اللَّهِ النَّارُ ، لَهُمْ فِيهَا دَارُ الْخُلْدِ ، جَزَاءً بِمَا كَانُوا بِآيَاتِنَا يَجْحَدُونَ).

"That is the recompense of the enemies of Allah: the Fire. Therein will be for them the eternal home, a recompense for that they used to deny Our signs."

(Qur'an 41:28)

---

[60] جحد

Some people confine their hearts' work to the mechanical function: pumping blood throughout their bodies. Such hearts, unfortunately, aren't better than the animals', for animals' hearts function in the same manner. It is also astonishing that disbelievers' hearts, regardless of their environments and times, react to Allah's messages and His miraculous universal signs in the same blind manner. Allah highlights this fact about disbelievers' hearts in the following ayah, from surah Al-Baqarah saying:

(وَقَالَ الَّذِينَ لاَ يَعْلَمُونَ لَوْلاَ يُكَلِّمُنَا اللَّهُ أَوْ تَأْتِينَآ ءَايَةٌ ، كَذَلِكَ قَالَ الَّذِينَ مِن قَبْلِهِم مِّثْلَ قَوْلِهِم ، تَشَابَهَتْ قُلُوبُهُم، قَدْ بَيَّنَّا الآيَاتِ لِقَوْمٍ يُوقِنُونَ).

"And those who have no knowledge say: 'Why does not Allah speak to us (face to face) or why does not a sign come to us?' So said those before them words of similar import. Their hearts are alike, We have indeed made plain the signs for people who believe with certainty."
(Qur'an 2:118)

Evidently, disbelievers' hearts are similar not only on a community level but also on an individual's. Prophet Noah's son, for instance, saw Allah's irresistible punishment had already started, yet when his father advised him to join the believers on board the Ark, he refused—arguing that he would find safe refuge on the top of a mountain. This dialogue, surprisingly enough, took place while the Ark was sailing on waves like mountains in height!

With respect to this and in reference to the Ark, Allah says:

(وَهِيَ تَجْرِي بِهِمْ فِي مَوْجٍ كَالْجِبَالِ وَنَادَى نُوحٌ ابْنَهُ وَكَانَ فِي مَعْزِلٍ يَا بُنَيَّ ارْكَب مَّعَنَا وَلاَ تَكُن مَّعَ الْكَافِرِينَ . قَالَ سَآوِى إِلَى جَبَلٍ يَعْصِمُنِي مِنَ الْمَآءِ)!

"So it (the ship) sailed with them amidst waves like mountains, and Noah called out to his son, who had separated himself (apart)): O my son! Embark with us and be not with the disbelievers. The son replied: 'I

*will betake myself to some mountain, it will save me
from the water!'"*   *(Qur'an 11:42—43)*

Pharaoh did the same: He saw the Red Sea had already split into two
halves when Prophet Musa hit it with his stick, yet he kept chasing
him!

Finally, the heart is the organ where *hasrah*[61] originates. According to
Ibn Manthoor (2008), hasrah refers to "the highest level of sorrow
that makes a person who experiences it like a *haseer* animal [such as a
horse] that has no benefit [because it can't move anymore]" (p. 116).
In other words, a person who experiences hasrah has no hope—
whatsoever!—to get out of the ugly situation he or she incurs.
Likewise, on the Day of Judgment, disbelievers' hearts will overflow
with this extremely painful sense of sorrow and despair, as a result of
facing their miserable destiny and their realization that they can do
nothing to avoid it.

This awful psychological feeling, in fact, represents a major ingredient
in the torment that these poor people will incur perpetually in the
Hereafter, again, as a result of their realization that it is too late to do
anything to avoid Hellfire.[62] In this regard, Allah says:

(وَقَالَ الَّذِينَ اتَّبَعُواْ لَوْ أَنَّ لَنَا كَرَّةً فَنَتَبَرَّأَ مِنْهُمْ كَمَا تَبَرَّؤُواْ مِنَّا ، كَذَلِكَ يُرِيهِمُ اللّـهُ أَعْمَالَهُمْ حَسَرَاتٍ عَلَيْهِمْ ، وَمَا هُم بِخَارِجِينَ مِنَ النَّارِ).

---

61 حسرة

62 Also in surah Mariam and in reference to the disbelievers' extremely terrible
destiny, Allah calls the Day of Judgment *"yawmu al hassrah,"* meaning the day of
extreme regret, grief, and hopelessness. He says:

(وَأَنذِرْهُمْ يَوْمَ الْحَسْرَةِ إِذْ قُضِيَ الْأَمْرُ وَهُمْ فِي غَفْلَةٍ وَهُمْ لَا يُؤْمِنُونَ).

*"And warn them of the Day of Regret, when the matter shall have
been decided; and they are (now) in negligence and they do not
believe."*   *(Qur'an 19:39)*

"And those who followed would say: 'If only We had one more chance, we would clear ourselves of them, as they have cleared themselves of us.' Thus will Allah show them (the fruits of) their deeds as (nothing but) regrets. Nor will they leave the Fire."   *(Qur'an 2:167)*

That is a brief discussion of the heart's positive and negative roles in people's life today and in their destiny on the Day of Judgment. As mentioned earlier, knowing the positive and the negative attributes that the heart can develop and adopt is important to believers, for it motivates them to cultivate their hearts in a way that helps them develop the positive attributes and prevent the growth of the negative ones. People, of course, do not come to this life with either good or bad hearts. The types of hearts they have are, of course, their own products—resulting from different factors, most of which are under their full control.

Ibn Al-Qayyim (2005) reported Ibn Mas'ud to have said:

"Check your heart in three situations: when you're listening to the Holy Qur'an, at the gathering of *thikr* (remembrances and glorification of Allah), and when you are alone. If you don't find it in these situations, then ask Allah to give you a heart, for you don't have one!" (p. 145)

"اطلب قلبك في ثلاثة مواطن: عند سماع القرآن، وفي مجالس الذكر، وفي أقات الخلوة،
فإن لم تجده في هذه المواطن، فسأل الله أن يمن عليك بقلب فإنه لا قلب لك."

The Heart's Role in Reflection

The brain's vital role in reflection is merely intellectual, and it is confined to the study, analysis, evaluation, and conclusion concerning specific phenomena, data, and events. The heart's role in this issue, however, is psycho-spiritual; that is, it translates the brain's intellectual work into different psychological feelings fundamental to the question of eiman and taqwa. If the heart fails to carry out its role in the early stages of reflection, the brain will also stop its work on this matter. And when this occurs—which is usually the case, unfortunately—it dramatically affects the quality of eiman and taqwa, for the quality of these two issues depends considerably on the quality of the heart's work on the information it receives from the brain in the early stages of reflection.

Analogically, the brain's and the heart's roles in the issue of reflection are similar to that of a camera and a film in photography. While the camera identifies the object to be photographed and allows control over the amount of the light needed, the film receives and keeps the image of the target object. Similarly, the process of reflection requires the heart to be available to the brain so that the latter can send it important messages. When this occurs, it can be said that the brain and the heart have started a dialogue in which the brain studies, analyses, evaluates, concludes, and sends messages to the heart. The heart, as mentioned earlier, translates the information in these messages into different psychological reactions that are crucial to the issues of eiman, taqwa, and worship.

Gradually, the heart becomes considerably affected by the brain's messages; accordingly, it develops more interest in the latter's work. The brain, as a result, becomes more motivated to coordinate, cooperate, and collaborate with the heart. In other words, both organs become more interested and more involved in each other's work. This improves their coordination, cooperation, and collaboration—an issue that enhances the quality of each one's work. All of this, in turn, improves the quality of reflection and its outcomes.

At an advanced stage, the heart's interest in the brain's work intensifies, so it starts to send frequent messages to the brain asking it to ponder over certain issues—Qur'anic messages, universal phenomena, ideas, events, or whatever it is interested in. The heart, for instance, may ask the brain to re-examine the same previous issues or objects again and again because it hasn't received the quality of impact it expects yet, or because it enjoys the effects of reflection on those particular issues or objects and wants to experience them again.

As a result of the repetition of this process, the heart gradually becomes in charge of the brain's activities. The relationship between the brain and the heart in this advanced phase of reflection resembles that between a ship and a captain, where the brain represents the ship, and the heart represents the captain. Eventually, the brain modifies itself in a way that enables it to handle all the demands of its master: the heart. At this very advanced stage of reflection, the brain and the heart become identical. This, though incredibly rare, may finally lead to the development of the ideal believer's mentality, psychology, and attitude that lead to the ideal believer's character and behaviour.

CHAPTER 4

The Psychology of Taqwa

People experience various psychological feelings as a result of different factors and experiences. These feelings, as indicated earlier, can be pleasant or unpleasant. Knowing the influence of such feelings on human behaviour and on behaviour modification, Allah has dedicated a huge portion of the Qur'an to excite them in the heart so that they help in the generation of the desired human response to both the Qur'anic messages and countless universal ones.[63]

The Element of Worry

Allah has revealed many Qur'anic messages that have strong power to make people worry about their destinies on the Day of Judgment. The objective of this is to help them develop taqwa, the key to a decent life today and the gate to Allah's Gardens of bliss. The following ayah, from the surah of Luqman, represents an example of the Qur'anic

---

[63] The expression "universal messages" in this context refers to all Allah's creation on earth and in the heavens through which He communicates to the human brain and heart countless, invaluable messages about Himself. He also recurrently recommends, in the Holy Qur'an, that humans reflect on His creation because if they do, they will not only believe in His existence and oneness, but they will also love Him. Early in surah Yunus and in reference to the significance of reflection, Allah, for example, says:

(إِنَّ فِي اخْتِلَافِ الَّيْلِ وَالنَّهَارِ وَمَا خَلَقَ اللَّهُ فِي السَّمَاوَاتِ وَالْأَرْضِ لَآيَاتٍ لِقَوْمٍ يَتَّقُونَ).

"Verily, in the alternation of the night and the day, and in all that Allah has created, in the heavens and the earth, are signs for those who fear Him."
(Qur'an 10:6)

speech that helps in the development of taqwa through the generation of worry. Highlighting humans' ignorance about their own future, Allah says:

$$\text{(وَمَا تَدْرِى نَفْسٌ مَّاذَا تَكْسِبُ غَداً)!}$$

"And no soul knows what it will earn tomorrow!"
(Qur'an 31:34)

The concept of "earning" in this ayah, according to the scholars of the Qur'anic exegesis, refers to future positive and negative things that people may do. It also refers to things that may happen to them. One inevitable event in every person's life is death. For conscientious believers, the way they end their lives is extremely important; therefore, it constitutes a major source of concern for them. More specifically, they want to make sure they will exit this life as good Muslims. So the message in this ayah can be extremely annoying to them. Such a reaction sharpens their sense of religiosity and makes them more obedient to Allah and more vigilant not to fall into the Satan's trap, even for a second, for—who knows?—that second might be the last in their lives.

Another ayah that has high potential for raising believers' level of taqwa through the excitation of worry in their hearts is this one, from surah Al-Baqarah, in which Allah warns saying:

$$\text{(وَلَنَبْلُوَنَّكُم بِشَيْءٍ مِّنَ الْخَوْفْ وَالْجُوعِ وَنَقْصٍ مِّنَ الْأَمْوَالِ وَالْأَنفُسِ وَالثَّمَرَاتِ ،}$$
$$\text{وَبَشِّرِ الصَّابِرِينَ).}$$

"And certainly, We shall test you with some fear, hunger, loss of wealth, lives and fruits, but give glad tidings to the patient."   (Qur'an 2:155)

In this ayah, the element of inevitable affliction in the future is more specific than that in the previous one, from surah Luqman. Here Allah warns that He will definitely test believers with five hard tests: fear, hunger, death (e.g., of family members, relatives, friends, etc.), a decrease in wealth, and a decrease in fruits. Grammatically speaking, this ayah has a strong emphatic tone, for Allah uses two Arabic grammatical devices to establish emphasis: the *lam* and the *noon* in the second word, which is, actually, a whole sentence—containing a subject, a verb, and an object. This strong emphatic tone functions in, at least, two ways. First, it suggests that the element of testing with these adversities is unavoidable. Second, it intensifies the potential feeling of insecurity in believers' hearts. Conscientious believers, as a result, are expected to become more motivated to hold firmly to the rope of Allah in order to protect themselves from being pushed far from His path by the strong, harsh waves of one or more of these testing adversities.

Believers' ideal reaction to the message in this ayah should be a strong determination to successfully handle all forms of hardship they may encounter, yet they won't be able to accomplish this unless they equip themselves with a substantially high level of taqwa. That is, when the level of taqwa is high enough, the effect of such adversities will be lightened. When the level of taqwa is low or when there is no taqwa at all, however, the consequences of these adversities will be regrettable. In the absence of taqwa, to be more specific, affliction with hardship may have serious, negative outcomes that can badly affect believers' Islamic identity today and their destiny on the Day of Judgment. Some people, for instance, may quit praying, start drinking alcohol, engage in taking drugs, or involve themselves in forbidden activities, just to forget or—even worse—to express their objection to Allah's decrees.

Also early in surah Al-Ankabut (The Spider), Allah reiterates His determination of testing believers with adversities. He says:

(أَحَسِبَ النَّاسُ أَن يُتْرَكُوا أَن يَقُولُوا آمَنَّا وَهُمْ لَا يُفْتَنُونَ . وَلَقَدْ فَتَنَّا الَّذِينَ مِن قَبْلِهِمْ فَلَيَعْلَمَنَّ اللَّهُ الَّذِينَ صَدَقُوا وَلَيَعْلَمَنَّ الْكَاذِبِينَ).

> *"Do people think that they will be left alone because they say: 'We believe' and they will not be tested? We indeed tested those who were before them so that Allah will know those who are true, and He will know those who are liars."* (Qur'an 29:2—3)

The message in these two ayahs reassures believers that their affliction with adversity tests is inevitable. This assurance is obvious in both the question form and the disapproving tone in the first ayah. The certainty of exposure to hardship and sufferings is also clear in the emphatic, informative statement in the second ayah. But, according to scholars, the level of testing matches the level of eiman: the stronger the eiman, the harder the test, and vice versa.

Imam Ahmed narrated that the Holy Prophet said:

> "Verily, those who suffered the most were Allah's Messengers, then those next to them, then those next to them [in rank with Allah]."[64]

The Element of Sorrow

Another distressing psychological feeling that the Qur'anic speech elicits in the heart to ignite the fire of taqwa in it is sorrow. When people experience this distressing feeling in reaction to particular Qur'anic messages, they become uncomfortable, and the more they reflect on this type of the Qur'anic speech, the more uncomfortable they become. Gradually, they will realize that repentance from whatever prohibited issues they're involved in is the only way to avoid this bothersome psychological feeling. Fortunately, repentance not only encourages repenters to refrain from evil deeds, but it also stimulates them to involve themselves—earnestly and perseveringly— in righteous activities. More precisely, believers' involvement in righteousness generates pleasurable psychological feelings in their hearts; these enjoyable feelings, in turn, increase their motivation to do more and more righteousness, an issue that reflects the dynamic nature of repentance.

One of the many ayahs that have the power to generate sorrow in the heart is this one from surah Al-Isra (The Night Journey):

(وَلاَ تَقْفُ مَا لَيْسَ لَكَ بِهِ عِلْمٌ ، إِنَّ السَّمْعَ وَالْبَصَـرَ وَالْفُؤَادَ كُـلُّ أُولَئِـكَ كَانَ عَنْـهُ مَسْؤُولاً).

> *"And follow not that of which you have no knowledge.*
> *Verily, the hearing, and the sight, and the heart of each*
> *of those ones will be questioned."*   *(Qur'an 17:36)*

---

[64] Musnad Imam Ahmed, p. 45, hadith no. 27078

This alarming ayah demands that people be in full control of three things: their hearing, their sight, and their hearts. These three human aspects are, unfortunately, the most difficult to control; thus, they are the worst troublemakers for people, especially on the Day of Judgment. First, the ears can be involved in listening to things that are thousands of miles away, such as listening to backbiting in a telephone conversation. Second, the eyes can be as problematic as the ears because there are always attractive things to see; some of them can be extremely harmful to believers' hearts, souls, and creed. For instance, seeing sexually arousing movies or pictures (pornography) undermines the Muslim's morality and character and mars his or her sense of purity. Third, the heart could be more harmful to people's relationship with Allah than the ears and the eyes combined, for—as previously mentioned—it is the organ that develops and harbours many evil feelings and intentions. Today, the media and modern technology—such as TV and Smartphones respectively—burden Muslims with an extremely high level of responsibility for their hearing, sight, and hearts than any time before.

As a comment on the above ayah, A. Y. Ali stated that three sculptures of "monkeys are shown [in a Japanese temple] as putting their hands to their ears, eyes, and mouths, respectively, to show that they weren't prepared to hear any evil, or see any evil, or speak any evil" (2008, p. 704).

Islam demands that believers' world of inner self be pure. Thus, Allah repeatedly warns against the incubation of negative thoughts that pervert the mind, the heart, the soul, and all the other human aspects. In a threatening tone, for example, He warns Muslims against the practice of evil thinking and bad intentions. He says:

(...وَاعْلَمُوا أَنَّ اللَّهَ يَعْلَمُ مَا فِي أَنْفُسِكُمْ فَاحْذَرُوهُ...)

"...and know that Allah knows what is in your minds, so fear Him..."   *(Qur'an 2:235)*

Also almost at the end of the same surah, Al-Baqarah, Allah reiterates the same previous warning but in a different way. He states:

(... وَإِن تُبْدُواْ مَا فِي أَنْفُسِكُمْ أَوْ تُخْفُوهُ يُحَاسِبْكُم بِهِ اللَّهُ ، فَيَغْفِرُ لِمَن يَشَآءُ وَيُعَذِّبُ مَن يَشَآءُ ، وَاللَّهُ عَلَى كُلِّ شَيْءٍ قَدِيرٌ).

> *"...and whether you disclose what is in yourselves or conceal it, Allah will call you to account for it. Then He forgives whom He wills and punishes whom He wills. And Allah is able to do all things."*   (Qur'an 2: 284)

The message in this ayah shows that Islam cares about the purity of the world of thoughts and feelings the way it does about the righteousness of conduct and speech, for purity or impurity of the inner self usually reflects on almost everything a person does. For instance, whereas positive thinking and positive feelings make people optimistic, happy, healthy, creative, productive, and positively influential, negative thinking and negative feelings mar their souls, corrupt their hearts, poison their brains, and interfere with their ability to think clearly and objectively.

When negative thinking and negative feelings become a social phenomenon, they create a poisonous social atmosphere that gradually afflicts most of the community members with—figuratively speaking—"moral asphyxia" that results in many social problems— such as injustice, hate, alcoholism, drug abuse, homicide, as well as different medical and mental problems. Imagine a community suffering from all these problems: What chance of a happy life would it dream of? What kind of relationship would it have with Allah? And, accordingly, what destiny would await it on the Day of Judgment?

Another alarming ayah that has great power to generate sorrow in believers' hearts is this extremely deterring one from surah Al-Zalzalah (The Earthquake):

(وَمَن يَعْمَلْ مِثْقَالَ ذَرَّةٍ شَرّاً يَرَهُ)!

> *"And whosoever does evil equal to the weight of a speck of dust shall see it!"*   (Qur'an 99:8)

Ibn Kathir reported Imam Ahmed to have said that Sasa'ah ibn Mu'awyiah came to the Holy Prophet who read the above ayah to him. Then Sasa'ah said, "This is enough; I don't need to listen to anything more" (2014, p. 538). Obviously, Sasa'ah meant that this ayah made him fully aware of how closely he had to observe Allah and how responsibly he had to live his entire life as a believer.

The Element of Sadness

Sadness, though abhorrent, can sometimes be an ideal, fertile soil for the growth, development, and blossom of the precious plant of taqwa in the heart. Because it is broken, a sad heart is easy to touch; therefore, the Qur'anic speech that triggers sadness occurs often. In the following ayah from surah Al-Imran, for instance, Allah warns people that on the Day of Judgment, they will, undoubtedly, reap the fruits of their own deeds. The message in it, in fact, has enough power to trigger sadness, but only when the heart listens carefully to it. It says:

(يَوْمَ تَجِدُ كُلُّ نَفْسٍ مَّا عَمِلَتْ مِنْ خَيْرٍ مُحْضَرًا وَمَا عَمِلَتْ مِن سُوءٍ ، تَوَدُّ لَوْ
أَنَّ بَيْنَهَا وَبَيْنَهُ أَمَدًا بَعِيدًا ، وَيُحَذِّرُكُمُ اللَّهُ نَفْسَهُ...)

"On the Day when every soul will be confronted with the good it has done, and all the evil it has done, it will wish that there were a great distance between it and its evil. And Allah warns you against Himself..."

(Qur'an 3:30)

This ayah begins with good news. Precisely, Allah acknowledges and approves believers' good deeds, and this, of course, instils hope and happiness into their hearts. But soon afterward, this good feeling vanishes away when a strong wave of sadness conquers their hearts in response to the second part of the ayah, in which Allah warns humans that all their evil deeds will also be present and that they will be fully accountable for them. He says:

(...وَمَا عَمِلَتْ مِن سُوءٍ...)

"...and all the evil it has done..."

The Arabic grammar that Allah uses in this part of the ayah, which is the indefinite form, emphasizes the fact that whatever evil that people did in this life—no matter how trivial—will be brought to their attention on the Day of Judgment, and they will be completely responsible for it. This horrible situation will, actually, take place while sinners and Hellfire are looking at each other—eye to eye! The guilty soul, in this case, will realize the miserable consequences of its nasty attitude and evil deeds in this life; it will also realize that Allah's punishment is inevitable. At that moment, the psychological reaction of such a guilty soul is an inexpressibly painful feeling of regret, which is "hasrah," as mentioned earlier.

That moment, such a guilty soul, according to this ayah, will wish that there were a great distance between it and the evil it had committed— a wish that, in fact, only multiplies this extremely awful feeling of sorrow and regret. With respect to this, Allah says:

$$(...تَوَدُّ لَوْ أَنَّ بَيْنَهَا وَبَيْنَهُ أَمَداً بَعِيْداً...)!$$

"...it will wish that there were a great distance between it and its evil...!"

Then Allah warns humans, not against His punishment—as usual— but, this time, against Himself! He says:

$$(...وَيُحَذِّرُكُمُ اللَّهُ نَفْسَهُ...)!$$

"...and Allah warns you against Himself..!"

In short, the warning in this ayah aims at motivating people to check themselves and to evaluate their current positions on Allah's message to them before it is too late. Only when they become mentally and psychologically affected by this extremely intimidating Qur'anic message and, indeed, other similar ones will they seriously consider their destinies in the Hereafter. Also only this way will they— hopefully—avoid such a horrible moment that may otherwise transform into a gateway to an indescribably miserable, eternal life in Hellfire! Hence, if a person has problems—and who doesn't?—such a person has an ample chance to address them today before it is too late.

In surah Fatir, Allah sheds light on the disbelievers' condition as they suffer from their extremely horrible chastisement in Hellfire. In that situation, they beg Allah to offer them another chance so that they would become good servants of Him, but the answer is, of course, extremely disappointing to them. Here is how the dialogue goes:

(وَهُمْ يَصْطَرِخُونَ فِيهَا رَبَّنَا أَخْرِجْنَا نَعْمَلْ صَالِحًا غَيْرَ الَّذِي كُنَّا نَعْمَلُ ، أَوَلَمْ نُعَمِّرْكُم مَّا يَتَذَكَّرُ فِيهِ مَن تَذَكَّرَ وَجَاءَكُمُ النَّذِيرُ فَذُوقُوا فَمَا لِلظَّالِمِينَ مِن نَّصِيرٍ).

"Therein they will cry: 'Our Lord! Bring us out, we shall do righteous good deeds, not (the evil deeds) that we used to do.' (Allah will reply): 'Did We not give you lives long enough, so that whosoever would receive admonition could receive it? And the warner came to you. So taste you (the evil of your deeds). For the polytheists and wrong-doers, there is no helper.'"

(Qur'an 35:37)

A. Al-Ghazali (2004) narrated the following:

Al-Rabia ibn Haitham dug himself a grave in his house. Whenever he sensed any level of hardness [65] in his heart, he would enter that grave, lie in it for a while, and recite the following ayah:

(حَتَّىٰ إِذَا جَاءَ أَحَدَهُمُ الْمَوْتُ قَالَ رَبِّ ارْجِعُونِ . لَعَلِّي أَعْمَلُ صَالِحًا فِيمَا تَرَكْتُ).

"Until, when death comes to one of them, he says: 'My Lord! Send me back (please) so that I may do good in that which I have left behind.'"

(Qur'an 23:99–100)

Then he would get out of the grave and say to himself, "Now, Al-Rabia, you've been returned back to life, so do righteousness [before it is too late]." (pp. 265–266)

---

[65] Here the concept of "heart hardness" is used figuratively, and it refers to heavy and continuous involvement in worldly affairs on the account of the preparation for the Day of Judgment.

The Element of Fear

Fear is an effective emotion in behaviour modification. In the traffic, fear of injury and fear of death, for example, motivate people to drive more responsibly. Likewise, fear of punishment prevents people from violating the rules and from committing crimes. Fear, in fact, functions not only on an individual level but also on a nation level. A country's leadership, for instance, may think twice before it afflicts another state with anything harmful because it fears that country's reaction and/or that of its allies, whether such a reaction is military, political, economic, or other.

So knowing this positive influence of fear on people's behaviour and on their lives in general, Allah speaks about it—more than once—as a favour. In surah Al-Baqarah, for instance, He says:

(وَلَوْلاَ دَفْعُ اللَّهِ النَّاسَ بَعْضَهُم بِبَعْضٍ لَفَسَدَتِ الارْضُ وَلَكِنَّ اللَّهَ ذُو فَضْلٍ عَلَى الْعَالَمِينَ).

"Had Allah not restrained mankind, some by means of others, the earth would have become chaotic. But Allah is Gracious towards His creation." (Qur'an 2:251)

Also in surah Al-Hajj, He declares:

(...وَلَوْلَا دَفْعُ اللَّهِ النَّاسَ بَعْضَهُم بِبَعْضٍ لَّهُدِّمَتْ صَوَامِعُ وَبِيَعٌ وَصَلَوَاتٌ وَمَسَاجِدُ يُذْكَرُ فِيهَا اسْمُ اللَّهِ كَثِيرًا...).

"...Had Allah not caused people to restrain one another, monasteries, churches, synagogues, and mosques, wherein the Name of Allah is mentioned much would surely have been destroyed..." (Qur'an 22:40)

Fortunately, Allah uses fear not only to aid humans to stay away from trouble in this life but also to help them avoid trouble in the Hereafter and become triumphant in it. The Qur'anic speech that addresses the emotion of fear has two categories: ayahs that warn about Allah's punishment today and others that warn about His punishment in the

Hereafter. The following are examples of fear-eliciting Qur'anic speech concerning these two categories.

Fear of Punishment in this Life

Allah can punish people in this life with different things. The following, however, is a brief explanation of His punishment with nature and with people.

Punishment with Nature

Sometimes Allah threatens to punish humans with natural disasters, such as the winds, floods, and earthquakes. In surah Al-A'raf (The Heights), for example, He warns disbelievers that His punishment may arrive at any time—perhaps at night, while they are sleeping, or during the day, as they are heavily involved in heedless activities. He says:

(أَفَأَمِنَ أَهْلُ الْقُرَى أَن يَأْتِيَهُم بَأْسُنَا بَيَاتاً وَهُمْ نَائِمُونَ . أَوَأَمِنَ أَهْلُ الْقُرَى أَن يَأْتِيَهُمْ بَأْسُنَا ضُحًى وَهُمْ يَلْعَبُونَ)؟

"Are the people of the cities confident that Our wrath will not strike them at night, while they sleep? Or are the people of the cities confident that Our wrath will not strike them in the morning while they amuse themselves?"
(Qur'an 7:97–98)

The question form and the disapproving tone in which Allah has expressed the above message invite critical thinking and serious consideration of the issue it raises; thus, it intensifies the sense of insecurity that Allah intends to ignite in people's hearts so that they may become mindful of Him.

Another similar threat occurs in surah Al-Nahl, where Allah says:

(أَفَأَمِنَ الَّذِينَ مَكَرُواْ السَّيِّئَاتِ أَن يَخْسِفَ اللَّهُ بِهِمُ الأَرْضَ أَوْ يَأْتِيَهُمُ الْعَذَابُ مِنْ حَيْثُ لاَ يَشْعُرُونَ . أَوْ يَأْخُذَهُمْ فِي تَقَلُّبِهِمْ فَمَا هُم بِمُعْجِزِينَ . أَوْ يَأْخُذَهُمْ عَلَى تَخَوُّفٍ فَإِنَّ رَبَّكُمْ لَرَؤُوفٌ رَحِيمٌ).

*"Do then those who devise evil plots feel secure that
Allah will not cause them to sink into the earth, or that
the torment will not seize them from directions they
perceive not? Or that He may catch them in the midst of
their going to and fro (their jobs), so that there be no
escape for them (from Allah's punishment)? Or might He
seize them while in a state of fearful expectancy? Truly!
your Lord id indeed full of Kindness Most Merciful."*
                                            (Qur'an 16:45—47)

It is narrated that whenever the Holy Prophet saw clouds, he would
engage in supplication in which he would pray Allah for His Mersey.
According to Al-Qurtubi (2014), Imam Al-Bukhari narrated that
Ayishah, the Holy Prophet's wife, said:

"Whenever the Holy Prophet saw clouds or the wind, his
face reflected discomfort, so she asked him, 'O Messenger of
Allah, when people see the clouds, they become happy,
hoping that they are bringing rain. But I noticed when you
see them, your face shows discomfort.' The Holy Prophet
answered, 'O Ayishah! What assurance do I have that these
clouds are not carrying torment? Some people were
punished with the wind. Seeing the punishment
[approaching them in a form of clouds], a group of people
said, *'These clouds will give us rain.'*"[66] (p.379)

"عَنْ عَائِشَةَ ، زَوْجِ النَّبِيِّ صَلَّى اللهُ عَلَيْهِ وَسَلَّمَ أَنَّهَا قَالَتْ : "كَانَ إِذَا رَأَى غَيْمًا أَوْ رِيحًا ،
عُرِفَ ذَلِكَ فِي وَجْهِهِ ." قَالَتْ: "يَا رَسُولَ اللهِ ، النَّاسُ إِذَا رَأَوُا الْغَيْمَ فَرِحُوا ، رَجَاءَ أَنْ يَكُونَ
فِيهِ الْمَطَرُ ، وَأَرَاكَ إِذَا رَأَيْتَهُ عَرَفْتُ فِي وَجْهِكَ الْكَرَاهِيَةَ." قَالَتْ: فَقَالَ: "يَا عَائِشَةُ مَا يُؤَمِّنُنِي
أَنْ يَكُونَ فِيهِ عَذَابٌ ؟ قَدْ عُذِّبَ قَوْمٌ بِالرِّيحِ ، وَقَدْ رَأَى قَوْمُ الْعَذَابَ ، فَقَالُوا : (هَذَا عَارِضٌ
مُمْطِرُنَا)" .

Also Ibn Kathir (2014) narrated that Ayishah said whenever the wind
blew, Allah's Messenger would say:

"O Allah! I ask you the best of it and the best in it as well as
the best of what it is sent with. And I seek refuge with you

---

[66] (Qur'an 46: 24)

from its evil, the evil in it, and the evil it is sent with." (p. 260)

"وعن عائشة رضي الله عنها قالت: كان رسول الله (ص) إذا عصفت الريح قال: "اللهم إني أسألك خيرها وخير ما فيها وخير ما أرسلت به ، وأعوذ بك من شرها ، وشر ما فيها وشر ما أرسلت به."

As indicated earlier, Allah recurrently reminds people of His employment of nature to obliterate different disbelieving communities in the past. Such a frequent recurrence of this matter, of course, is meant to help disbelievers reconsider their negative attitude and to also aid believers to observe the Islamic teachings more seriously. The ayahs below represent a few examples of this.

First, in reference to His obliteration of Prophet Hud's argumentative community, the All-Mighty declares:

(فَأَنْجَيْنَاهُ وَالَّذِينَ مَعَهُ بِرَحْمَةٍ مِّنَّا ، وَقَطَعْنَا دَابِرَ الَّذِينَ كَذَّبُواْ بِآيَاتِنَا ، وَمَاكَانُواْ مُؤْمِنِينَ).

"So We saved him and those who were with him out of mercy from Us, and We severed the roots of those who belied Our revelations; and they were not believers."
(Qur'an 7:72)

Second, with regard to His merciless eradication of the dirty community of Lut, He states:

(فَأَخَذَتْهُمُ الصَّيْحَةُ مُشْرِقِينَ . فَجَعَلْنَا عَالِيَهَا سَافِلَهَا وَأَمْطَرْنَا عَلَيْهِم حِجَارَةً مِّن سِجِّيلٍ).

"So the blast overtook them at the time of sunrise. And We turned them upside down and rained stones of baked clay upon them."   *(Qur'an 15:73–74)*

Third, sometimes Allah's punishment with the power of nature can be inflicted on individuals, rather than on a whole community. Allah, for example, punished Qarun (Korah) in the same manner He punished the whole disbelieving community of Prophet Lut. Precisely, He made the earthquake swallow him and his entire luxurious, massive home. With respect to this issue, He says:

(فَخَسَفْنَا بِهِ وَبِدَارِهِ الْأَرْضَ فَمَا كَانَ لَهُ مِن فِئَةٍ يَنصُرُونَهُ مِن دُونِ اللَّهِ
وَمَا كَانَ مِنَ الْمُنتَصِرِينَ).

"So, We caused the earth to swallow him and his dwelling place. Then he had no group to help him against Allah, nor was he one of those who could save themselves."   *(Qur'an 28:81)*

Punishment with Humans

Besides His threat to punish with nature, Allah threatens to punish at the hands of humans. Because humans have lots of evil attributes, the sufferings they may inflict on each other could sometimes be more painful than those caused by nature. Some evils that stigmatize humans and make them extremely dangerous are anger, hatred, thirst for revenge, violence, cruelty, homicide, and even genocide, to mention a few. The Muslim nation, at different times, had, unfortunately, suffered a great deal from this type of punishment at both the brothers' and the enemies' hands.

In the following ayah, from surah Al-An'am, Allah threatens His enemies that He may punish them by nature or by each other's evil. He says:

(قُلْ هُوَ الْقَادِرُ عَلَى أَن يَبْعَثَ عَلَيْكُمْ عَذَاباً مِّن فَوْقِكُمْ أَوْ مِن تَحْتِ أَرْجُلِكُمْ
أَوْ يَلْبِسَكُمْ شِيَعاً وَيُذِيقَ بَعْضَكُم بَأْسَ بَعْضٍ ، انْظُرْ كَيْفَ نُصَرِّفُ الآيَاتِ
لَعَلَّهُمْ يَفْقَهُونَ).

"Say: 'He has the power to send torment on you from above or from under your feet, or to divide you into discordant factions, and make you taste the violence of one another.' See how variously We explain our revelation so that they may understand.'"

(Qur'an 6:65)

According to Ibn Ashoor (1984), the threatening message in this ayah was [originally] directed to the Makkan disbelievers, and it was meant to help them fear Allah. He also mentioned that examples of Allah's punishment that attacks from above are thunder as well as the wind, and examples of His punishment that comes from underneath are earthquakes and floods. Further, in reference to Allah's threat *"and make you taste the violence of one another,"* Ibn Ashoor added that this is a threat to the disbelievers of Makkah, which, actually, became a fact at the Battle of Badr and other battles, where they suffered badly at the Muslims' hands (pp. 283–284).

Fear of Punishment in the Hereafter

In many surahs and in a recurrent manner, Allah talks about the torment He has prepared to punish His enemies in the Hereafter. He sometimes refers to it in general; other times, however, He describes it in horrifying detail, such as in the surahs of Al-Hajj and Al-Waqi'ah (The Inevitable Event). This terrifying description of Allah's punishment in the Hereafter aims at, of course, helping humans to believe in Him, His final Book, and His final Messenger; it also aims at helping people to observe His teachings. All of these—with Allah's mercy—will qualify them for the entrance of His Gardens of bliss.

This section examines only one slide of Allah's horrible punishment that He describes in surah Al-Hajj. In this regard, He states:

(هَذَانِ خَصْمَانِ اخْتَصَمُواْ فِى رَبِّهِمْ ، فَالَّذِينَ كَفَرُواْ قُطِّعَتْ لَهُمْ ثِيَابٌ مِّن نَّارٍ يُصَبُّ مِن فَوْقِ رُءُوسِهِمُ الْحَمِيمُ . يُصْهَرُ بِهِ مَا فِى بُطُونِهِمْ وَالْجُلُودُ. وَلَهُم مَّقَامِعُ مِنْ حَدِيدٍ . كُلَّمَا أَرَادُواْ أَن يَخْرُجُواْ مِنْهَا مِنْ غَمٍّ أُعِيدُواْ فِيهَا، وَذُوقُواْ عَذَابَ الْحَرِيقِ)!

"These two opponents dispute with each other about their Lord; then as for those who disbelieved, garments of fire will be cut out for them; boiling water will be poured down over their heads. With it will melt (or vanish away) what is within their bellies, as well as (their) skins. And for them are hooked rods of iron. Every time they seek to get away therefrom, from

> *anguish, they will be driven back therein: Taste the*
> *torment of burning!"*   *(Qur'an 22: 19—22)*

This torment, as the first ayah indicates, is prepared for disbelievers. Nevertheless, its exceptionally terrifying nature makes believers oversee this fact and react to the message as if it were directed exclusively to them. Now before discussing the different aspects of Allah's torture in this ayah, let's consider the following.

First, there is no comparison between the fire we use today and the fire that Allah has prepared to punish His enemies, which is, according to the hadith, seventy times as hot![67] Second, consider the following question: How sensitive a disbeliever's skin is going to be on the Day of Judgment? In this life, Allah has made the human skin sensitive enough to help people realize the concept of physical pain and thus learn to avoid physically harmful situations. Fortunately, besides helping people to avoid harmful situations, the experience of physical pain in this life aids them in avoiding the All-Mighty's punishment in the Hereafter. In other words, if people didn't experience physical pain in this life, they wouldn't fear Hellfire, of course.[68] Third, what does it mean to live in Hellfire everlastingly? The overwhelming majority of people have, unfortunately, chosen to do so! Further, people cannot bear putting their fingers' tips on a burning stove for a few seconds. The majority of them, however, seem indifferent about Allah's endless and unspeakably horrible torture in Hellfire, which is even painful to just think about it. It is a place that is not only entirely empty of Allah's mercy, but it is also completely full of His wrath!

---

[67] Imam Al-Bukhari and Imam Muslim

[68] In surah Al-Waqi'ah and in reference to this life's fire, Allah says:

(نَحْنُ جَعَلْنَاهَا تَذْكِرَةً وَمَتَاعًا لِّلْمُقْوِينَ).

"We have made it a Reminder (of the Hell-fire in the Hereafter), and an article of use for the travellers (and all the others, in this world)."   *(Qur'an 56:73)*

Scholars of the Qur'anic exegesis, such as Al-Shawkani (2012), claimed that in this ayah, the word *"tathkirah,"* which is "reminder," means Allah has made the fire in this life a reminder of that in Hellfire (p. 197). Thus, again, the realization of the danger of today's fire can be of great help for humans to avoid Allah's fire in the Hereafter.

Allah begins the previous ayahs, from surah Al-Hajj, with an extremely dreadful description of His punishment. He says:

$$(\ldots \text{فَالَّذِينَ كَفَرُوا قُطِّعَتْ لَهُمْ ثِيَابٌ مِّن نَّارٍ} \ldots)!$$

> *"…but those who deny their Lord, for them will be cut out a garment of fire…!"*

That is how disbelievers will relate to Hellfire: They will not only live in it, but they will also wear its fire, as garments covering their entire bodies! In other words, Allah's fire will perfectly encircle both their souls and their bodies! In addition, they will suffer from this horrible torment perpetually.

The All-Mighty sheds light on another extremely awful type of His torture in Hellfire. He declares:

$$(\ldots \text{يُصَبُّ مِن فَوْقِ رُءُوسِهِمُ الْحَمِيمُ . يُصْهَرُ بِهِ مَا فِي بُطُونِهِمْ وَالْجُلُودُ} \ldots)$$

> *"…over their heads will be poured out hameem (boiling water). With it will melt (or vanish away) what is within their bellies, as well as (their) skin…"*

It seems that *hameem* is a liquid that resembles lava in its heat and water in its density, but it is, actually, infinitely hot. Or it might be fire turned into a liquid! In any case, the hameem's temperature must be high enough to match Allah's anger and His ability to revenge for Himself. As this ayah explains, as soon as this extremely boiling liquid touches disbelievers' heads and runs down their bodies, their skins and whatever in their bellies will melt. If people read these two ayahs thoughtfully, they will experience some level of psychological pain; this psychological pain will, indeed, increase if they imagine themselves suffering from this torment in Hellfire. But an important question to ask in this context is this: How would people feel if they literally find themselves in the middle of this unspeakably ugly place?

Yet there is another different type of torment. Specifically, the angels will continuously and everlastingly hit the Hellfire's dwellers on their heads with extremely heavy iron rods. In this regard, the All-Mighty says:

$$(\dots \text{وَلَهُمْ مَّقَامِعُ مِنْ حَدِيدٍ} \dots)$$

"...and for them are hooked rods of iron..."

According to Al-Shawkani (2102), Imam Ahmed narrated that Allah's Holy Messenger said, "If one of these rods were put on the floor, the entire human and jinn populations wouldn't be able to pick it up" (p. 555). Thus, imagine—if you can—the strength of the angels who use these rods to hit disbelievers on their heads. These angels will raise these hammers high enough, and—with all their anger and power—they will push them down against these poor people's heads. Perhaps these poor humans will flatten momentarily, but Allah will instantaneously recreate them for other even more painful hits, again, and again, and over again—endlessly!

The disbelievers will try in vain to escape from this extremely miserable place. Scholars of the exegesis of the Qur'an, such as Al-Tabari (2010), reported that each time they try to flee their torture, the angels will force them back, using those extremely heavy rods (p. 166). These poor people's attempts to escape from the Fire are, certainly, meant to humiliate them more and more and to increase their psychological pain, for Allah can force them to stay constantly in one place, without allowing them to move for even a fraction of an inch.

With respect to this aspect of their sufferings, Allah says:

$$(\dots \text{كُلَّمَا أَرَادُوا أَن يَخْرُجُوا مِنْهَا مِنْ غَمٍّ أُعِيدُوا فِيهَا ، وَذُوقُوا عَذَابَ الْحَرِيقِ})!$$

"...every time they seek to get away therefrom, from anguish, they will be driven back therein: Taste the torment of burning!"

The Arabic word *gham*[69] in this ayah connotes far more distressing meanings than those suggested by its English equivalents, such as "anguish" and "distress." According to Ibn Manthoor (2008), gham means *karb*,[70] which refers to an extremely high level of sadness and distress that fill the entire heart (p. 88 & p. 41). Grammatically

---

[69] غَمٌّ

[70] كرب

speaking, the indefinite form of the word "gham" in this context suggests that the sources of distress and anguish from which disbelievers will suffer in that extremely terrible, ugly place are infinite in number and level of pain.

Further, the range of torture that disbelievers will experience in Hellfire extends to include even their food and drinks. In other words, as food and drinks represent an essential source of happiness and pleasure for the righteous in Allah's Gardens of bliss, they are also fundamental in disbelievers' punishment in Hellfire. Surah Al-Ghashiyah (The Overwhelming Event) introduces the following awful menu of food from which disbelievers will eat. In reference to them, it says:

(لَّيْسَ لَهُمْ طَعَامٌ إِلاَّ مِن ضَرِيعٍ . لاَّ يُسْمِنُ وَلاَ يُغْنِي مِن جُوعٍ).

"No food will there be for them but a poisonous thorny plant. It will neither nourish nor satisfy hunger."
(Qur'an 88: 6–7)

Also surah Al-Waqi'ah has a different menu that includes another variety of unutterably terrible food. Addressing disbelievers in this regard, the All-Mighty threatens them emphatically saying:

(ثُمَّ إِنَّكُمْ أَيُّهَا الضَّالُّونَ الْمُكَذِّبُونَ. لَآكِلُونَ مِن شَجَرٍ مِّن زَقُّومٍ . فَمَالِئُونَ مِنْهَا الْبُطُونَ)!

"Then moreover, verily you the erring-ones, the deniers (of Resurrection)! You verily will eat of the trees of zaqqum. Then you will fill your bellies therewith."
(Qur'an 56:51–53)

Surah Al-Saffat (Those Ranged in Ranks), in addition, provides more information on the above-mentioned food, namely the "zaqqum." According to Ibn Kathir (2014), zaqqum is a tree that grows at the bottom of Hellfire, and it has extremely dreadful, ugly crops that resemble the devils' heads. He added that notwithstanding the addressee's unfamiliarity with the devils' look, Allah likens the crops of this tree to their heads because people have an assumption that the devils are extremely ugly (p. 147). Describing this tree, the environment where it grows, and its fruits, Allah says:

$$\text{(إِنَّهَا شَجَرَةٌ تَخْرُجُ فِي أَصْلِ الْجَحِيمِ . طَلْعُهَا كَأَنَّهُ رُؤُوس الشياطين)!}$$

"Verily, it is a tree that springs out of the bottom of Hell-fire. The shoots of its fruit-stalks are like the heads of demons!" (Qur'an 37:64-65)

The way the crops of the zaqqum look as well as the place where their tree grows—the bottom of Hellfire!—imply that the bitter taste of these crops as well as the anguish that this taste causes exceed the human imagination. Further, although this food is extremely awful, Allah's enemies will not just eat from it; they will, actually, be forced to fill their stomachs with it. With regard to this ugly fate, Allah says:

$$\text{(فَإِنَّهُمْ لَآكِلُونَ مِنْهَا فَمَالِئُونَ مِنْهَا البطون).}$$

"Truly, they will eat thereof and fill their bellies therewith." (Qur'an 37:66)

Allah goes on to describe the disbelievers' suffering in Hellfire in order to frighten them more and more so that they may choose to overcome their denial of His existence or their rejection of His oneness and thus believe in Him, His final Book, His last Messenger, and observe His teachings, which are in their own best interests. So in surah Al-Haqqah (The Inevitable Hour), He adds another even more awful dish to the previous, ugly menu; perhaps it will be more effective in helping them avoid this miserable situation in Hellfire. He says:

$$\text{(وَلاَ طَعَامٌ إِلاَّ مِنْ غِسْلِينٍ . لَا يَأْكُلُهُ إِلاَّ الْخَاطِئُونَ).}$$

"Nor any food (will be offered to them) except filth from the washing of wounds. None will eat it except the sinners." (Qur'an 69:36-37)

The food in the above ayah reflects the extremely high level of humiliation and torture that the dwellers of Hellfire will eternally incur. Imagine humans eating—abundantly, continuously, and ceaselessly—

from the pus that comes out of badly festering wounds on humans' bodies.

These are only a few types of disbelievers' food, which, again, they will be forced to eat and with which they will fill their stomachs in that extremely ugly place—Hellfire. But what about their beverages? Of course, there must be drinks for them so that their meals will be complete. From surah Al Waqi'ah, we learn that Allah will honour these special people with a special drink from hameem. In reference to this issue, He addresses them saying:

(فَشَارِبُونَ عَلَيْهِ مِنَ الْحَمِيمِ . فَشَارِبُونَ شُرْبَ الْهِيمِ).

"And [you will] drink Boiling water on top of it. Indeed you shall drink like diseased camels raging with thirst!"
(Qur'an 56:54–55)

According to different exegetes of the Qur'an, such as Ibn Kathir (2014), *alheem* in this ayah refers to ailing camels that—due to a specific disease—are always thirsty, and their thirst for water can never be satisfied, no matter how much water they may drink (p. 353). Accordingly, the message in the second ayah above is that dwellers of Hellfire will continuously and endlessly drink from that extremely hot liquid, and as they will have no choice but eating from the zaqqum's crops, pus, and other ugly types of food, they will also have no option but drinking—abundantly—from this "hameem" and other similar awful drink!

The surah of The Cave sheds light on the context in which this horrible drink will be offered to these wretched people. Precisely, it will be given to them when they feel overwhelmed with the torture of Hellfire and the pain of thirst. In reference to this, Allah states:

(...وَإِن يَسْتَغِيثُوا يُغَاثُوا بِمَاءٍ كَالْمُهْلِ يَشْوِى الْوُجُوهَ ، بِئْسَ الشَّرَابُ وَسَاءَتْ مُرْتَفَقًا)!

"...then if they implore relief, they will be granted water like melted brass that will scald their faces. How dreadful a drink and an evil dwelling resting place!"
(Qur'an 18:29)

It seems that this extremely hot liquid that these people will drink is similar to that which will be poured over their heads. But how can humans drink water hot enough to burn their faces even before it reaches their mouths? The result of drinking such extremely hot—so-called—water is the cutting of their bowels into pieces,[71] according to the following message from surah of Mohammad:

$$(...وَسُقُوا مَاءً حَمِيماً فَقَطَّعَ أَمْعَاءَهُمْ)!$$

"...and are given to drink boiling water that cuts up their bowels!"   *(Qur'an 47:15)*

That is a brief account of the Qur'anic speech that describes Allah's extremely merciless punishment in Hellfire. Such a description is meant to, again, generate fear in peoples' hearts that helps them avoid all these forms of wretchedness by believing in Allah, His Book, and His Holy Messenger, which—with Allah's mercy—will hopefully qualify them for the enjoyment of the Gardens of endless bliss.

Hope and Glad Tidings of Forgiveness

The issue of hope and glad tidings in this section is confined to Allah's forgiveness. But before discussing this topic, it is important to mention that in Islam, there is no place for despair and that the torch of hope to win Allah's forgiveness must always keep burning in believers' hearts. Two of Allah's many names and attributes are *Al-Ghaffar* [72] (The Oft-Forgiving) and *Al-Afwu* [73] (The Oft-Pardoning). According to Al-Qahtani (2010), "Al-Afwu" means "the one who has

---

[71] It is previously indicated that this so-called "water," which is mentioned in surah Al-Hajj, will melt whatever in these poor people's bellies. Again, in reference to this issue, Allah says:

$$(يُصْهَرُ بِهِ مَا فِي بُطُونِهِمْ وَالْجُلُودُ)!$$

"With it will melt what is within their bellies, as well as (their) skins!"   *(Qur'an 22:20)*

[72] الغفّار

[73] العفوّ

the inclusive and entire forgiveness that encompasses the sins of all His slaves, especially those who meet the requirements for His forgiveness, such as believing in Him, doing good deeds, repenting, and seeking His forgiveness" (p. 73).

Asking Allah His forgiveness (*istighfar*[74]) is a result of a particular mental and psychological condition. The main characteristics of it are belief in Allah and the Day of Judgment, fear of Allah, sadness, sorrow, worry, regret, and hope. Therefore, praying Allah for forgiveness is beloved of Him for different reasons. First, it inspires believers with hope, without which they become desperate, apathetic, and easily lured into unethical practices and behaviour that may gradually strip them of most of their Islamic values. Second, when people pray Allah for forgiveness, they prove that they believe His knowledge encompasses everything and that He holds them accountable for whatever they do, say, or even think of. Third, seeking Allah's forgiveness suggests that seekers of His forgiveness are certain that He is the only one who can forgive their sins and that He fulfils His promise of forgiving the sinful if they repent. Fourth, people's prayer for Allah's pardon indicates that they experience a strong sense of guilt about something they have or haven't done; thus, they seek His forgiveness to rid themselves of this distressing feeling and to avoid His punishment, which might take place soon in this life or later in the Hereafter or in both. Finally, praying Allah for forgiveness sharpens believers' conscience and makes their observance of Him persistent and stronger; as a result, it improves their Islamic character and the quality of their lives as Muslims.

The issues of istighfar (seeking Allah's forgiveness) and *maghfirah*[75] (Allah's forgiveness) occur frequently in the Qur'an due to different factors that make humans vulnerable to the violation of Allah's rules. Such factors, as mentioned before, are human nature (with all its shortcomings), daily challenging circumstances, and the Satan's continuous, relentless plot to seduce and take people astray from Allah's path. As a result, Allah has compassionately left the door to His mercy always open for people who acknowledge their mistakes, regret them, and seek His forgiveness.

---

[74] إستغفار

[75] مغفرة

In the following ayah, from the surah of Al-Muzzammil (The One Wrapped up in Garments), for example, Allah commands and encourages believers to seek His forgiveness. At the same time, He confirms that He is "Oft-Forgiving and Most Merciful to those who seek His forgiveness" (Ibn Kathir, 2014, p. 458). In this ayah, Allah says:

$$ (\ldots \text{وَاسْتَغْفِرُوا اللَّهَ ، إِنَّ اللَّهَ غَفُورٌ رَحِيمٌ}). $$

"...and seek the Forgiveness of Allah. Verily Allah is Oft-Forgiving, Most Merciful."   *(Qur'an 73: 20)*

Also in the surah of Al-Hajj, Allah promises to forgive the sins of believers who are engaged in righteousness. With regard to this, He declares:

$$ (\text{فَالَّذِينَ آمَنُوا وَعَمِلُوا الصَّالِحَاتِ لَهُمْ مَغْفِرَةٌ وَرِزْقٌ كَرِيمٌ}). $$

"Those who believe and do righteousness, for them is forgiveness and a sustenance most generous."
(Qur'an 22:50)

Al-Saadi (2011) argued:

> The bottom line, according to this ayah, is that Allah will forgive all the sins of those who strongly believe in Him and His Holy Messenger and who also translate their belief into good deeds. In addition, He will grant them an excellent, bountiful provision in the Garden. (p. 484)

Further, the surah of Al-Nisa' carries remarkably beautiful and heartening news to all sinners. Specifically, Allah promises to forgive them on condition that they regret their sins, repent, and seek His forgiveness. With respect to this, He announces:

$$ (\text{وَمَنْ يَعْمَلْ سُوءًا أَوْ يَظْلِمْ نَفْسَهُ ثُمَّ يَسْتَغْفِرِ اللَّهَ يَجِدِ اللَّهَ غَفُورًا رَحِيمًا}). $$

"And whoever does evil or wrongs himself but afterwards seeks Allah's forgiveness, he will find Allah Oft-forgiving, Most Merciful."   *(Qur'an 4:110)*

In reference to this message, Al-Qurtubi said that the promise of forgiveness in this ayah includes all humans (2014, p. 254). Also the conditional statement in this ayah is, actually, strongly motivating; it should, therefore, stimulate sinners to react to its beautiful message in two positive ways: acknowledging their sins and seeking Allah's forgiveness urgently and earnestly.

Ibn Kathir (2014) quoted Abu-Bakr to have said that Allah's Holy Messenger said:

> "If a Muslim commits a sin, then he [she] makes *wdhu'* [ablution], establishes salah, and asks Allah His forgiveness, Allah will forgive him [her]." (p. 349)

Another Qur'anic message that carries similar glad tidings regarding Allah's forgiveness is this exceptionally lovely one from surah Al-Nahl, in which Allah mercifully offers this extremely beautiful promise:

(ثُمَّ إِنَّ رَبَّكَ لِلَّذِينَ عَمِلُواْ السُّوءَ بِجَهَالَةٍ ثُمَّ تَابُواْ مِن بَعْدِ ذَلِكَ وَأَصْلَحُواْ إِنَّ رَبَّكَ مِن بَعْدِهَا لَغَفُورٌ رَحِيمٌ).

"Then, your Lord for those who did evil out of ignorance and afterward repent and do righteous deeds-verily, after that, your Lord is Pardoning, Most Merciful."
(Qur'an 16:119)

According to Al-Saadi (2011), in this message, Allah invites and motivates His slaves who have committed sins to return back to Him in repentance. If they do and follow their repentance with righteous deeds, He will forgive them and will bestow His mercy on them (p. 398).

Furthermore, surah Al-Hijr (The Rocky Tract) carries a beautiful, emphatically expressed message concerning Allah's forgiveness. It says:

(نَبِّئْ عِبَادِي أَنِّي أَنَا الْغَفُورُ الرَّحِيمُ).

"Declare to My servants that I am truly the Oft-Forgiving, the Most Merciful." *(Qur'an 15:49)*

In their exegeses, Al-Qurtubi, Al-Tabari, and Ibn Kathir stated that Abd Allah ibn Omar narrated that one day the Holy Prophet saw him and other companions laughing. He said:

"Why do you laugh? Let me not see you laugh again!" Then he left and came back to say, "When I left, Gabriel came to me and said, 'Allah says to you, O Mohammad! Why do you make my servants despair of My mercy? Declare to My servants that I am truly the Oft-Forgiving, the Most Merciful, and that My torment is, indeed, the most painful one.'" (2014, p. 274; 2010, p. 94; 2014, p. 248)

"مَالِكُمْ تَضْحَكُونَ ؟ لَا أَرَاكُمْ تَضْحَكُونَ . " ثُمَّ أَدْبَرَ حَتَّى إِذَا كَانَ عِنْدَ الْحِجْرِ رَجَعَ الْقَهْقَرَى فَقَالَ لَنَا : "إِنِّي لَمَّا خَرَجْتُ جَاءَنِي جِبْرِيل فَقَالَ إِنَّ الله يقول لك : "يَا مُحَمَّد لِمَ تُقَنِّط عِبَادِي مِنْ رَحْمَتِي؟ (نَبِّئْ عِبَادِي أَنِّي أَنَا الْغَفُورُ الرَّحِيم . وَأَنَّ عَذَابِي هُوَ الْعَذَاب الْأَلِيم). "[76]

Moreover, the Holy Qur'an carries good news of forgiveness, even for people who have extremely wronged themselves—to a degree that they have become overwhelmed with despair that Allah may never forgive them. In an exceptionally generous message, expressed in a remarkably kind, merciful, and hope-inspiring tone, Allah addresses these desperate people saying:

(قُلْ يَا عِبَادِيَ الَّذِينَ أَسْرَفُوا عَلَىٰ أَنْفُسِهِمْ لَا تَقْنَطُوا مِنْ رَحْمَةِ اللَّهِ ، إِنَّ اللَّهَ يَغْفِرُ الذُّنُوبَ جَمِيعاً ، إِنَّهُ هُوَ الغَفُورُ الرَّحِيمْ).

"Say: 'O my Servants who have transgressed against their souls! Despair not of the mercy of Allah: for Allah forgives all sins: for He is Oft-Forgiving, Most Merciful.'" *(Qur'an 39:53)*

---

[76] (Qur'an 15:49–50)

Ibn Kathir (2014) said that this ayah represents a generous invitation to the disobedient to repent; if they do, Allah will forgive all their sins (p. 182). He also cited Ibn Mas'ud to have said, "This ayah has the best glad tiding in Allah's entire Book [the Holy Qur'an]" (p. 183). Al-Tirmithi, in addition, narrated that Anas ibn Malik said he heard Allah's Holy Messenger say that Allah said:

> "O son of Adam! If you hopefully pray Me to forgive you, I will forgive you, no matter what you have done. O son of Adam! If your sins [accumulate until they] reach the sky, and you seek my forgiveness, I will forgive you. O son of Adam! If you meet me with sins that cover the entire face of the earth, I will still forgive you, as far as you don't associate others with me."

"يا بن آدم ، إنك ما دعوتني ورجوتني غفرت لك ما كان منك ولا أبالي . يا بن آدم ، لو بلغت ذنوبك عنان السماء ثم استغفرتني غفرت لك. يا بن آدم ، إنك لو أتيتني بقراب الأرض خطايا ثم لقيتني لا تشرك بي شيئاً ، لأتيتك بقرابها مغفرة."

As a result of the beautiful messages in the previous ayah (from surah Al-Zumar) and the beautiful message in this hadith, despair will, obviously, have no chance to exist in the human heart if people believe and repent.

Certainly, Allah neither loves torturing His servants nor does He enjoy seeing them suffer. This is why, as a kind invitation in an unexpected context, He reminds the disbelievers of His forgiveness and His mercy so that they may reconsider their negative position on His message to them and repent. Examine the following ayahs from the surah of Al-Ahqaf:

(وَإِذَا تُتْلَىٰ عَلَيْهِمْ آيَاتُنَا بَيِّنَاتٍ قَالَ الَّذِينَ كَفَرُوا لِلْحَقِّ لَمَّا جَاءَهُمْ هَٰذَا سِحْرٌ مُبِينٌ . أَمْ يَقُولُونَ افْتَرَاهُ ، قُلْ إِنِ افْتَرَيْتُهُ فَلَا تَمْلِكُونَ لِي مِنَ اللَّهِ شَيْئًا هُوَ أَعْلَمُ بِمَا تُفِيضُونَ فِيهِ ، كَفَىٰ بِهِ شَهِيدًا بَيْنِي وَبَيْنَكُمْ ، وَهُوَ الْغَفُورُ الرَّحِيمُ).

"When Our clear signs are recited to them, the disbelievers say, of the Truth (the Qur'an) when it

*comes to them: 'This is plain magic!' Or do they say,
'He (Prophet Mohammad) has forged it?' Say: 'Had I
forged it, then you have no power to support me against
Allah. He knows best of what you say among yourselves
concerning it. Sufficient is He as witness between me
and you! And He is the Oft-Forgiving, the Most
Merciful.'"*   *(Qur'an 46:7–8)*

The occurrence of Allah's forgiveness and mercy in this context takes
the thoughtful audience by surprise, for the ayahs speak about the
Makkan disbelievers' nasty attitude towards both the Holy Qur'an and
the Holy Prophet. More precisely, the first ayah declares that these
disbelievers claimed that the Holy Qur'an was mere magic; the second
reports that they accused the Holy Prophet of faking and attributing it
to Allah. Logically speaking, in such a situation, one would expect a
threat or, at least, a strong warning from Allah to these people.
Instead, He reminds them of His forgiveness and His mercy to
encourage them to repent so that He may bestow His forgiveness and
mercy on them. He says:

$$(\text{...وَهُوَ الْغَفُورُ الرَّحِيمُ}).$$

"...and He is Oft-Forgiving, the Most Merciful."

The Excitation of the Appreciation of Allah

Allah has revealed a considerable portion of the Holy Qur'an to excite
people's thankfulness to Him. One of the different methods He uses
in this regard is reminding them of some of the infinite favours He
bestows on them. Immediately after the opening of surah Al-Nahl, for
example, He—in an extensive manner[77]—highlights many of these
favours. Also in the middle of the same surah, He resumes reminding
people of the same issue by highlighting other different favours that
He grants them.

In each of these segments of this surah, interestingly, Allah repeatedly

---

[77] Ayahs 5 –16

uses a special Arabic expression beloved to the human heart—namely, *lakum*, [78] which means "for you"—to enjoy, O humankind!

In the first segment, this expression—"lakum" [79]—occurs six times. In two consecutive ayahs, for instance, it recurs twice to remind people of the blessing of the water that He sends down from the sky for them to drink, and with it, He grows all kinds of crops for them to enjoy and vegetation for their livestock to graze. He says:

(هُوَ الَّذِى أَنْزَلَ مِنَ السَّمَاءِ مَآءً لَّكُم مَّنْهُ شَرَابٌ وَمِنْهُ شَجَرٌ فِيهِ تُسِيمُونَ. يُنبِتُ لَكُم بِهِ الزَّرْعَ وَالزَّيْتُونَ وَالنَّخِيلَ وَالأَعْنَابَ وَمِن كُلِّ الثَّمَرَاتِ إِنَّ فِي ذَلِكَ لآيَةً لِّقَوْمٍ يَتَفَكَّرُونَ).

"He it is Who sends water down from the sky; from it you drink and from it (grows) the vegetation on which you send your cattle to pasture. With it He causes crops to grow for you, the olives, the date-palms, the grapes,

---

[78] With respect to the excitation of Allah's appreciation by the usage of the Arabic expression "lakum," this section focuses on surah Al-Nahl, where this expression recurs remarkably. The same expression, however, occurs in other surahs to accomplish the same honourable objective. In one ayah in surah Al-Baqarah, for instance, Allah uses it twice to create special, positive effects on people's hearts in a way that motivates them to become thankful to Him. He says:

(الذي جَعَلَ لَكُمُ الأَرْضَ فِرَاشاً وَالسَّمَاء بِنَاءً وَأَنزَلَ مِنَ السَّمَاءِ مَاءً فَأَخْرَجَ بِهِ مِنَ الثَّمَرَاتِ رِزْقاً لَّكُمْ ، فَلاَ تَجْعَلُواْ لله أَنداداً وانتم تعلمون).

"Who has made the earth a resting place for you, and the sky as a canopy, and sent down water (rain) from the sky and brought forth therewith fruits as a provision for you. Then do not set up rivals to Allah (in worship) while you know (that He Alone has the right to be worshipped)." (Qur'an 2:22)

[79] Also in the same surah, Allah uses the same Arabic expression "lakum" to call people's attention to an amazing fact capable of overwhelming the listening heart with a deep sense of gratitude to Him. He says:

(هُوَ الَّذِي خَلَقَ لَكُم مَّا فِي الأَرْضِ جَمِيعاً...)

"It is He Who has created for you all things that are on earth...." (Qur'an 2:29)

*and every kind of fruit. Verily, in this there is indeed an
evident proof and a manifest sign for people who give
thought."*   *(Qur'an 16:10-11)*

In the ayah next to this one, Allah employs the same previous
expression, "lakum," to, again, remind people that He is the One Who
has subjugated different universal phenomena and gigantic entities of
His creation for their service—namely, the daytime, the nighttime, the
sea, the moon, the sun, and the stars. With respect to this, He declares:

(وَسَخَّرَ لَكُمُ الَّيْلَ وَالنَّهَارَ وَالشَّمْسَ وَالْقَمَرَ ، وَالنُّجُومُ مُسَخَّرَاتٌ بِأَمْرِهِ ، إِنَّ فِي
ذَلِكَ لَآيَاتٍ لَّقَوْمٍ يَعْقِلُونَ).

*"And He has subjected the night and the day for you,
and the sun and the moon; and the stars are subjected by
His command. Surely, in this are proofs for people who
understand."*   *(Qur'an 16:12)*

Then using the same expression, "lakum," in the ayah following the
above one, He reminds humans of all the things that He has created
on earth for them to enjoy. He states:

(وَمَا ذَرَأَ لَكُمْ فِي الأَرْضِ مُخْتَلِفًا أَلْوَانُهُ ، إِنَّ فِي ذَلِكَ لَآيَةً لَّقَوْمٍ يَذَّكَّرُونَ).[80]

*"And whatsoever He has created for you on the earth of
varying colours (and qualities from vegetation and fruits*

---

[80] The same expression, "lakum," occurs in surah Al-Mulk in association with the
Planet Earth. In this surah, Allah calls people's attention to the fact that it is He Who
has made this whole planet under their control. Here He uses the adjective *"thalool,"*
which in this context, means completely succumbing and obedient to humans.
People's easy and enjoyable life on this amazing, generous planet is, certainly, due to
the fact that Allah has made it under their control—that is, *"thalool."* Imagine the
countless things that humans do and can do on this planet and the infinite number
of things it furnishes them with. In this surah and with regard to this issue, Allah
says:

(وَهُوَ الَّذِى جَعَلَ لَكُمُ الأَرْضَ ذَلُولًا...)

"...and it is He Who has made the earth subservient to you!"
(Qur'an 67:15)

*(botanical life) and from animal (zoological life). Verily,
in this is a sign for people who remember!"*

(Qur'an 16:13)

Also in the middle of this surah—where, again, Allah highlights more
different favours He bestows on humans—the expression "lakum"
recurs six times. In one ayah, for instance, He employs it twice to
highlight some more special blessings that He always favours humans
with: having spouses, children, grandchildren, and good sustenance.
He says:

(وَاللَّهُ جَعَلَ لَكُمْ مِّنْ أَنفُسِكُمْ أَزْوَاجًا وَجَعَلَ لَكُمْ مِّنْ أَزْوَاجِكُم بَنِينَ وَحَفَدَةً
وَرَزَقَكُم مِّنَ الطَّيِّبَاتِ...)

*"And Allah has made for you spouses of your own
nature, and made for you, out of them, children and
grandchildren, and provided for you sustenance of the
best..."*   *(Qur'an 16:72)*

As previously mentioned, the human journey in this life is difficult and
full of countless challenges of various nature. At different stages in
their lives, therefore, people need others to help and support them. So
the above ayah highlights a great favour that Allah bestows on people
at a certain stage of their lives, namely having a spouse. Spouses not
only split concerns, responsibilities, duties, and burdens with each
other, but they also provide one another with comfort, security,
tranquillity, peace of mind, support, care, love, and sexual
gratification.[81]

---

[81] In the context of the messages in the following ayahs, the Arabic root *s-k-n*
suggests most of the above-mentioned meanings:

(...وَجَعَلَ مِنْهَا زَوْجَهَا لِيَسْكُنَ إِلَيْهَا...)

*"...and from it He made its mate so that he might find comfort in
her..."*   *(Qur'an 7:189)*

(وَمِنْ آيَاتِهِ أَنْ خَلَقَ لَكُم مِّنْ أَنفُسِكُمْ أَزْوَاجًا لِّتَسْكُنُوا إِلَيْهَا وَجَعَلَ بَيْنَكُم مَّوَدَّةً وَرَحْمَةً ، إِنَّ فِي ذَلِكَ لَآيَاتٍ
لِّقَوْمٍ يَتَفَكَّرُونَ).

In addition, children represent one of the best and most beloved fruits that a couple can have from a marital bond. According to the Holy Qur'an itself, having children constitutes half of the allurement of this life. No matter how successful, accomplished, rich, famous, or admirable spouses are, they still feel sad and deprived if they don't have children. In fact, this strong, intuitive, human desire for having children and being a parent motivates many people who don't have children to adopt some. Also the natural human desire for survival seems to be one of the reasons underlying this inflamed human passion for having one's own children.

Thus, to generate a strong sense of appreciation in the heart, the previous ayah calls people's attention to the invaluable blessing of having children so that they may appreciate their Merciful and Generous Lord. Again, using the same beloved Arabic expression, "lakum," Allah addresses all humanity saying:

(...وَجَعَلَ لَكُم مِّنْ أَزْوَاجِكُم بَنِينَ وَحَفَدَةً...)

"...and has made for you, from your spouses, children, and grandchildren..."

Certainly, the pleasure of having children and grandchildren increases when the person who has them enjoys a good provision—*tayyibat,*[82] as Allah refers to it in the previous ayah. Parents sitting around a dinner table full of a variety of nice, delicious food, for instance, are, indeed, happier than they are if such a dinner table has little or no food on it. Accordingly, in this ayah, Allah calls people's attention to the good provision that He bestows on them to enjoy with their spouses, children, and grandchildren so that, again, they may become grateful to Him. He says:

(...وَرَزَقَكُم مِّنَ الطَّيِّبَاتِ)

"And among His signs is this, that He created for you mates from among yourselves, that you may dwell in tranquillity with them, and He has put between you affection and mercy. Verily in that are signs for those who reflect."   *(Qur'an 30:21)*

"...and provided for you sustenance of the best."

Moreover, in the same surah, Allah reminds humans that when they came to this life, they were empty-headed. But, fortunately, He has equipped them with different, invaluable faculties and organs without which their lives would become impossible: the hearing, the vision, and the brain. With respect to this, He says:

(وَاللَّهُ أَخْرَجَكُم مِّن بُطُونِ أُمَّهَاتِكُمْ لاَ تَعْلَمُونَ شَيْئًا وَجَعَلَ لَكُمُ السَّمْعَ وَالأَبْصَارَ وَالأَفْئِدَةَ لَعَلَّكُمْ تَشْكُرُونَ). [83]

"And Allah has brought you out from the wombs of your mothers while you knew nothing, and He gave you hearing, sight, and the minds, that you might give thanks."   (Qur'an 16:78)

Immediately after their births,[84] babies start to learn by using these and other amazing organs; accordingly, their knowledge and skills increase every day. And when they become adults, they have enough knowledge, skills, and experience that make them strong and independent. The professions they choose, in addition, may bring them personal gratification, recognition, and social prestige. They may even become charismatic and highly admired people, who are positively effective not only locally but also globally. So the underlying message in the above ayah is that a person's gifts, knowledge, experience, skills, expertise, power, and success, for example, are from Allah, and thus they deserve appreciation.

Further, in only one ayah in this segment of this surah, Allah, once again, uses the previously mentioned expression, "lakum," three times to highlight three different favours He bestows on humans. He says:

(وَاللَّهُ جَعَلَ لَكُم مِّمَّا خَلَقَ ظِلالاً وَجَعَلَ لَكُم مِّنَ الْجِبَالِ أَكْنَاناً وَجَعَلَ لَكُمْ سَرَابِيلَ

---

[83]According to Ibn Ashoor (1984), in this context, the word "fu'ad"—the singular form of "af'idah"—in this ayah, refers to the brain (p. 232). Al-Shawkani (2012), however, argued that it means "heart;" for, according to him, "fu'ad" refers to the middle of the heart (p. 228).

[84]It is proven that babies strat learning even before they are born.

تَقِيكُمُ الْحَرَّ وَسَرَابِيلَ تَقِيكُم بَأْسَكُمْ ، كَذَلِكَ يُتِمُّ نِعْمَتَهُ عَلَيْكُمْ لَعَلَّكُمْ تُسْلِمُونَ).

"And Allah has made shade for you out of that which He has created, and He has made places of refuge in the mountains for you, and He has made garments for you to protect you from the heat, and coats of mail to protect you from your violence. Thus does He perfect His favour for you, that you may submit yourselves to His will."

(Qur'an 16:81)

Furthermore, in surah Ibrahim, Allah recurrently employs the same expression, "lakum," to remind people of His unlimited kindness to them and thus to spark the virtue of thankfulness in their hearts. Precisely, in only two successive ayahs, He employs this expression five times to underscore different favours He bestows on them. The message in these ayahs, in fact, could have been expressed using this expression only twice. Its repetition in this manner, nevertheless, emphasizes these favours and touches the listening heart in a way that makes it overflow with a deep sense of gratitude to Allah, which is fundamental in the issues of eiman and taqwa.

In these two ayahs, Allah states:

(اللَّهُ الَّذِي خَلَقَ السَّمَاوَاتِ وَالْأَرْضَ وَأَنزَلَ مِنَ السَّمَاءِ مَاءً فَأَخْرَجَ بِهِ مِنَ الثَّمَرَاتِ رِزْقاً لَكُمْ ، وَسَخَّرَ لَكُمُ الْفُلْكَ لِتَجْرِيَ فِي الْبَحْرِ بِأَمْرِهِ ، وَسَخَّرَ لَكُمُ الْأَنْهَارَ . وَسَخَّرَ لَكُمُ الشَّمْسَ وَالْقَمَرَ دَائِبَيْنِ ، وَسَخَّرَ لَكُمُ اللَّيْلَ وَالنَّهَارَ).

"Allah is He Who has created the heavens and the earth and sends down water from the sky, and thereby brought forth fruits as provision for you; and He has made the ships to be of service to you, that they may sail through the sea by His command; and He has made rivers [also] to be of service to you. And He has made the sun and the moon, both constantly pursuing their courses, to be of service to you; and He has made the night and the day to be of service to you." (Qur'an 14:32–33)

Interestingly, after highlighting different blessings in the surahs of Al-Nahl and Ibrahim, Allah reminds humans that the blessings He bestows on them are certainly beyond their ability to name and count. In each of these two surahs, He challenges humankind saying:

$$\text{(وَإِن تَعُدُّواْ نِعْمَةَ اللَّهِ لاَ تُحْصُوهَآ...)!}$$

"And if you would try to count the favours of Allah, you would never be able to count them...!"
(Qur'an 14:34) & (Qur'an 16:18)

The Appreciation of Beauty

According to Ibn Al-Qayyim (2005), Imam Muslim narrated that the Holy Prophet said:

"Verily, Allah is beautiful, and He loves beauty" (p. 172).

$$\text{"إن الله جميل، يحب الجمال."}$$

In fact, Allah's love for beauty reflects clearly on this overwhelmingly wonderful universe He has created. Our planet, for example, teems with endless, beautiful things that attract the eye to look, force the brain to reflect, and compel the heart to appreciate, love, and glorify the Creator. Allah, in addition, has created humans not only in a way that makes them appreciate and enjoy beauty but also in a fashion that makes them always in search for it. He has also enriched the earth with an endless spectrum of material that generously satisfies this inflamed human longing for beauty. Most importantly, He recurrently raises the issue of beauty in the Qur'an to address people's strong desire for it so that they may acknowledge, appreciate, and glorify Him.

A beautiful view of a clear night sky with billions of glittering stars, for instance, can have dramatic effects on the human brain, soul, heart, and attitude when beholders go beyond what their eyes can observe to what their hearts can see—the Creator. Allah, in fact, calls people's attention to the sky's beauty many times in the Qur'an. In surah Al-Saffat, for example, He emphatically declares:

$$\text{(إِنَّا زَيَّنَّا السَّمَآءَ الدُّنْيَا بِزِينَةٍ الْكَوَاكِبِ).}$$

"Verily, We have adorned the nearest heaven with the stars."   *(Qur'an 37:6)*

In surah Al-Mulk, He repeats the same previous invitation so that people may reflect on this extremely wonderful beauty of the sky. He indicates:

(وَلَقَدْ زَيَّنَّا السَّمَاءَ الدُّنْيَا بِمَصَابِيحَ...)

"And indeed We have adorned the nearest heaven with lamps..."   *(Qur'an 67:5)*

Surah Al-Hijr, in addition, carries a similar message to all people who can see so that they may reflect on the amazing beauty in the sky and thus appreciate its Creator. It says:

(وَلَقَدْ جَعَلْنَا فِي السَّمَاءِ بُرُوجًا وَزَيَّنَّاهَا لِلنَّاظِرِينَ).

"And indeed, We have put the big stars in the heaven and We have beautified it for the beholders."
(Qur'an 15:16)

Obviously, the sky's beautification for beholders that Allah indicates in this ayah suggests its expected positive effects on the human attitude towards Him. In other words, this amazing ornamentation of the sky is supposed to attract people to look, reflect, enjoy, and thus appreciate, love, and glorify Allah—its Originator. When people experience the unique joy of reflection on the sky's beauty, they become motivated to reflect on it more often in order to experience this pleasurable feeling again and again. As a result, they become attracted to the sky more than any time before. Gradually, this recurrent, thoughtful reflection on the sky's beauty transcends their longings from being earthly and inferior to being heavenly and superior. That is, they become more focused on the upper world than on the lower one, which is under their feet, an issue that gradually ties their hearts' strings to—figuratively speaking—the Throne of Allah!

Interestingly, all the previous ayahs highlight the beauty in the sky only, which is represented by the *kawakib* (constellations), *massabeeh* (lamps), and *burooj* (the signs of the Zodiac). [85] In the following ayahs, from surah Qaf, however, Allah calls the human attention to the issue of beauty in the sky and on the earth. He says:

(أَفَلَمْ يَنظُرُواْ إِلَى السَّمَاءِ فَوْقَهُمْ كَيْفَ بَنَيْنَاهَا وَزَيَّنَّاهَا وَمَا لَهَا مِن فُرُوجٍ. وَالْأَرْضَ مَدَدْنَاهَا وَأَلْقَيْنَا فِيهَا رَوَاسِيَ وَأَنبَتْنَا فِيهَا مِن كُلِّ زَوْجٍ بَهِيجٍ . تَبْصِرَةً وَذِكْرَى لِكُلِّ عَبْدٍ مُّنِيبٍ . وَنَزَّلْنَا مِنَ السَّمَاءِ مَاءً مُّبَارَكاً فَأَنبَتْنَا بِهِ جَنَّاتٍ وَحَبَّ الْحَصِيدِ . وَالنَّخْلَ بَاسِقَاتٍ لَّهَا طَلْعٌ نَّضِيدٌ).

"Have they not looked at the heaven above them, how We have made it and adorned it, and there are no cracks in it. And the earth! We have spread it out, and set thereon mountains standing firm, and We planted in it every lovely pair. An insight and a reminder for every servant who turns to Allah in repentance. And We send down blessed water from the sky, then We produce therewith gardens and grain that are reaped. And tall date-palms, with arranged clusters."

(Qur'an 50:6–10)

The beauty of the sky in the first ayah above appears at night only. Yet during the day, the sky reveals another aspect of beauty—for example, when the sky is clear and even when it is partially cloudy, it reveals an agreeable view, at least to some people in some cultures. At sunrise and sunset, in addition, the sky's beautiful view has always attracted the human eye and left its remarkably strong effects on the human heart. People have, in fact, reflected this sentimental effect of the sky's beauty on various creative, artistic works—such as poetry, songs, paintings, and wonderful photographs, to mention only a few.

In the rest of the ayahs, the element of beauty is confined to that on the earth, and it is represented by the view of the mountains and the scene of an infinite number of plants carrying endless kinds of fruits

---

[85] This translation of the word *burooj* has been quoted from A. Y. Ali's (2001, p. 224 & p. 530).

and crops. This is clear in this eloquent, stirring, and compelling Qur'anic sentence:

(...وَأَنبَتْنَا فِيهَا مِن كُلِّ زَوْجٍ بَهِيجٍ)!

"..and We planted[86] in it every lovely pair!"[87]

The human natural love for greenery and crops, in fact, makes such a beautiful view even more enjoyable and more beloved. Of the countless, amazing plants He has created, Allah singles out the date-palm trees, which represent only one of the uncountable, attractive ones that He has adorned our amazing planet with. Besides being slender and remarkably tall, the date-palm trees are significantly distinctive, elegant, beautiful, amazing, graceful, and attractive. The view of their dates hanging down—like chandeliers—in neat and well-organized clusters—a fact that the last ayah highlights—offers these outstandingly beautiful trees an additional dimension of splendour and glamour.

Allah could have pointed to the date-palm trees without using the word *basiqat*. But this word, which means considerably tall,[88] has a special role to play in the message of this ayah. Precisely, it helps

---

[86] The word "planted" in this translation does not convey the actual meaning of the Arabic verb in this ayah, the literal translation of which is "grew," which is more accurate than its translations in the following. Abdel Haleem (2008) translated it as "caused" (p. 340), Asad (2012), as "caused it to bring forth" (p. 908), and A. Y. Ali (2008) as "produced" (p. 1411).

[87] (وَأَنبَتْنَا فِيهَا مِن كُلِّ زَوْجٍ بَهِيجٍ)!

[88] Allah could've used another Arabic plural form for this noun; specifically, He could have said "*basiqah*," instead of "*basiqat*." In fact, each of these two words has three syllables. However, whereas ba-si-qah has only one *alif*, basiqat has two *alifs*, so the quick repetition of the *alif* sound in *basiqat* helps in the creation of a mental picture of palm trees that seem taller, compared to those in the mental picture created by the word *basiqah*. Even the way these two words are written in Arabic provides two visuals in which the view of the word *basiqat* is closer to the view of the date-palm trees than that of *basiqah*. Based on this, you may now view, below, the way each of these words is written in Arabic.

basiqat باسِقات
basiqah باسقة

create—in the audience's minds—a beautiful mental picture of this exceptionally elegant tree. This mental image, in turn, leads to the creation of special mental and psychological effects that excite the glorification of the Creator deep in the heart, the actual addressee of this Qur'anic message. Further, the question form and the disapproving tone in this message suggest that the beauty in the sky and that on the earth can have a remarkably positive influence on the heart, but only if beholders reflect. Again, Allah starts this whole message saying:

$$\text{؟(}\ldots\text{أَفَلَمْ يَنظُرُواْ)}$$

"Have they not looked...?"

Furthermore, in these ayahs, each of the Arabic words *yanthuroo, zayiannaha, baheej, basiqat,* and *nadheed*[89] forcefully points to the element of beauty both in the sky and on the earth, and each of them invites an excellent quality of reflection that forces beholders to appreciate, love, and glorify the Creator. Similarly, another couple of words, namely *tabssirah*[90] and *thikra*,[91] in the third ayah, suggest that the creation of all the things mentioned in these ayahs—the sky, the earth, the mountains, the rain, the different lovely pairs of fruits and crops, as well as the palm trees—and the issue of beauty highlighted in them are supposed to elicit acknowledgement and glorification of the Creator.

In addition, Allah employs the Arabic root *n-th-r*[92] many times in the Qur'an to direct humans to use their eyes and ponder over different things in the universe so that they may realize His Greatness and His infinite ability to create and do whatever He pleases. In one ayah in the surah of Al-An'am, for example, Allah uses this root in the imperative form to encourage people to reflect on His amazing power, represented by His creation of endless types of plants from the water of the sky. At the end of this ayah, interestingly, He singles out the

---

[89] ينظروا (they look) ، زيّنّاها (We have adorned it.) ، بهيج (lovely)، باسقات (considerably tall)

[90] تبصرة (insight)

[91] ذكرى (reminder)

[92] Allah has predominantly employed this root as a verb in the present and in the imperative forms. The English equivalent of the present form from this Arabic root, for example, is look."

element of beauty associated with different crops' ripeness and invites people to reflect on it saying:

$$(...\text{انْظُرُوا إِلَى ثَمَرِهِ إِذَآ أَثْمَرَ وَيَنْعِهِ}...)$$

"...look at their fruits as they grow and ripen..."

Most importantly, in the last sentence in this ayah, Allah emphatically declares that such a phenomenon—the creation of different plants, crops, and fruits, as well as their beauty—represents a compelling sign of His amazing, unlimited power, but only for those who believe. Here is the whole text of the ayah, so you may read it thoughtfully:

$$(\text{وَهُوَ الَّذِي أَنزَلَ مِنَ السَّمَآءِ مَآءً فَأَخْرَجْنَا بِهِ نَبَاتَ كُلِّ شَيْءٍ فَأَخْرَجْنَا مِنْهُ}$$
$$\text{خَضِراً نُّخْرِجُ مِنْهُ حَبّاً مُّتَرَاكِباً وَمِنَ النَّخْلِ مِن طَلْعِهَا قِنْوَانٌ دَانِيَةٌ وَجَنَّاتٍ مِّنْ}$$
$$\text{أَعْنَابٍ وَالزَّيْتُونَ وَالرُّمَّانَ مُشْتَبِهاً وَغَيْرَ مُتَشَابِهٍ ، انْظُرُوا إِلَى ثَمَرِهِ إِذَآ أَثْمَرَ وَيَنْعِهِ ،}$$
$$\text{إِنَّ فِي ذِلِكُمْ لَآيَاتٍ لَّقَوْمٍ يُؤْمِنُونَ}).$$

"It is He Who sends down water from the sky, and with it We bring forth vegetation of all kinds, and out of it We bring forth green stalks, from which We bring forth thick clustered grain. And out of the date palm and its sprouts come forth clusters of dates hanging low and near, and gardens of grapes, olives and pomegranates, each similar, yet different. Look at their fruits when they begin to bear, and the ripeness thereof.[93] *Verily, in these things there are signs for people who believe."*   (Qur'an 6:99)

Also at the beginning of surah Al-Nahl, Allah mentions the element of beauty more often using three different words that connote beauty: *jamal*, *zeenah*, and *hilyah*.[94] First, He draws people's attention to the view of livestock, as a source of beauty for their owners, especially—as the ayah indicates—when these animals pasture during the day, and when

---

[93] Compared to A. Y. Ali's, A. Ali's, Asad's, and Khalidi's, Abdel Haleem's translations of this imperative is more accurate. He rendered it as *"Watch their fruits as they grow and ripen"* (2008, p. 87).

[94] جمال (beauty) ، زينة (adornment) ، حلية (ornament)

they lay down to rest at the end of it. The aspect of beauty that these animals represent to their owners can be looked at from two different angles. First, livestock's owners may see nothing as beautiful as the view of their animals when they are happily and peacefully grazing during the day and when they are relaxing at home at the end of it. Second, the ownership of these animals offers the owners special social beauty and glamour: They are beautiful people because they are economically strong, socially influential, and prestigious.

In reference to the aspect of beauty that Allah bestows on these livestock's owners, He states:

$$^{95}\ (\text{وَلَكُمْ فِيهَا جَمَالٌ حِينَ تُرِيحُونَ وَحِينَ تَسْرَحُونَ}).$$

"And there is beauty in them for you, when you bring them home in the evening, and when you lead them forth to pasture (in the morning)."   (Qur'an: 16:6)

Second, people take pride in the means of transportation they possess or use. In this surah, Allah points to a variety of domestic animals that—besides being a means of transportation—represent an essential source of beauty for their owners. He says:

$$(\text{وَالْخَيْلَ وَالْبِغَالَ وَالْحَمِيرَ لِتَرْكَبُوهَا وَزِينَةً}...)$$

"And (He has created) horses, mules and donkeys for you to ride, and as an adornment..."   (Qur'an 16:8)

---

[95] Here it is important to note that in the second ayah above, Allah emphasizes this special type of beauty He has bestowed on livestock's owners. This emphasis stems from the repetition of the Arabic word *"heen,"* meaning "when," to equally highlight the beauty of these livestock as they're grazing in the daytime and as they're resting at home at the end of the day. In fact, Allah could've used this word only once to express the same message, but without emphasis. In other words, its usage twice here makes the ayah's underlying message thus: "You have beauty in these livestock not only when you bring them home to rest but also when you take them out to pasture," so acknowledge their Creator, your Merciful Lord, Who has given them to you, and be always thankful to Him.

In the past, people used only animals to travel from place to another—many still do. Today, however, most of them use different types of modern means of transportation, which sometimes represent a distinctive aspect of their social beauty. The message in this ayah should, therefore, remind people that their modern means of transportation—e.g., cars, buses, trains, and planes—are also a source of beauty for them, and thus they should appreciate Allah for making their current means of transportation faster, safer, and more beautiful. Third, this surah reminds people of another matter of beauty that Allah has made available to them, namely the beautification objects they obtain from the sea. Here the Holy Qur'an sheds light on people's extreme fondness of beauty and their natural, extraordinary eagerness to obtain it: They search for it wherever it exists. Even if it lies at the bottom of the sea or it requires fighting with extremely dangerous waves, they are still willing to risk their lives to possess it!

Examine the following Qur'anic message that projects humans in the middle of the sea looking for matter to beautify themselves. It sates:

(وَهُوَ الَّذِى سَخَّرَ الْبَحْرَ لِتَأْكُلُواْ مِنْهُ لَحْمًا طَرِيًّا وَتَسْتَخْرِجُواْ مِنْهُ حِلْيَةً تَلْبَسُونَهَا وَتَرَى الْفُلْكَ مَوَاخِرَ فِيهِ وَلِتَبْتَغُواْ مِن فَضْلِهِ وَلَعَلَّكُمْ تَشْكُرُونَ).

"And He it is Who subjected the sea [to you], that you may eat from the fresh tender meat, and that you bring forth out of it ornaments to wear. And you see the ships ploughing through it, that you may seek from His bounty and that you may perhaps be grateful."
(Qur'an 16:14)

Also in this ayah, Allah draws people's attention to the view of the ships in the middle of the sea saying:

(...وَتَرَى الْفُلْكَ مَوَاخِرَ فِيهِ...)

"...and you see the ships ploughing through it..."

In addition to the highlighted kindness of Allah to people, represented by His enabling their little, helpless ships to sail safely and gracefully in the danger of the endless sea, the Qur'anic expression (وَتَرَى), meaning *"and you see,"* in this ayah, carries a subtle, underlying message of beauty, specifically the beautiful view of the ships as they plough the surface of the sea (Qutb, 1992, p. 2163).

Interestingly, the element of beauty in the Holy Qur'an and its relationship with the subject of taqwa extends to include even rocks. In surah Fatir, for example, Allah points to this issue saying:

(... وَمِنَ الْجِبَالِ جُدَدٌ بِيضٌ وَحُمْرٌ مُخْتَلِفٌ أَلْوَانُهَا وَغَرَابِيبُ سُودٌ).

"...and in the mountains are tracts white and red, of various shades of colour, and black intense in hue."
(Qur'an 35: 27)

A. Y. Ali (2008) wrote the following reflection on the above ayah:

These wonderful colours and shades of colours are to be found not only in vegetation but in rocks and mineral products. There are the white veins of marble and quartz or chalk, and red laterite, the blue basaltic rocks, the ink-black flints, and all the variety, shade, and gradation of colours. Speaking of mountains, we think of their "azure hue" from a distance due to atmospheric effects, and these atmospheric effects lead our thoughts to the glories of clouds, sunsets, the zodiacal light, the aurora borealis, and all kinds of nature's gorgeous pageantry. (p. 1161)

Again, such recurrent reminders of the element of beauty in the Holy Qur'an prove people's extreme fondness for it. Most importantly, it suggests the potential role that beauty can play in their appreciation of the Creator and in their connection with Him. Nevertheless, people shouldn't confine their love for beauty to physical things. They should go beyond its tangible, earthly form to its abstract, spiritual, ethical, and invaluable one—the excellent Islamic principles, values, morals, and conduct. In surah Al-A'raf, therefore, Allah advises people to transcend their love for beauty from being worldly to being heavenly. He also assures them that they look more beautiful when they obey Him than when they don't, even if they wear the most beautiful worldly attires. He says:

(يَا بَنِي آدَمَ قَدْ أَنزَلْنَا عَلَيْكُمْ لِبَاسًا يُوَارِي سَوْءَاتِكُمْ وَرِيشًا ، وَلِبَاسُ التَّقْوَى

ذَلِكَ خَيْرٌ ، ذَلِكَ مِنْ آيَاتِ اللّهِ لَعَلَّهُم يَذَّكَّرُون). [96]

"O Children of Adam! We have bestowed raiment upon you to cover your shame, as well as to be an adornment to you. But the raiment of righteousness, that is the better. Such are among the Signs of Allah, that they may receive admonition."   (Qur'an 7:26)

The Excitation of Longing

Longing is a special psychological feeling associated with what we love and what we desire to achieve, access, or possess. One of the different methods that Allah uses in the Holy Qur'an to ignite the fire of taqwa in the heart is the excitation of longing. Specifically, He has revealed numerous ayahs that describe His Gardens in a way that excites and intensifies the human longing for the bliss He has prepared in them for His obedient, beloved servants. He has, in fact, dedicated huge portions of different surahs to the achievement of this. Examples of such surahs are AL-Rahman (The Most Gracious), Al-Waqi'ah, and Al-Insan (The Human Being). This section casts a little light on two ayahs that address the issue of longing in the Holy Qur'an, one from surah Al-Mutaffifeen and another from surah Al-Sajdah (The Prostration). It also sheds light on the surah of Al-Insan, as a model that addresses the element of longing intensively.

The Element of Longing in Surah Al-Mutaffifeen

Today, people spend a lot of time and money to travel to different places, in the same country or abroad, just to visit specific places where they can enjoy the splendour of certain, spectacular views. Some of these places are, for example, Rainbow Mountains of Zhangye Danxia, China; Aogashima Volcano, Japan; and the Grand

---

[96] In reference to the issue of taqwa in this ayah, Allah uses the Arabic word *thalik*, the equivalent of the English demonstrative pronoun "that." Grammatically, this demonstrative pronoun is used to refer to something or someone in a remote or a high position. Its usage in this ayah, therefore, suggests the highness of taqwa as well as the great effort one needs to exert before he or she may acquire its attire that the ayah recommends.

Canyon National Park, the US. Also on different occasions, cities around the world organize numerous activities to entertain their residents and visitors. On the 4th of July, for instance, people in many cities throughout the US start gathering at specific places and wait for many hours in order to watch and enjoy the incredible shows of fireworks.

Allah, of course, knows people's love for exceptionally beautiful and wonderful things; He also knows the great joy they derive from seeing them. Therefore, what He has prepared for the fortunate dwellers of His Gardens to watch for pleasure and fun is, indeed, beyond human imagination. With respect to this, in surah Al-Mutaffifeen, for example, He says:

$$\text{(إِنَّ الْأَبْرَارَ لَفِي نَعِيمٍ . عَلَى الْأَرَائِكِ يَنْظُرُونَ)!}$$

"Truly, the righteous will be in Bliss. On couches, watching!" (Qur'an 83: 22–23)

Based on the message in the second ayah, fortunate believers who succeed in entering the Gardens of bliss will experience special delight through their sense of seeing. Precisely, they will be sitting on raised couches, and they will be watching. But what they will watch isn't specified in this ayah. Perhaps the unspecificity of this issue in this context is due to the infinite number of the inexpressibly spectacular things that these fortunate people will watch in that particular setting. It is also possibly due to the fact that what they will watch in that place is beyond human cognition and imagination.

By and large, this message is meant to excite the emotion of longing in people's hearts by sparking the flames of curiosity in their minds, again, as a result of lack of specificity in the second ayah. The message is, indeed, extremely exciting, and the more that people ponder over it, the more overwhelmed with wonder and longing for that setting they become.

In reference to this ayah, scholars of the exegesis of the Holy Qur'an claimed that these fortunate people will be watching the endless bliss that Allah has prepared for them in His Gardens. They also claimed that believers at that moment will be looking at Allah Himself (Al-

Qurtubi, 2014, p. 171).[97] Ibn Kathir added that the most honourable among them will have the honour of seeing Allah twice a day (2014, p. 498). So, based on this, one may ask: Is there anything more exciting and more motivating than this?

The Element of Longing in Surah Al-Sajdah

Like the previous ayah, from surah Al Mutaffifeen, the following one, from surah Al-Sajdah, addresses and excites the human emotion of longing, but from a different perspective. It challengingly declares:

(فَلَا تَعْلَمُ نَفْسٌ مَّآ أُخْفِيَ لَهُم مِّن قُرَّةِ أَعْيُنٍ جَزَآءً بِمَا كَانُواْ يَعْمَلُونَ).

"No person knows what is kept hidden for them of delights of eyes as a reward for what they used to do."
(Qur'an 32:17)

This ayah is significantly forceful in the ignition of the emotion of longing in the heart for the Gardens of Allah. Unlike many other ayahs that address this issue, this one suggests that the element of bliss in these Gardens is not only unspecific, but it is also unlimited. In other words, while many other ayahs mention specific elements of bliss in the Gardens of Allah, such as food, drinks, and clothing, this one declares that the bliss in those Gardens is beyond human knowledge, imagination, and expectation. The only specific issue in this ayah in this regard is that the bliss that Allah has prepared for His honourable servants is but *"quratu aiun"*[98]—ultimate and perfect happiness!

The Element of Longing in Surah Al-Insan

On the surah's level, Al-Insan represents an ideal model that forcefully and effectively addresses the sentiment of longing to attract people to Allah's Gardens. Allah has, in fact, dedicated a huge portion of this surah—almost its half—to exclusively speak about the bliss He has prepared in His Gardens for His devout, beloved, honourable servants. Besides its exceptionally beautiful promise, this surah has

---

[97]Al-Saadi (2011, p. 867) and Al-Shawkani (2012, p. 505) provided the same meaning above.

[98] قُرَّة أعين

different factors that make it not only vivid but also unique, beautiful, fascinating, beloved, enjoyable, and extraordinarily influential.

First, it has captivating rhythms and soft rhymes. The rhyme in its first two-thirds is generally *"ra, ra, ra."* In most of the last third of the surah, nonetheless, this rhyme changes smoothly and unnoticeably to *"la, la, la,"* maintaining the surah's same overwhelming authority and sweet melody that attracts the ear and captures the heart.

Second, this surah enjoys a unique linguistic texture represented by a remarkably charming diction, beautiful expressions, elegant words, and special Arabic grammar. This special grammar helps in the achievement of three important issues: the maintenance of the surah's beautiful rhythms and rhymes, the creation of a delighting psychological atmosphere in which it deeply immerses its audience's hearts, and—most importantly—the effective delivery of its beautiful, beloved message. Some of the grammatical features used in the creation and the achievement of these special aspects of the surah, for example, are the objective case,[99] the adjectivals,[100] the adverbials,[101] the predicate of *can*, and the passive voice.

Third, the ayahs' lengths are similar throughout the surah, a feature that re-energizes its melodious, heart-capturing nature. The ayahs' lengths, in other words, aren't too extensive to make the audience forget the last word's sound in the preceding ayah, but they are perfectly measured to help them remember that specific sound before it recurs again in the end of the subsequent ayah in an effective, regular pattern, which overflows the listening heart with great delight.

These different factors work together, hand in hand, to generate the musical, the mental, the psychological, the spiritual, and the inspirational atmosphere needed to attract the heart to listen to the surah's beautiful message not only attentively but also eagerly, lovingly, and joyfully.

Besides the sentiment of longing it sparks in the listening heart, this surah, in fact, generates other psychological feelings fundamental to the issues of eiman and taqwa—namely, hope, happiness, and love. It also creates two important mental effects in its audience. First, it

---

[99] The objective case is a noun or a pronoun functioning as an object of the verb.
[100] An adjectival is a structure (group of words) that functions as an adjective.
[101] An adverbial is a structure (group of words) that functions as an adverb.

makes them perceive this life as a road or as a bridge to the other eternal, perfect one in Allah's Gardens of bliss. Second, it makes them determine to live their lives today according to the excellent Islamic values and rules so that they may enjoy the everlasting bliss in that perfect place.

Here—as explained earlier—we will confine our discussion to the element of longing as a major psychological emotion that Allah addresses in this surah to ignite the fire of taqwa deep in the human heart. First, let's read the text carefully.

(إِنَّ الْأَبْرَارَ يَشْرَبُونَ مِن كَأْسٍ كَانَ مِزَاجُهَا كَافُوراً . عَيْناً يَشْرَبُ بِهَا عِبَادُ اللَّهِ يُفَجِّرُونَهَا تَفْجِيراً . يُوفُونَ بِالنَّذْرِ وَيَخَافُونَ يَوْماً كَانَ شَرُّهُ مُسْتَطِيراً . وَيُطْعِمُونَ الطَّعَامَ عَلَى حُبِّهِ مِسْكِيناً وَيَتِيماً وَأَسِيراً . إِنَّمَا نُطْعِمُكُمْ لِوَجْهِ اللَّهِ لَا نُرِيدُ مِنكُمْ جَزَاءً وَلَا شُكُوراً . إِنَّا نَخَافُ مِن رَّبِّنَا يَوْماً عَبُوساً قَمْطَرِيراً . فَوَقَاهُمُ اللَّهُ شَرَّ ذَلِكَ الْيَوْمِ وَلَقَّاهُمْ نَضْرَةً وَسُرُوراً . وَجَزَاهُم بِمَا صَبَرُوا جَنَّةً وَحَرِيراً . مُتَّكِئِينَ فِيهَا عَلَى الْأَرَائِكِ لَا يَرَوْنَ فِيهَا شَمْساً وَلَا زَمْهَرِيراً . وَدَانِيَةً عَلَيْهِمْ ظِلَالُهَا وَذُلِّلَتْ قُطُوفُهَا تَذْلِيلاً . وَيُطَافُ عَلَيْهِم بِآنِيَةٍ مِّن فِضَّةٍ وَأَكْوَابٍ كَانَتْ قَوَارِيرَا . قَوَارِيرَ مِن فِضَّةٍ قَدَّرُوهَا تَقْدِيراً . وَيُسْقَوْنَ فِيهَا كَأْساً كَانَ مِزَاجُهَا زَنجَبِيلاً . عَيْناً فِيهَا تُسَمَّى سَلْسَبِيلاً . وَيَطُوفُ عَلَيْهِمْ وِلْدَانٌ مُّخَلَّدُونَ إِذَا رَأَيْتَهُمْ حَسِبْتَهُمْ لُؤْلُؤاً مَّنثُوراً . وَإِذَا رَأَيْتَ ثَمَّ رَأَيْتَ نَعِيماً وَمُلْكاً كَبِيراً . عَالِيَهُمْ ثِيَابُ سُندُسٍ خُضْرٌ وَإِسْتَبْرَقٌ وَحُلُّوا أَسَاوِرَ مِن فِضَّةٍ وَسَقَاهُمْ رَبُّهُمْ شَرَاباً طَهُوراً . إِنَّ هَذَا كَانَ لَكُمْ جَزَاءً وَكَانَ سَعْيُكُم مَّشْكُوراً).

"Verily, the righteous shall drink of a cup mixed with kafur. A spring wherefrom the servants of Allah will drink, causing it to gush forth abundantly. They fulfil (their) vows, and they fear a Day whose evil will be wide-spreading. And they give food, in spite of their love for it, to the poor, the orphan, and the captive (saying): 'We feed you seeking Allah's Face only. We wish for no reward, nor thanks from you. Verily, We fear from our Lord a Day that is hard and distressful.' So, Allah saved them from the evil of that Day and gave them a light of beauty and joy. And

their recompense shall be Paradise, and silken garments, because they were patient. Reclining therein on raised couches, they will see there neither the excessive heat nor the excessive cold. And the shade thereof is close upon them, and the bunches of fruit thereof will hang low within their reach. And among them will be passed round vessels of silver and cups of crystal, crystal-clear, made of silver. They will determine the measure thereof. And they will be given to drink there of a cup (of wine) mixed with ginger. A spring there, called Salsabil. And round about them will (serve) boys of everlasting youth. If you see them, you would think them scattered pearls. And when you look there (in Paradise), you will see a delight (that cannot be imagined), and a great dominion. Their garments will be of fine green silk and Istabraq. They will be adorned with bracelets of silver, and their Lord will give them a purifying drink. And it will be said to them: 'Verily, this is a reward for you, and your endeavour has been accepted.'"   (Qur'an 76:5–22)

A wide spectrum of soft drinks in any society indicates its affluence and luxury. In rich countries, for example, it is difficult—if not impossible—to count the number of drinks that the marketplace makes available to consumers to enjoy every day. Conversely, in many poor countries, the majority of people drink almost only water, which might sometimes be difficult to access, and it may have many health problems. So in this surah, interestingly, Allah recurrently speaks about the element of the drinks—as a source of luxury and delight—He has prepared for His beloved servants in His amazing Gardens of bliss. He mentions it five times; each time, He introduces a different type, an issue that, of course, stresses the extraordinarily high level of luxury that the inhabitants of His Gardens will enjoy.

The first drink that Allah mentions in this surah has the flavour of *kafur*.[102] Obviously, there is no comparison between the kafur we know and the one in Allah's Gardens. What we need to understand with respect to this issue is that the flavour of that "kafur" must be indescribably pleasurable since Allah Himself has chosen it to be an ingredient of that drink in that cup that He will offer His honourable

---

[102] According to Abdel Haleem (2008), "kafur is a fragrant herb" (p. 4001).

guests in His high Gardens of bliss. Further, here Allah states only the flavour of that drink, but the drink itself remains unknown, a matter that intensifies the element of longing in the heart and makes the ayah's message even more exciting. With regard to this, He declares:

(إِنَّ الأَبْرَارَ يَشْرَبُونَ مِن كَأْسٍ كَانَ مِزَاجُهَا كَافُوراً).

"Verily, the righteous shall drink of a cup mixed with choicest fragrance."

The second ayah that speaks about the element of the drinks that Allah will offer His honourable guests in His Gardens of bliss says:

(عَيْناً يَشْرَبُ بِهَا عِبَادُ اللَّهِ يُفَجِّرُونَهَا تَفْجِيراً).

"A spring wherefrom the servants of Allah will drink, causing it to gush forth abundantly."

The third ayah states:

(وَيُطَافُ عَلَيْهِمْ بِآنِيَةٍ مِّن فِضَّةٍ وَأَكْوابٍ كَانَتْ قَوَارِيرَا . قَوَارِيرَا مِنْ فِضَّةٍ قَدَّرُوهَا تَقْدِيراً).

"And among them will be passed round vessels of silver and cups of crystal, Crystal-clear, made of silver. They will determine the measure thereof."

The fourth one proclaims:

(ويُسْقَوْنَ فِيهَا كَأْساً كَانَ مِزَاجُهَا زَنجَبِيلاً).

"And they will be given to drink there of a cup (of wine) mixed with ginger."

Grammatically, the passive voice [103] in the above ayah renders the actual subject of the verb "give" in the verb string *"will be given"*

---

unknown. So we don't know who serves that drink to the righteous. That is, this special grammar in this Qur'anic sentence draws the addressees' entire attention to that beverage; at the same time, it tells them nothing about those who serve it because the message's focal point is the blessing in that cup, not the servant who serves it.

In reference to the ginger flavour in this ayah, Al-Qurtubi (2014) said:

> The Arabs used to enjoy drinks that were mixed with ginger, due to the ginger's nice flavour and its role in digestion. Therefore, they were addressed in this manner to motivate them with . . . [things] they thought were the ultimate types of bliss. (pp. 92–93)

The fifth ayah that speaks about the element of the drink in this surah reveals an additional type of drink. It announces:

$$(\text{...عَيْناً فِيهَا تُسَمَّى سَلْسَبِيلاً}) \;.$$

"...a spring there, called Salsabil."

Above all, Allah—as a gesture of honour—associates Himself with the last drink He mentions in this surah. He says:

$$(\text{...وَسَقَاهُمْ رَبُّهُمْ شَرَاباً طَهُورا}).$$

"...and their Lord will give them a pure drink."

Further, looking beautiful and attractive is a major factor in human happiness—everyone wants to look nice and appealing to the eye. This surah, therefore, excites the addressee's emotion of longing for the Gardens of Allah through the light it sheds on their dwellers' looks. Their faces, in particular, shine with a special light of beauty that Allah favours them with, and their hearts overflow with permanent, deep-rooted gladness, which reflects on their beautiful faces and makes them even more alluring. With respect to this, Allah says:

$$(\text{...وَلَقَّاهُمْ نَضْرَةً وَسُرُوراً}).$$

(1996, p. 57). An example of this is The book was written.

> *"...and gave them a light of beauty and joy."*

People usually recline when they have peace of mind, but when they are stressed or distressed, they may not be able to. To shed light on the Garden inhabitants' peace of mind, Allah portrays them in a beloved, relaxing posture. He states:

(مُّتَّكِئِينَ فِيهَا عَلَى الأَرَائِكِ لاَ يَرَوْنَ فِيهَا شَمْساً وَلاَ زَمْهَرِيرا).

> *"Reclining therein on raised couches, they will experience there neither the excessive heat, nor the excessive cold."*

Since Allah Himself designs them,[104] these couches—on which these fortunate people will recline—must be astonishingly beautiful, exceptionally luxurious, and extraordinarily comfortable. Allah has, actually, mentioned them five times in the Holy Qur'an—once in each of the surahs of The Cave, Ya-Sin,[105] this one, and twice in the surah of Mutaffifeen. He also mentions this reclining posture seven times in the Holy Qur'an: once in the surahs of Al-Kahf, Sad,[106] Al-Tur (The Mount), Al-Waqi'ah, this one, and twice in the surah of Al-Rahman. Such a frequent recurrence of this issue indicates the happy, relaxing, and easy life that these successful people will enjoy in that perfect

---

[104] Of course, Allah does not prepare the things in His Gardens manually, but with His word "Be!"

[105] Like the message in this ayah, the one in the ayah from the surah of Ya-Sin portrays the honourable people of the Gardens reclining on these couches too, but, this time, with their spouses. In this regard, Allah says:

(هُمْ وَأَزْوَاجُهُمْ فِي ظِلَالٍ عَلَى الأَرَآئِكِ مُتَّكِئُونَ).

> *"They and their wives will be in pleasant shade, reclining on thrones."* (Qur'an 36:56)

Obviously, the presence of each person's spouse in this setting adds a romantic dimension to the ayah's message, and thus it becomes more exciting and more motivating to both genders.

[106] Sad, the name of this surah, refers to the fourteenth Arabic letter *sad*; therefore, it shouldn't be confused with the English word "sad."

place, compared to this demanding, stressful life that people have on the earth today.

Human happiness seems to be impossible in bad weather conditions. Humanity has, certainly, suffered considerably from the summer heat and winter cold. Allah, of course, knows the temperature's role in people's happiness, so in this surah, He assures them that in His Gardens of bliss, the temperature is neither hot nor cold—it is just perfect! He declares:

$$(\text{...}\ \text{لاَ يَرَوْنَ فِيهَا شَمْساً وَلاَ زَمْهَرِيراً})\ .$$

"...they will see there neither the excessive heat, nor the excessive cold."

Also the different items that the triumphant inhabitants of the Gardens use to eat and drink reveal another aspect of their luxury and extravagant lifestyle. In this surah, Allah mentions only a few of them, namely the silver vessels and the crystal cups. In reference to these fortunate people and the bliss they will enjoy, He says:

$$(\text{وَيُطَافُ عَلَيْهِمْ بِآنِيَةٍ مِّن فِضَّةٍ وَأَكْوابٍ كَانَتْ قَوَارِيرَا})\ .^{107}$$

"And amongst them will be passed round vessels of silver and cups of crystal."

As previously explained, in a similar context, the passive voice grammar in this message plays a special communication role. Precisely, it places emphasis on the vessels and the crystal cups rather than on the servants, who are, of course, purposefully ignored. In other words, the employment of this specific grammar in this context heightens the value of the blessings that will be served and thus excites the audience's sentiment of longing, which is, again, a major objective of this part of the surah.

Hypothetically speaking, Allah could've expressed this message thus:

---

[107] The special mental and psychological effects that this surah can create in the attentive addressees make them almost see these cups glittering and hear them jingling!

> *"Servants will pass round vessels of silver and cups of crystal amongst them."*

In this case, the focus will be divided between the subject of the verb—"servants," and its object—*"vessels of silver and cups of crystal,"* which are both underlined in this hypothetical sentence for clarity. But, perhaps Allah—the best communicator—has decided to ignore the servants and to mention only "the vessels and the cups" so that, again, the focus will be on the blessings that will be served in them, whether these blessings are "only drinks," as some scholars of the Qur'anic exegesis argued, or "both food and drinks," as other scholars claimed.[108]

Another issue that reflects the luxury of the residents of the Gardens of Allah is expressed in the beautiful message in the following ayah:

(وَيَطُوفُ عَلَيْهِمْ وِلْدَانٌ مُّخَلَّدُونَ إِذَا رَأَيْتَهُمْ حَسِبْتَهُمْ لُؤْلُؤاً مَّنثُوراً)!

> *"And round about them will (serve) boys of everlasting youth. If you see them, you would think them scattered pearls!"*

According to Al-Tabari (2010), Abd Allah ibn Amr narrated that in this setting, everyone of these fortunate people will be served by a thousand of these young boys, and each of them will be serving something completely different from the things that the rest of these servants will be serving at that moment (p. 280). Surprisingly, each of these triumphant dwellers of Allah's Gardens will be able to enjoy all of these countless types of bliss simultaneously!

Further, these extremely polite, obedient, elegant, and pearl-like boys, who are scattered all over that beautiful place, are, in fact, an indispensable part of the beauty parade that characterizes that wonderful setting in that amazing environment. Most importantly, their unprecedented number—again, one thousand per person!—

---

[108] Al-Qurtubi and Al-Shawkani claimed that these vessels and cups will be used to provide only drinks (2014, p. 92; 2012, p. 436). On the other hand, Ibn Ashoor (1984) and Ibn Kathir (2014) argued that these vessels and cups will be used to serve both food and beverages (p. 391; p. 472).

reflects Allah's extraordinary honour to His righteous servants and His indescribable hospitality to them.

From a grammatical perspective, unlike the case in the previous couple of ayahs—where the subject of the verb is ignored—in this message, it is, in fact, the object of the verb that is ignored. In other words, here Allah mentions these young servants—the subject, but He doesn't mention what they serve—the object. Hypothetically speaking, Allah could have said:

> *"And round about them will be <u>boys</u> of everlasting youth who serve <u>food and drinks</u> in vessels of silver and cups of crystal."*

In this case, the focus will be divided between the subject, <u>boys</u>, and the object, <u>food and drinks</u>. But to focus the entire light of the message on these elegant, pearl-like servants, who, again, represent a major element of honour to the dwellers of His Gardens, Allah does not mention the blessings they serve.

Also to provide a general idea of the bliss of unlimited quantity and indescribable quality that He has prepared for His beloved servants and to intensify the audience's longing for it, Allah says:

$$\text{(وَإِذَا رَأَيْتَ ثَمَّ رَأَيْتَ نَعِيماً وَمُلْكاً كَبِيْراً)!}$$

> *"And when you look there (in Paradise), you will see a delight (that cannot be imagined), and a great dominion!"*

The message in this ayah denotes an infinite range of bliss in the Gardens, for Allah, the Greatest, Himself describes the dominion in them as "great" and "magnificent." Besides its power that inflames the heart's yearning for this infinite bliss, this ayah reflects a special, incredible hospitality of Allah towards these special, honourable people. As if it says, "All the amazing bliss mentioned in this surah is, in fact, too little compared to what Allah has prepared for His celebrated guests in His high Gardens of bliss."

Today, especially in civilized, urban communities, people pay considerable attention to their clothing. Textile factories around the world, therefore, produce numerous kinds of fabrics of different material, qualities, textures, patterns, and colours. Likewise, the apparel industry continuously overwhelms the marketplace with countless, beautiful styles and fashions. Knowing the role of clothing in people's luxury and happiness, Allah speaks twice about it in this surah. First, He mentions silk as one material of which the clothes of His Garden's dwellers are made. He says:

$$\text{(وَجَزَاهُم بِمَا صَبَرُواْ جَنَّةً وَحَرِيراً)} .$$

"And their recompense shall be Paradise, and silken garments, because they were patient."

Second, of the countless, extraordinarily beautiful attires that the dwellers of the Gardens will wear, Allah specifies two different apparels of silk that He has prepared for these beloved, honourable guests to enjoy: a thick garment—to be worn on top, and a lighter one—to be worn underneath. With respect to this, He proclaims:

$$\text{(عَالِيَهُمْ ثِيَابُ سُندُسٍ خُضْرٌ وَإِسْتَبْرَقٌ)} .$$

"Upon them will be green garments of fine and thick silk."

Through many things they do, make, possess, and use, humans have proven to have a significantly high quality of taste. For instance, the endless, beautiful designs of houses, gardens, furniture, utensils, devices, clothing, shoes, vehicles, trains, and planes represent strong evidence for the amazing human taste. But if humans are this tasteful, then—figuratively speaking—how is the taste of the Creator Himself? In other words, the splendour of the Garden dwellers' clothes is left to Allah and His infinitely marvellous ability to amaze.

Who can imagine the beauty of the garments that the righteous will wear in Allah's Gardens, their infinite variety of textile, their feel, their unprecedented excellent quality, their extremely wonderful colours, and their uncountable, gorgeous designs that Allah Himself—not anyone else—prepares for His honourable, beloved guests? So in the light of this, imagine—and, of course, you can't!—the quality and beauty of all things that the residents of Allah's Gardens will possess and enjoy: their cities, public places, recreational facilities, gardens, streets, homes, furniture, devices, housewares, clothing, shoes, and vehicles.

What is more, Allah doesn't confine the luxury of His Gardens' inhabitants to their garments, furniture, tableware, vessels, food, and drinks. Their luxury extends to include everything, even jewellery. Their wrists, for example, will be adorned with special silver bracelets. In fact, this specific issue of the Garden inhabitants' beautification has a prominent presence in the Holy Qur'an. Allah mentions it in different surahs, a matter that suggests its significance as an item of adornment for the affluent dwellers of His Gardens.[110] In this surah and with respect to this issue, He says:

(...وَحُلُّواْ أَسَاوِرَ مِن فِضَّةٍ...)

"...they will be adorned with bracelets of silver..."

In the final ayah in this part of the surah, Allah sends this special, honorary message to His beloved, righteous guests. He says:

---

[109] The adornment of the wrists of the Garden's dwellers is mentioned in the following ayahs:

First, in surah Al-Kahf, Allah says:

(...يُحَلَّوْنَ فِيهَا مِنْ أَسَاوِرَ مِن ذَهَبٍ).

"...they will be adorned with bracelets of gold."

(Qur'an 18:31)

Second, in surah, Al-Hajj, He states:

(...يُحَلَّوْنَ فِيهَا مِنْ أَسَاوِرَ مِن ذَهَبٍ وَلُؤْلُؤاً وَلِبَاسُهُمْ فِيهَا حَرِيرٌ).

"...wherein they will be adorned with bracelets of gold and pearls and their garments therein will be of silk."

(Qur'an 22:23)

Third, in surah Fatir, He declares:

(...يُحَلَّوْنَ فِيهَا مِنْ أَسَاوِرَ مِن ذَهَبٍ وَلُؤْلُؤاً وَلِبَاسُهُمْ فِيهَا حَرِير).

"...therein will they be adorned with bracelets of gold and pearls, and their garments therein will be of silk."

(Qur'an 35:33)

(إِنَّ هَذَا كَانَ لَكُمْ جَزَاءً وَكَانَ سَعْيُكُم مَّشْكُوراً). [110]

> *"Verily, this is a reward for you, and your endeavour has been accepted."*

Before closing the discussion of the issue of longing in this surah, it is important to mention that Allah stresses different aspects of taqwa as requirements for the enjoyment of the bliss He describes. First, believers must fulfil their vows, for fulfilling one's promises—if they don't conflict with the Islamic teachings—is fundamental in Islam. Concerning this, Allah says:

(يُوفُونَ بِالنَّذْرِ...)

> *'They fulfil (their) vows...'*

Second, as mentioned earlier, fear of Allah represents a main aspect of taqwa because it helps believers observe Him closely and continuously. So like many other surahs, this one stresses the role of fear of Allah in believers' security and happiness on the Day of Judgment. With respect to this, Allah describes the righteous saying:

(...وَيَخَافُونَ يَوْمًا كَانَ شَرُّهُ مُسْتَطِيرًا) .

> *"...and fear a day the evil of which shall be spreading far and wide."*

Third, Allah demands that believers do righteousness based on pure intentions—that is, *ikhlass*. In other words, all believers' good deeds should be done solely for His sake. This essential requirement is signified in the following virtuous declaration that the righteous have made. They say:

(إِنَّمَا نُطْعِمُكُمْ لِوَجْهِ اللَّهِ لَا نُرِيدُ مِنكُمْ جَزَاءً وَلَا شُكُورًا).

---

[110] Here the word "*mashkura*" is translated as "accepted." Other translators, namely Pickthall and A. Y. Ali provided similar interpretation: "hath found acceptance," "shall be recompensed," and "accepted and recognized," respectively. The literal translation of it is "appreciated," which seems more accurate. See Al-Qurtubi, 2014, p. 96.

> *"We feed you for the sake of Allah alone: no reward do we desire from you, nor thanks."*

Fourth, because—as mentioned before—the course of Islam is long and sometimes prickly, Allah demands that believers be patient. He has, actually, repeatedly stressed the significance of the virtue of patience in the Holy Qur'an, and He has associated it with many attractive issues, such as victory in this life and on the Day of Judgment. In this surah, He points to this virtue as a requirement for the admission to His Gardens. He says:

$$(وَجَزَاهُم بِمَا صَبَرُوا جَنَّةً وَحَرِيراً).$$

> *"And their recompense shall be Paradise, and silken garments, because they were patient."*

That is a brief discussion of the element of longing in the Holy Qur'an exemplified by three examples from the Qur'anic speech that addresses this unique human emotion. The objective of it is, again, to demonstrate how this special Qur'anic speech ignites the fire of taqwa in the heart by sparking the sentiment of longing for Allah's Gardens of bliss. If people listen thoughtfully to this type of the Qur'anic speech, their hearts will indeed overflow with strong waves of longing for those Gardens. If they fail to experience any level of longing, however, their hearts are to blame.

Seeing Allah Himself!

In His blissful Gardens, Allah will offer His honourable guests something that will outweigh everything else. They will, in fact, never receive or enjoy anything better than it. Precisely, He will allow them to see Him—face to face! In the entire Holy Qur'an, Allah has favoured only the surah of Al-Qiyamah (The Resurrection) to explicitly deliver this inexpressibly good news to His beloved servants.[111] He declares:

---

[111] Surah Qaf carries the same good news, but the message in it is expressed implicitly. It is narrated that successful believers will be invited to see Allah every Friday, which is called *Yawm Almazeed*—The Day of Extra Grant. In this regard Allah says:

(وُجُوهٌ يَوْمَئِذٍ نَّاضِرَةٌ . إِلَى رَبِّهَا نَاظِرَةٌ)!

*"Some faces that Day shall be shining and radiant.
Looking at their Lord!"*   *(Qur'an 75:22–23)*

The quality and intensity of longing that this ayah can generate in believers' listening hearts exceed all that which the other ayahs may create. The offer in it is, indeed, beyond human expectations; perhaps this is why—mistakenly—some people advise that the message in this ayah shouldn't be understood literally.

In reference to this inexpressibly beloved Qur'anic message, Ibn Kathir (2014) reported that one day, the Holy Prophet looked at the full moon and said:

"You will see your Lord the way you see this moon" (p. 467).

Al-Qurtubi (2014), in addition, narrated a similar hadith on this issue. Citing Al-Nisa'ee, he said that Suhayb narrated that the Holy Messenger of Allah said:

"Then He [Allah] will reveal Himself to them, and they will look at Him! By the name of Allah, He will give them nothing more beloved to them than seeing His face" (p. 72).

"فيكشف الحجاب فينظرون إليه ! فو الله ما أعطاهم الله شيئاً أحب إليهم من النظر إلى
وجهه".

(لَهُمْ مَا يَشَاءُونَ فِيهَا وَلَدَيْنَا مَزِيدٌ).

"There they will have all that they desire—and We have more."
(Qur'an 50:35)

CHAPTER 5

—— — ——

The Dynamic Nature of Taqwa

Taqwa, as previously mentioned, demands continuous, conscientious observance of Allah, even in the world of thoughts and feelings. This extremely demanding nature of taqwa makes it unattractive to people who—due to their human nature—prefer to be free in all situations, throughout their lives. Allah, of course, knows this irresponsible human inclination. He has, therefore, addressed it in the early Makkan Holy Qur'an. Precisely, in surah Al-Qiyamah, He says:

(بَلْ يُرِيدُ الْإِنْسَانُ لِيَفْجُرَ أَمَامَهُ).

"Nay! Man (denies Resurrection and Reckoning. So he) desires to continue committing sins."   *(Qur'an 75:5)*

Also knowing the demanding nature of taqwa and the negative human attitude towards it, Allah has, fortunately, repeatedly associated it with numerous attractive stimuli that make it appealing to believers and dynamic in their lives. Using a few examples from the Holy Qur'an, this section casts some light on this issue.

The Promotion of Unity

The Muslim community's unity, both locally and globally, is imperative. Without it, the Muslim society will not only fail, but it will also collapse. The five pillars of Islam, fortunately, emphasize the significance of this unity and support it. First, shahadah,[112] the first

---

[112] Believing and witnessing that there is no god but Allah and that Mohammad is His final Messenger.

pillar of Islam, represents the foundation of this nation's unity: All Muslims believe in the same one God, Allah; and all of them believe in His final Book, the Holy Qur'an, and in His final Holy Messenger, Mohammad. In other words, the issue of *tawheed,*[113] unites Muslims' hearts, values, ethics, concerns, goals, longings, and destiny. Second, salah, the second pillar of Islam, unites Muslims spiritually, morally, socially, and physically. They all pray to Allah, shoulder to shoulder, and wherever they exist, they're supposed to pray under one leadership——the *imam.* Also in different parts of the world, all Muslims turn their faces in the direction of the same place: Al-Kabah. Third, *zakah,* the third pillar of Islam, signifies the Muslims' solidarity and mutual caring. The advantaged concern themselves with the welfare of the disadvantaged and help improve their quality of life. Fourth, the fast of Ramadan, the fourth pillar of Islam, reflects the nation's unity in different ways. The whole nation, for instance, is supposed to begin and end the fast of this Holy month together. In addition, the Muslims' objectives of fasting are the same—the development of taqwa and the achievement of Allah's approval. Finally, *hajj,* the fifth pillar of Islam, unifies Muslims, who congregate from different parts of the world to establish this important pillar of Islam together. During the performance of this Islamic worship, the Muslims' unity reflects on many things they do, say, and even on the way they dress.[114]

Knowing the significant role of unity in the Muslim nation's success, Allah has enjoined on Muslims to establish a strong bond between them. In surah Al-Anfal and with a special stress on the issue of taqwa, He calls upon them to unite saying:

$$(\ldots \text{فَٱتَّقُواْ ٱللَّهَ وَأَصْلِحُواْ ذَاتَ بَيْنِكُمْ} \ldots)$$

"...so be mindful of Allah and settle all matters of difference among you..."   *(Qur'an 8:1)*

Though this command was revealed in the context of after-war, it should govern Muslims' relationships in all circumstances. According to scholars of the exegesis of the Holy Qur'an, this ayah was revealed to initially address a definite issue on a specific occasion. Particularly,

---

[113] The belief that Allah is only one and that He has no partner.
[114] This, of course, is a very brief account of the five pillars of Islam.

soon after the end of the Battle of Badr, the Holy Prophet's companions had a dispute as who had the right of the spoils.

According to Al-Shawkani (2012), Ubadah ibn Al-Samit said:

> This ayah was about us—the people of Badr—when we disputed about the spoils and our manners became bad. As a result, Allah took the spoils from our hands and put them in the Prophet's; then he divided them equally among the Muslims. (p. 353)

With respect to this incident, it is advisable here to have a look at the complete text of the above ayah. Allah says:

$$ \text{(يَسْأَلُونَكَ عَنِ الأَنْفَالِ قُلِ الأَنْفَالُ لِلّهِ وَالرَّسُولِ فَاتَّقُواْ اللّهَ وَأَصْلِحُواْ ذَاتَ بِيْنِكُمْ} $$
$$ \text{وَأَطِيعُواْ اللّهَ وَرَسُولَهُ إِن كُنتُم مُّؤْمِنِينَ).} $$

"They ask you about Al-Anfal (the spoils of war). Say: "Al-Anfal are for Allah and the Messenger." So have Taqwa of Allah and settle all matters of difference among you, and obey Allah and His Messenger, if you are believers."   *(Qur'an 8:1)*

Based on the message in this ayah, one of the most significant roles that taqwa can play in the Muslim community is to unite it. To realize the importance of the Muslims' unity in Islam, we need to remember that soon after building his mosque in Al-Madinah, the Holy Prophet established brotherhood amongst the immigrant believers and their Muslim brothers in that city. It is also important to remember that the Holy Prophet achieved all of his subsequent success on the foundation of that strong brotherhood he had established.

In reference to the strong unity that the Holy Prophet established among his companions who had immigrated to Al-Madinah and the Ansar (Helpers), Al-Mubarakpuri stated the following:

> The Helpers were extremely generous to their brethren-in-faith. Abu Hurairah reported that they once approached the Holy Prophet with the request that their orchards of palm trees should be distributed equally between the Muslims of Madinah and brethren in Makkah. But the Holy Prophet was hesitant to put

this heavy burden upon them. It was, however, decided that the Emigrants would work in the orchards along with the Helpers and the yield would be divided equally among them.

Such examples point directly to the spirit of cordiality, sacrifice and selflessness on the part of the Helpers, and also to the feeling of appreciation, gratitude and self-respect that the Emigrants held dear to their hearts. They took only what helped them make a reasonable living. In short, this policy of mutual brotherhood was so wise and timely that many obstinate problems were resolved wonderfully and reasonably. (1979/2008 p. 229)

Also in another ayah in the same surah, Allah commands believers to keep united. He even warns them that if they don't, the result will be undoubtedly regrettable: weakness and failure. He says:

(وَأَطِيعُواْ اللَّهَ وَرَسُولَهُ وَلاَ تَنَازَعُواْ فَتَفْشَلُواْ وَتَذْهَبَ رِيحُكُمْ وَاصْبِرُواْ إِنَّ اللَّهَ مَعَ الصَّابِرِينَ).

"And obey Allah and His Messenger, and do not dispute [with one another] lest you lose courage and your strength departs, and be patient. Surely, Allah is with the patient."   *(Qur'an 8:46)*

In addition, the Holy Prophet has, actually, stressed the significance of Muslims' unity in different hadiths. The following one, for example, demonstrates the crucial role of taqwa in this issue. Ibn Kathir (2014) cited Anas ibn Malik to have said the following:

While the Holy Messenger of Allah was sitting, we saw him smiling. . . . Then Omar asked him, ". . . what made you smile, O Messenger of Allah?" The Holy Prophet answered, "Two men from my nation sat on their knees in front of Allah, and one of them said, 'My Lord, please let this brother of mine give me my dues.'" Then Allah said, "Give him his dues." The man answered, "O my Lord, none of my *hasanat* [good deeds] has remained with me." The other man [the complainant] said, "He may take from my sins, Lord!" The Holy Prophet started to cry; then he said, "That's a horrifying day, on which people need others to lift their sins from them."

Then [in continuation of the two men's story] the Prophet said, "Allah said to the man [the complainant], "Raise your eyes and look at the Gardens." The man looked and said, "O my Lord, I see cities of silver and palaces of gold decorated with pearls. Which Prophet do they belong to? Which Siddiq [a sincere servant of Allah]? Which martyr?" Allah said, "They are for whoever has their price." Then the man asked, "O my Lord, but who has their price!" Allah answered him, "You!" The man exclaimed, "What!" Then Allah said, "Their price is to forgive your brother." "I've forgiven him," said the man. Then Allah said, "Take your brother, and— both of you—enter the Garden."

Then the Messenger of Allah said, "Observe taqwa of Allah and keep good relationship among you, for Allah adjusts all matters of difference among believers on the Day of Judgment." (p. 65)

عن أنس بن مالك ، قال: "بينا رسول الله صلى الله عليه وسلم جالس إذ رأيناه ضحك حتى بدت ثناياه." فقال له عمر : "ما أضحكك يا رسول الله بأبي أنت وأمي ؟ " قال : "رجلان من أمتي جثيا بين يدي رب العزة . فقال أحدهما : " يا رب خذ لي مظلمتي من أخي." فقال الله تبارك وتعالى : " أعط أخاك مظلمته ." قال : " يا رب لم يبق من حسناتي شئ." قال : "يا رب فليحمل من أوزاري ." قال : "ففاضت عينا رسول الله صلى الله عليه وسلم بالبكاء." ثم قال: "إن ذلك ليوم عظيم، يوم يحتاج الناس إلى من يتحمل عنهم من أوزارهم ." فقال الله تعالى للطالب: " ارفع بصرك وانظر في الجنان ." فرفع رأسه فقال: "يا رب أرى مدائن من فضة وقصورا من ذهب مكللة باللؤلؤ ، لأي نبي هذا ؟ لأي صديق هذا ؟ لأي شهيد هذا ؟" قال: "هذا لمن أعطى الثمن ." قال: "رب ومن يملك ثمنه ؟" قال : "أنت تملكه ." قال: "ماذا يا رب ؟" قال: "تعفو عن أخيك ." قال: "يا رب فإني قد عفوت عنه ." قال الله تعالى : "فخذ بيد أخيك فادخلا الجنة ." ثم قال رسول الله صلى الله عليه وسلم :" (اتقوا الله وأصلحوا ذات بينكم)، فإن الله تعالى يصلح بين المؤمنين يوم القيامة ."

The Consideration of the Day of Judgment

To help humankind in general and believers in specific acquire taqwa, Allah recurrently links it with an exceptionally powerful stimulus—the Day of Judgment, on which He punishes mercilessly and rewards lavishly. In surah Al-Baqarah, for instance, He says:

(وَاتَّقُواْ يَوْمًا تُرْجَعُونَ فِيهِ إِلَى اللَّهِ، ثُمَّ تُوَفَّ كُلُّ نَفْسٍ مَّا كَسَبَتْ وَهُمْ لاَ يُظْلَمُونَ).

"And fear a Day in which you shall return to Allah, when each soul shall be paid back that which it has earned. And they shall not be wronged."

(Qur'an 2:281)

With some reflection, one can see how strongly this ayah motivates people to develop taqwa and adhere strongly to it. The fact that Allah's knowledge encompasses all things and that He will resurrect all people after death and hold them accountable for all their deeds leave no chance for believers to behave irresponsibly. In fact, this ayah has, at least, two factors that intensify the warning it carries.

First, grammatically speaking, the usage of the word *yawman*,[115] meaning "a day," in the indefinite form stresses the infinitely horrible nature of the Day of Judgment, for it suggests that the evil nature of that day lies beyond the power of human imagination. Second, according to Al-Tabari (2010), Ibn Abbas reported that this was "the last ayah revealed" (p. 22). Also in his exegesis, Al-Shawkani (2012) cited Saeed ibn Jubair to have mentioned that this ayah was revealed only nine days before the Holy Prophet's death (p. 378). Hence, the fact that this ayah was the last that Allah revealed and the fact that it was revealed in the very last few days in the Holy Prophet's life make the warning it carries even stronger and more frightening. As if it says to all humanity, "This is the last warning!"

Another similar threatening message occurs in the following ayah from surah Al-Hashr (The Gathering). The issue of taqwa in this ayah arises twice; each time, Allah uses the imperative to warn believers not against Hellfire but against Himself! He says:

---

[115] يوما

(يَا أَيُّهَا الَّذِينَ آمَنُوا اتَّقُوا اللَّهَ وَلْتَنْظُرْ نَفْسٌ مَا قَدَّمَتْ لِغَدٍ ، وَاتَّقُوا اللَّهَ إِنَّ اللَّهَ خَبِيرٌ بِمَا تَعْمَلُونَ).

"O you who believe! Fear Allah, and let every soul consider what it has laid in stock for the tomorrow, and be pious before Allah. Verily, Allah is All-Aware of what you do." (Qur'an 59:18)

In addition, the surah of Luqman carries the same previous warning against the wrath of Allah and His horrible, merciless punishment on the Day of Judgment. But whereas the previous message warns the believers, this one warns all humankind. It says:

(يَا أَيُّهَا النَّاسُ اتَّقُوا رَبَّكُمْ وَاخْشَوْا يَوْمًا لَا يَجْزِي وَالِدٌ عَن وَلَدِهِ وَلَا مَوْلُودٌ هُوَ جَازٍ عَن وَالِدِهِ شَيْئًا ، إِنَّ وَعْدَ اللَّهِ حَقٌّ ، فَلَا تَغُرَّنَّكُمُ الْحَيَاةُ الدُّنْيَا وَلَا يَغُرَّنَّكُم بِاللَّهِ الْغَرُورُ).

"O people! Guard against (the punishment of) your Lord and dread the day when no father can avail aught for his son, nor a son avail aught for his father. Verily, the promise of Allah is true, therefore let not this world's life deceive you, nor let the chief deceiver (Satan) deceive you about Allah." (Qur'an 31:33)

The Key to Knowledge Acquisition

Taqwa represents a key factor in knowledge acquisition. The following ayah, from surah Al-Baqarah, stresses this fact clearly; the message in it, however, attracts only those who honour knowledge and understand its significance and its role in Islam. Concerning this issue, Allah says:

(...وَاتَّقُوا اللَّهَ وَيُعَلِّمُكُمُ اللَّهُ...)

"... so have taqwa of Allah; and Allah will teach you..." (Qur'an 2:282)

In reference to this Qur'anic message, Al-Qurtubi said that this is a promise from Allah to those who observe taqwa that He will educate them. That is, Allah will put light in their hearts with which they understand, and He will offer them a distinguishing power with which they differentiate between right and wrong (2014, p. 268).

Perhaps this light that Al-Qurtubi indicated is what Imam Ali ibn Abi-Talib was referring to in his response to a question that a man asked him saying:

> "Did the Holy Messenger of Allah favour you [the Holy Prophet's family] with anything special . . . ?" Ali answered, "No, . . . except an understanding of the Qur'an that Allah might give to one [of His servants]."

عن مطرف عن الشعبي عن أبي جحيفة قال : "سألنا علياً هل خصكم رسول الله (صلى الله عليه وسلم) بشيئ بعد القرآن؟" قال :"لا والذي فلق الحبة وبرأ النسمة ، إلا فهم يؤتيه اللَّه عز وجل رجلاً في القرآن."

This special understanding of the Holy Qur'an, which Imam Ali pointed to in this hadith, occurs as a result of taqwa, which enables its people to see what others cannot. Examine Allah's extremely beautiful promise in the following ayah and notice the condition that believers need to meet before they may enjoy the promised reward in it:

(يا أَيُّهَا الَّذِينَ ءَامَنُواْ اتَّقُواْ اللَّهَ وَءَامِنُواْ بِرَسُولِهِ يُؤْتِكُمْ كِفْلَيْنِ مِن رَّحْمَتِهِ وَيَجْعَل لَّكُمْ نُوراً تَمْشُونَ بِهِ).

> *"O you who believe! Have taqwa of Allah, and believe in His Messenger, He will give you a double portion of His mercy, and He will give you a light by which you shall walk (straight)."*   (Qur'an 57:28)

According to Al-Saadi, in this ayah, the light that Allah promises to offer those who have eiman and taqwa is knowledge (2011, p. 787).

Further, A. Al-Ghazali (1992) has argued that the story of Prophet Musa with Al-Khadir proves that knowledge can be earned without the traditional ways of learning (pp. 31–33). Here Al-Ghazali is referring to the following ayah from the surah of Al-Kahf:

(فَوَجَدَا عَبْدًا مِّنْ عِبَادِنَا ءَاتَيْنَاهُ رَحْمَةً مِّنْ عِندِنَا وَعَلَّمْنَاهُ مِن لَّدُنَّا عِلْماً).

"Then they found one of Our servants, on whom We had bestowed mercy from Us, and whom We had taught knowledge from Us."

(Qur'an 18:65)

According to this surah, Al-Khadir had knowledge that Prophet Musa himself didn't. Upon his meeting with Al-Khadir, Prophet Musa requested the former to allow him to be his companion because he wanted to learn from him. Al-Khadir agreed but on condition that Prophet Musa wouldn't ask him any question, so Prophet Musa agreed. Soon thereafter, Al-Khadir started doing things that were apparently criminal. Prophet Musa couldn't tolerate Al-Khadir's actions, so he impatiently started to question him. His first two questions were, in fact, not only interrogative but also condemning.

Here is the Holy Qur'an narrating the whole story of these two great men, where the reasons underlying Al-Khadir's actions are explained:

(فَوَجَدَا عَبْدًا مِنْ عِبَادِنَا آتَيْنَاهُ رَحْمَةً مِنْ عِنْدِنَا وَعَلَّمْنَاهُ مِن لَّدُنَّا عِلْمًا . قَالَ لَهُ مُوسَىٰ هَلْ أَتَّبِعُكَ عَلَىٰ أَن تُعَلِّمَنِ مِمَّا عُلِّمْتَ رُشْدًا . قَالَ إِنَّكَ لَن تَسْتَطِيعَ مَعِيَ صَبْرًا . وَكَيْفَ تَصْبِرُ عَلَىٰ مَا لَمْ تُحِطْ بِهِ خُبْرًا . قَالَ سَتَجِدُنِي إِن شَاءَ اللَّهُ صَابِرًا وَلَا أَعْصِي لَكَ أَمْرًا . قَالَ فَإِنِ اتَّبَعْتَنِي فَلَا تَسْأَلْنِي عَن شَيْءٍ حَتَّىٰ أُحْدِثَ لَكَ مِنْهُ ذِكْرًا . فَانطَلَقَا حَتَّىٰ إِذَا رَكِبَا فِي السَّفِينَةِ خَرَقَهَا قَالَ أَخَرَقْتَهَا لِتُغْرِقَ أَهْلَهَا لَقَدْ جِئْتَ شَيْئًا إِمْرًا . قَالَ أَلَمْ أَقُلْ إِنَّكَ لَن تَسْتَطِيعَ مَعِيَ صَبْرًا . قَالَ لَا تُؤَاخِذْنِي بِمَا نَسِيتُ وَلَا تُرْهِقْنِي مِنْ أَمْرِي عُسْرًا . فَانطَلَقَا حَتَّىٰ إِذَا لَقِيَا غُلَامًا فَقَتَلَهُ قَالَ أَقَتَلْتَ نَفْسًا زَكِيَّةً بِغَيْرِ نَفْسٍ لَقَدْ جِئْتَ شَيْئًا نُكْرًا . قَالَ أَلَمْ أَقُلْ لَكَ إِنَّكَ لَن تَسْتَطِيعَ مَعِيَ صَبْرًا . قَالَ إِن سَأَلْتُكَ عَن شَيْءٍ بَعْدَهَا فَلَا تُصَاحِبْنِي، قَدْ بَلَغْتَ مِن لَّدُنِّي عُذْرًا . فَانطَلَقَا حَتَّىٰ إِذَا أَتَيَا أَهْلَ قَرْيَةٍ اسْتَطْعَمَا أَهْلَهَا فَأَبَوْا أَن يُضَيِّفُوهُمَا فَوَجَدَا فِيهَا جِدَارًا يُرِيدُ أَن يَنقَضَّ فَأَقَامَهُ ، قَالَ لَوْ شِئْتَ لَاتَّخَذْتَ عَلَيْهِ أَجْرًا . قَالَ هَٰذَا فِرَاقُ بَيْنِي وَبَيْنِكَ سَأُنَبِّئُكَ بِتَأْوِيلِ مَا لَمْ تَسْتَطِع عَّلَيْهِ صَبْرًا . أَمَّا السَّفِينَةُ فَكَانَتْ لِمَسَاكِينَ يَعْمَلُونَ فِي الْبَحْرِ فَأَرَدتُّ أَنْ أَعِيبَهَا وَكَانَ وَرَاءَهُم مَّلِكٌ يَأْخُذُ كُلَّ سَفِينَةٍ غَصْبًا . وَأَمَّا الْغُلَامُ فَكَانَ أَبَوَاهُ مُؤْمِنَيْنِ فَخَشِينَا أَن

يُرْهِقَهُمَا طُغْيَانًا وَكُفْرًا . فَأَرَدْنَا أَنْ يُبْدِلَهُمَا رَبُّهُمَا خَيْرًا مِنْهُ زَكَاةً وَأَقْرَبَ رُحْمًا.
وَأَمَّا الْجِدَارُ فَكَانَ لِغُلَامَيْنِ يَتِيمَيْنِ فِي الْمَدِينَةِ وَكَانَ تَحْتَهُ كَنْزٌ لَهُمَا وَكَانَ أَبُوهُمَا
صَالِحًا فَأَرَادَ رَبُّكَ أَنْ يَبْلُغَا أَشُدَّهُمَا وَيَسْتَخْرِجَا كَنْزَهُمَا رَحْمَةً مِنْ رَبِّكَ ، وَمَا فَعَلْتُهُ
عَنْ أَمْرِي ، ذَٰلِكَ تَأْوِيلُ مَا لَمْ تَسْطِعْ عَلَيْهِ صَبْرًا).

*"Then they found one of Our slaves, on whom We have
bestowed mercy from Us, and whom We had taught
knowledge from Us. Moses said to him: 'May I follow you
so that you teach me something of that knowledge which
you have been taught?' (The other) said: 'Verily you will
not be able to have patience with me, and how can you
have patience about things of which your understanding
is not complete?' Moses said: 'You will find me, if Allah
so wills, patient, and I will not disobey you in aught.' The
other said: 'Then if you follow me, ask me no questions
about anything until I myself speak to you concerning it.'
So they both proceeded, until, when they embarked the
ship, he scuttled it. Moses Said: 'Have you scuttled it in
order to drown its people? Truly, you have done a
dreadful thing.' He answered: 'Did I not tell you that you
would not be able to have patience with me?' Moses said:
'Rebuke me not for forgetting, nor grieve me by raising
difficulties in my case.' Then they proceeded, until, when
they met a boy, and he killed him. Moses said: 'Have you
killed an innocent person who had killed none? Verily,
you have committed an evil thing.' He answered: 'Did I
not tell you that you can have no patience with me?'
Moses said: 'If ever I ask you about anything after this,
keep me not in your company; you have received an
excuse from me.' Then they proceeded, until, when they
came to the inhabitants of a town, they asked them for
food, but they refused them hospitality. They found there
a wall on the point of falling down, but he set it up
straight. Moses said: 'If you had wished, surely, you
could have taken wages for it.' He answered: 'This is the
parting between me and you. Now will I tell you the
interpretation of (those things) over which you were
unable to hold patience. As for the ship, it belonged to*

certain needy people working in the sea, so I wished to render it unserviceable, for there was after them a certain king who seized every ship by force. As for the boy, his parents were people of Faith, and we feared that he would grieve them by obstinate rebellion and ingratitude (to Allah and man). So we desired that their Lord would give them in exchange (a son) better in purity (of conduct) and closer in affection. As for the wall, it belonged to two orphan boys, in the town; there was, beneath it, a buried treasure, to which they were entitled: their father had been a righteous man, so your Lord desired that they should attain their age of full strength and get out their treasure as a mercy from your Lord. I did it not of my own accord. Such is the interpretation of those things over which you could not hold patience.'"

(Qur'an 18: 65–82)

Certainly, one cannot acquire such astonishing knowledge—like Al-Khadir's—through the conventional ways of learning. It must be the fruit of a significantly advanced level of taqwa. The previous message from surah Al-Baqarah substantiates this allegation. Again, it says:

(...وَاتَّقُوا اللهَ وَيُعَلِّمُكُمُ اللهُ...)

"...so fear Allah, and Allah will teach you..."

(Qur'an 2:282)

Surah Al-Naml (The Ants), in addition, carries further evidence that supports the theory of knowledge acquisition through taqwa, rather than through the traditional methods of learning only. One day, Prophet Suleiman wanted to have the Queen of Sheba's throne as quickly as possible, so He referred to his special men and jinns in this matter. Prophet Suleiman was then in Jerusalem, Palestine. Astoundingly, one servant of Allah brought it to him in no time—less than a blink of an eye! Allah attributes this man's incredible power to his knowledge of the Book.

But what kind of knowledge is this? And where in the world can people acquire it? Again, it must have been a special offer from Allah to a special servant of His who had reached a significantly high level of taqwa. According to Ibn Kathir (2014), this man was a "*siddeeq*," meaning a sincere believer. After giving his promise to Prophet Suleiman, he made ablution then prayed Allah to bring the throne (p. 540).

Now carefully read the dialogue between Prophet Suleiman, the jinni, and the man who had the knowledge of the Book:

(قَالَ يَا أَيُّهَا المَلَأُ أَيُّكُمْ يَأْتِينِي بِعَرْشِهَا قَبْلَ أَن يَأْتُونِي مُسْلِمِينَ . قَالَ عِفْرِيتٌ مِّنَ الْجِنِّ أَنَا آتِيكَ بِهِ قَبْلَ أَن تَقُومَ مِن مَّقَامِكَ ، وَإِنِّي عَلَيْهِ لَقَوِيٌّ أَمِينٌ . قَالَ الَّذِي عِندَهُ عِلْمٌ مِّنَ الْكِتَابِ أَنَا آتِيكَ بِهِ قَبْلَ أَن يَرْتَدَّ إِلَيْكَ طَرْفُكَ...)!

"He said: O chiefs! Which of you can bring to me her throne before they come to me in submission? One audacious among the jinn said: I will bring it to you before you rise up from your place; and most surely I am strong (and) trusty for it. One with whom was knowledge of the Scripture, said: I will bring it to you within the twinkling of an eye...!"   *(Qur'an 27:38–40)*

Furthermore, Omar ibn Al-Khattab said and did many things that were products of a significantly high level of taqwa. Thousands of miles away, for example, he was once able to sense a dangerous situation that a Muslim army was about to face. He was in Al-Madinah when he screamed to warn the army's leader, Sariyah, about the enemy's army that was about to attack from the mountainside. Omar shouted, "O Sariyah, the mountain!" Surprisingly, Sariyah heard him and reacted accordingly (A. Al-Ghazali, 2004, p. 33). In this context, it is natural and common sense to ask the following questions: How did Omar see the enemy's army? And how did he make Sariyah hear him?

In fact, there were many other occasions when Omar said things that the Holy Qur'an subsequently approved. For instance, he suggested that the Holy Messenger of Allah use the *Maqam*[116] of Prophet

---

116 One of the different things exegetes of the Holy Qur'an said about the *Maqam* of Ibrahim is that it was a stone on which the Holy Prophet Ibrahim used to stand while he was building the Kabah with his son Ismai'l.

Ibrahim as a spot to establish salah at Al-Kabah, the House of Allah. Amazingly, Allah revealed an ayah commanding the Holy Prophet to do so. He said:

$$(...وَاتَّخِذُواْ مِن مَّقَامِ إِبْرَاهِيمَ مُصَلًّى...)$$

"...and take the station of Abraham as a place of prayer..."   *(Qur'an 2:125)*

Also the Holy Prophet himself, according to Imam Al-Bukhari, witnessed that Omar was a *muhaddath*. He said:

"Verily, my *ummah* [nation] has *muhaddatheen* [inspired ones] . . . and Omar is one of them." (A. Al-Ghazali, 2004, p. 32)

$$"إِنَّ مِن أُمَّتِي مُحَدَّثِين ومعلمين و مكلمين ، وإِنَّ عمر منهم"$$

Obviously, Omar's unique and extraordinary inspiration occurred as a result of his considerably high level of taqwa that qualified him to enjoy this amazing, supernatural power that enabled his heart to see even far-future events and extremely far-away issues. According to Ibn Al-Uthaymeen (1415), these people (those of Omar's type) are inspired to see and say the right thing, which indicates that Allah honours them (pp. 78–79).

This, of course, is not to suggest that people stop seeking knowledge through the conventional methods of learning, for Islam itself emphasizes the importance of knowledge acquisition and the role of effort in the accomplishment of all good goals. But the point is that a considerably high level of taqwa may open doors not only to knowledge acquisition but also to the creation of knowledge that is beyond the traditional ways of teaching, learning, and knowledge generation. Allah has, unlimited ways of teaching; the traditional way, however, is only one.

When Allah wants to teach His servants through the conventional ways of learning, for instance, He may set them to learn with and without their intention. He may also create all the required conditions and situations for them to learn—the need and eagerness for learning, willingness to sacrifice for the sake of knowledge acquisition, and the availability of different sources and means of knowledge gaining, e.g., scholars, books, technology, and easy access to them. Most importantly, Allah will open their minds and hearts so that they can learn quickly and profoundly. At the end, Allah will fulfil His promise if humans meet His condition, as the previous ayah indicates:

$$ (...\text{وَاتَّقُواْ اللَّهَ وَيُعَلِّمُكُمُ اللَّهُ}...) $$

"...and fear Allah and Allah teaches you..."
						(Qur'an 2:282)

The Qualification for Allah's Support

To encourage believers to observe taqwa, which is, again, thorny and challenging, Allah recurrently stresses the fact that He is with those who adhere to it. The messages in the following ayahs, for instance, guarantee Allah's support to those who observe taqwa.

The first ayah comes from surah Al-Baqarah. It says:

$$ (...\text{وَاتَّقُواْ اللَّهَ وَاعْلَمُواْ أَنَّ اللَّهَ مَعَ الْمُتَّقِينَ}). $$

"...and fear Allah, and know that Allah is with those who have taqwa."			*(Qur'an 2:194)*

The second occurs in the last ayah in surah Al-Nahl. It emphatically declares:

$$ (\text{إِنَّ اللَّهَ مَعَ الَّذِينَ اتَّقَواْ وَّالَّذِينَ هُم مُّحْسِنُونَ}). $$

"For Allah is with the pious, and those who do good."
						(Qur'an 16:128)

Having Allah on one's side reflects on many good things. Specifically, when true believers succeed in having Allah on their side, as a result of an advanced level of taqwa, they will enjoy countless fruits of this, both explicit and implicit. The most valuable of such fruits is that Allah will help them to always obey Him—by doing all that He commands and by avoiding whatever He forbids. Scholars, in fact, argue that the best duwa' (supplication) that believers may make is asking Allah to help them achieve what He has, actually, created them for. In this regard, Ibn Taymiyyah (1978) narrated that the Holy Messenger of Allah advised Mu'ath ibn Jabal to pray Allah at the end of each prayer saying,

> "O Allah, [please] help me remember, appreciate, and worship You in the best manner." (p. 68)[117]

Further, when Allah becomes on His servants' side, He certainly gives them victory over the Satan and over the negative side of their own "selves." He also, in this case, helps them to distinguish between right and wrong, even in situations where these two issues are extremely intricate and confusing to most people. In short, the closer believers observe taqwa, the more they enjoy Allah's support, and the more they experience this, the firmer they hold to the rope of taqwa.

The Safety Boat in this Life

In the Holy Qur'an, Allah frequently addresses people's intuitive need for safety in a way that motivates them to seek and acquire taqwa. In different occasions, for example, He shows humankind that taqwa is the safety boat on which He delivers the righteous at times of hardship and fatal disasters. A couple of surahs that highlight this issue are Al-Naml and Fussilat in which Allah demonstrates that eiman and taqwa saved Prophet Salih and his followers from the horrible punishment He inflicted on the rest of their disbelieving community.

In the former surah and with regard to this issue, He says:

(وَأَنجَيْنَا الَّذِينَ ءَامَنُواْ وَكَانُواْ يَتَّقُونَ).

"And We saved those who believed and were pious."
(Qur'an 27:53)

With only a slight change in the first word, the All-Mighty repeats—for emphasis—the same previous message in surah Fussilat. He declares:

---

[117] "اللهم أعني على ذكرك وشكرك وحسن عبادتك".

(وَنَجَّيْنَا الَّذِينَ ءَامَنُواْ وَكَانُواْ يَتَّقُونَ).

"And We saved those who believed and were pious."
(Qur'an 41:18)

The Qualification for Allah's Love

Taqwa crowns its people with the best reward: Allah's love. In fact, in one surah, Allah repeats this extraordinarily motivating and beloved message twice—in two ayahs that are close to each other. In the surah of Al-Tawbah, to be exact, He declares:

(...إِنَّ اللَّهَ يُحِبُّ الْمُتَّقِينَ). [118]

"...surely, Allah loves the pious."
(Qur'an 9:4&7)

When believers seriously and consistently do their best to live according to the teachings of Islam, Allah will love them. The ayah of love—as scholars refer to it—sheds light on this most desirable issue. It declares that the obedience to the Holy Prophet, which is a product of an advanced level of taqwa, wins the love of Allah as well as His forgiveness. In this ayah, Allah says:

(قُلْ إِن كُنتُمْ تُحِبُّونَ اللَّهَ فَاتَّبِعُونِي يُحْبِبْكُمُ اللَّهُ وَيَغْفِرْ لَكُمْ ذُنُوبَكُمْ ، وَاللَّهُ غَفُورٌ رَّحِيمٌ).

"Say: O Muhammad to mankind: 'If you love Allah, then follow me, Allah will love you and forgive you your sins. And Allah is Oft-Forgiving, Most Merciful.'"
(Qur'an 3:31)

The Holy Qur'an highlights different attributes that crown believers with the love of Allah, such as *ihsan*, repentance, patience, and purification. These excellent attributes, interestingly, represent some of the many major components of taqwa. Based on this, you may reflect

---

[118] The same message recurs in surah Al-Imran, ayah 76.

on the following ayahs that highlight Allah's love for His servants who have these attributes.

The first ayah in this group comes from surah Al-Imran, and it declares "ihsan" as a requirement for the love of Allah. It says:

(الَّذِينَ يُنفِقُونَ فِي السَّرَّاءِ وَالضَّرَّاءِ وَالْكَاظِمِينَ الْغَيْظَ وَالْعَافِينَ عَنِ النَّاسِ ، وَاللَّهُ يُحِبُّ الْمُحْسِنِينَ).

"Those who spend (in Allah's cause) in prosperity and in adversity, who restrain anger, and who pardon people; verily, Allah loves those who do good."
(Qur'an 3:134)

The second comes from the same surah—Al-Imran—and it also emphasizes "ihsan" as a qualification for Allah's love. It states:

(فَآتَاهُمُ اللَّهُ ثَوَابَ الدُّنْيَا وَحُسْنَ ثَوَابِ الْآخِرَةِ ، وَاللَّهُ يُحِبُّ الْمُحْسِنِينَ).

"So Allah gave them the reward of this world, and the excellent reward of the Hereafter. And Allah loves those who do good."   *(Qur'an 3:148)*

The third comes from surah Al-Ma'idah. It also proclaims "ihsan" as a requirement for the love of Allah:

(فَبِمَا نَقْضِهِم مِّيثَاقَهُمْ لَعَنَّاهُمْ وَجَعَلْنَا قُلُوبَهُمْ قَاسِيَةً ، يُحَرِّفُونَ الْكَلِمَ عَن مَّوَاضِعِهِ وَنَسُواْ حَظًّا مِّمَّا ذُكِّرُواْ بِهِ ، وَلاَ تَزَالُ تَطَّلِعُ عَلَى خَائِنَةٍ مِّنْهُمْ إِلاَّ قَلِيلاً مِّنْهُمْ ، فَاعْفُ عَنْهُم وَاصْفَحْ ، إِنَّ اللَّهَ يُحِبُّ الْمُحْسِنِينَ).

"So, because of their breach of their covenant, We cursed them and made their hearts grow hard. They changed the words from their (right) places and have abandoned a good part of the Message that was sent to them. And you will not cease to discover deceit in them, except a few of them. But forgive them and overlook (their misdeeds). Verily, Allah loves the doers of good."   *(Qur'an 5:13)*

The fourth ayah comes from surah Al-Imran. It declares patience as a qualification for the love of Allah. It says:

(...وَاللَّهُ يُحِبُّ الصَّابِرِينَ) .

"...and Allah loves the patient."

(Qur'an 3:146)

The last comes from surah Al-Baqarah, and it highlights two attributes that qualify for Allah's love, namely repentance and self-purification. It is also obvious from the ayah that each of these two characteristics leads to Allah's love. In this ayah, Allah proclaims:

(...إِنَّ اللَّهَ يُحِبُّ التَّوَّابِينَ وَيُحِبُّ المُتَطَهِّرِينَ) .

"...truly, Allah loves those who turn unto Him in repentance and loves those who purify themselves."

(Qur'an 2:222)

Al-Tabari (2010) confined the issue of purification in this ayah to its physical meaning, which is ablution—the cleaning of the body with water (p. 438). Al-Saadi, nevertheless, argued that the question of purification in this ayah should be construed more extensively and more generally. According to him, it refers to different forms: physical, spiritual, moral, and behavioural (2011, p. 76).

The Qualification for Allah's Honour

Taqwa qualifies believers for the enjoyment of Allah's Honour. The ayah below expresses this fact clearly, and the message in it has enough power to motivate believers to live on earth with morals similar to those of Paradise's dwellers. Imagine a society where everyone observes Allah and behaves according to His teachings. How ideal and happy would such a society be?

The message in this ayah, in addition, reflects Allah's fairness, for it declares that the scale that Allah uses to judge amongst His servants is taqwa—the higher the level of taqwa a person enjoys, the more honourable such a person is with Him. In this ayah, Allah emphatically declares:

(...إِنَّ أَكْرَمَكُمْ عَندَ اللَّهِ أَتْقَاكُمْ...)

"...Verily, the most honourable of you with Allah are the most pious..." (Qur'an 49:13)

Thus, no one can claim he or she doesn't have means to help him or her gain the honour of Allah. The rich, the poor, the strong, the weak, the young, the old, the privileged, the unprivileged, the Arab, the non-Arab, the white, and the black all have the same opportunity to achieve the highest level of taqwa that may crown them with the honour of Allah.

Inspired by the message in this ayah and by similar messages in other ayahs, the Holy Prophet advised his own beloved daughter Fatimah that being his daughter wouldn't help her on the Day of Judgment, and thus she had to build her own fortune with Allah. He addressed her saying:

"O Fatimah, daughter of Mohammad! Save yourself from Hellfire, for I have no power to interfere with Allah in your favour" (Al-Mubarakpuri, 2007, p. 68).

"يا فاطمة بنت محمد! أنقذي نفسك من النار ، فإني لا أملك لك من الله شيئاً."

In this context, it is worth mentioning that the enjoyment of Allah's honour based on the individual's high quality of taqwa should comfort those who don't belong to a social class whose members are automatically held in high regards. For example, Bilal, who was badly persecuted and was, actually, treated like dirt, had climbed the ladder of fortune and become not only above the noble Arabs who failed to believe in Islam but also above many believers of Arab origin contemporary with him. The bottom line is that Bilal—the one who was once a worthless slave—had won the honour of Allah through taqwa.

The surah of Mariam (Mary), in addition, highlights the role of taqwa in the enjoyment of Allah's honour on the Day of Judgment. In particular, it shows that taqwa is the only qualification that a person needs to have in order to join the fortunate, honourable delegation of believers who will receive Allah's honour on that day. It states:

(يَوْمَ نَحْشُرُ الْمُتَّقِينَ إِلَى الرَّحْمَنِ وَفْدًا)!

"Upon a Day when We muster the pious towards the All-Merciful, all in one delegation!"   *(Qur'an 19:85)*

The Security on the Day of Judgment

Allah assures people who have taqwa that on the most terrifying day, they will enjoy perfect peace and security. So when disbelievers come out of their graves with hearts full of woe and horror, the righteous, nevertheless, will be not only secure but also cheerful. In surah Yunus, for example, Allah favours these honourable servants of His with an exceptionally beautiful promise. In reference to them, He declares:

(أَلَا إِنَّ أَوْلِيَآءَ اللَّهِ لاَ خَوْفٌ عَلَيْهِمْ وَلاَ هُمْ يَحْزَنُونَ . الَّذِينَ ءَامَنُواْ وَكَانُواْ يَتَّقُونَ. لَهُمُ الْبُشْرَى فِي الْحَيَاةِ الدُّنْيَا وَفِي الأُّخِرَةِ...).

"Behold! For those who are on Allah's side, no fear shall come upon them nor shall they grieve. Those who believed, and were pious. For them is good news, in the life of the present world, and in the Hereafter..."
(Qur'an 10:62–64)

In addition, Allah has sent the surah of Al-Zumar to deliver the same previous glad tidings to the same preceding group of people: those who have taqwa. In this surah, He assures them that on the Day of Judgment, they will enjoy perfect peace and full security. He says:

(وَيُنَجِّى اللَّهُ الَّذِينَ اتَّقَوْا بِمَفَازَتِهِمْ لاَ يَمَسُّهُمُ السُّوءُ وَلاَ هُمْ يَحْزَنُونَ).

"And Allah will deliver those who were pious to their places of success. Evil shall touch them not, nor shall they grieve."   *(Qur'an 39:61)*

Further, surah Al-A'raf carries the same beloved news for the same previous, fortunate group—the people of taqwa. In this regard, Allah announces:

(يَا بَنِي آدَمَ إِمَّا يَأْتِيَنَّكُمْ رُسُلٌ مِّنكُمْ يَقُصُّونَ عَلَيْكُمْ آيَاتِي فَمَنِ اتَّقَى وَأَصْلَحَ فَلاَ خَوْفٌ عَلَيْهِمْ وَلاَ هُمْ يَحْزَنُونَ).

"O Children of Adam! If there come to you messengers from among you, reciting to you My revelations, then whosoever is pious and becomes righteous, on them shall be no fear nor shall they grieve."

(Qur'an 7:35)

Also the last third of the surah of Mariam carries a strong warning and a recurrent threat from Allah to his enemies. In the midst of this alarming and intimidating atmosphere, however, this surah brings glad tidings—like a beautiful oasis in the middle of an endless desert—only to those who observe taqwa. In this threatening part of the surah, in fact, the issue of taqwa occurs twice. In its first occurrence,[119] taqwa functions as the only saviour from Hellfire. Here, Allah declares:

(فَوَرَبِّكَ لَنَحْشُرَنَّهُمْ وَالشَّيَاطِينَ ثُمَّ لَنُحْضِرَنَّهُمْ حَوْلَ جَهَنَّمَ جِثِيًّا . ثُمَّ لَنَنزِعَنَّ مِن كُلِّ شِيعَةٍ أَيُّهُمْ أَشَدُّ عَلَى الرَّحْمَنِ عِتِيًّا . ثُمَّ لَنَحْنُ أَعْلَمُ بِالَّذِينَ هُمْ أَوْلَى بِهَا صِلِيًّا . وَإِن مِّنكُمْ إِلَّا وَارِدُهَا كَانَ عَلَى رَبِّكَ حَتْمًا مَّقْضِيًّا . ثُمَّ نُنَجِّي الَّذِينَ اتَّقَوا وَّنَذَرُ الظَّالِمِينَ فِيهَا جِثِيًّا).

"By your Lord [Prophet] We shall gather them and the devils together and set them on their knees around Hell; We shall seize out of each group those who were most disobedient towards the Lord of Mercy—We know best who most deserves to burn in Hell—but every single one of you will approach it, a decree from your lord which must be fulfilled. We shall save the devout and leave the evildoers there on their knees."

(Qur'an 19:68 –72)

---

[119] The second occurrence of the issue of taqwa in this part of the surah of Mariam is already discussed under "The Qualification for Allah's Honour."

The Key to the Gardens of Bliss

Allah frequently associates the entry of His Gardens with taqwa. He also sometimes repeats this association in the same surah, a matter that stresses the significance of taqwa and its role in people's success in the Hereafter. In surah Al-Imran, for instance, He praises those who have taqwa and promises them His Gardens of bliss. He states:

(قُلْ أَؤُنَبِّئُكُمْ بِخَيْرٍ مِنْ ذَٰلِكُمْ ، لِلَّذِينَ اتَّقَوْا عِنْدَ رَبِّهِمْ جَنَّاتٌ تَجْرِي مِنْ تَحْتِهَا الْأَنْهَارُ خَالِدِينَ فِيهَا وَأَزْوَاجٌ مُطَهَّرَةٌ وَرِضْوَانٌ مِنَ اللَّهِ ، وَاللَّهُ بَصِيرٌ بِالْعِبَادِ . الَّذِينَ يَقُولُونَ رَبَّنَا إِنَّنَا آمَنَّا فَاغْفِرْ لَنَا ذُنُوبَنَا وَقِنَا عَذَابَ النَّارِ . الصَّابِرِينَ وَالصَّادِقِينَ وَالْقَانِتِينَ وَالْمُنْفِقِينَ وَالْمُسْتَغْفِرِينَ بِالْأَسْحَارِ).

"Say: 'Shall I give you glad tidings of things far better than those?' For the righteous are Gardens in nearness to their Lord, with rivers flowing beneath; therein is their eternal home; with companions pure (and holy); and the good pleasure of Allah. For in Allah's sight are (all) His servants. Those who say: 'Our Lord! we have indeed believed: forgive us, then, our sins, and save us from the agony of the Fire.' Those who show patience, those who are true (in faith, words, and deeds), those who are obedient with sincere devotion in worship to Allah. Those who spend (in the way of Allah), and who pray for forgiveness in the early hours of the morning."
(Qur'an 3:15–17)

Based on this message, eiman and taqwa have qualified these people for the admission to Allah's Gardens of bliss. The message, in addition, sheds light on the dynamic nature of taqwa, which is represented by these people's characteristics that Allah highlights in these ayahs. Particularly, besides their belief in Allah, they enjoy major attributes of taqwa: fear of Hellfire, engagement in regular prayer for Allah's forgiveness, patience, sincerity, devotion, obedience to Allah, and expenditure in His cause (Al-Qurtubi, 2014, pp. 309–320; Ibn Kathir, 2014, p. 217).

Later, in another message in the same surah, Allah assures the same previous group of believers that He will admit them to His Gardens of bliss; this time, however, this beautiful promise comes in contrast to the miserable destiny of disbelievers. Explicitly, the message projects disbelievers suffering from the misery in Hellfire, while believers are swimming in endless oceans of bliss in the Gardens of Allah. Evidently, this effective method of communication is supposed to help disbelievers reconsider their negative position on Islam; at the same time, it motivates careless believers to become more responsible for their Islamic duties and more committed to their Islamic values. It also aids the dedicated ones to observe taqwa even more closely.

Here is the message from surah Al-Imran, so notice the effective contrast between the two destinies in it:

(لاَ يَغُرَّنَّكَ تَقَلُّبُ الَّذِينَ كَفَرُواْ فِي الْبِلاَد . مَتَاعٌ قَلِيلٌ ثُمَّ مَأْوَاهُمْ جَهَنَّمُ ، وَبِئْسَ الْمِهَادُ. لَكِنِ الَّذِينَ اتَّقَوْاْ رَبَّهُمْ لَهُمْ جَنَّاتٌ تَجْرِي مِن تَحْتِهَا الأَنْهَارُ خَالِدِينَ فِيهَا نُزُلاً مِّنْ عِندِ اللَّهِ وَمَا عِندَ اللَّهِ خَيْرٌ لِّلأَبْرَارِ).¹²⁰

"Let not the free disposal (and affluence) of the disbelievers throughout the land deceive you. A brief enjoyment! Then Hell shall be their refuge—and what a wretched place! But, for those who fear their Lord, are Gardens under which rivers flow; therein are they to dwell, an entertainment from Allah; and that which is with Allah is the best for the most righteous."

(Qur'an 3:196-198)

Further, surah Al-Zumar sheds a bright light on the righteous servants of Allah adorned with their distinguished, beautiful attire of taqwa, while the angels are honourably escorting them to their homes of perfect happiness in the Gardens of bliss. It pronounces:

(وَسِيقَ الَّذِينَ اتَّقَوْاْ رَبَّهُمْ إِلَى الْجَنَّةِ زُمَراً...)

---

[120] Possessions and social prestige do not necessarily indicate Allah's approval. Ironically, sometimes power and affluence could be the very tools that Allah uses to both blindfold His enemies and coax them into Hellfire. Qarun's wealth and arrogance, for instance, transformed into an earthquake that swallowed him and his entire beautiful, extensive palace!

"And those who feared their Lord in piety shall be herded
to the Garden in groups..."   *(Qur'an 39:73)*

Furthermore, surah Al-Naba' (The Great News) points to the issue of
taqwa as, again, the requirement that people need to fulfil before they
are admitted to the Gardens of bliss. It emphatically proclaims:

(إِنَّ لِلْمُتَّقِينَ مَفَازًا . حَدَائِقَ وَأَعْنَابًا . وَكَوَاعِبَ أَتْرَابًا . وَكَأْسًا دِهَاقاً . لَّا
يَسْمَعُونَ فِيهَا لَغْوًا وَلَا كِذَّابًا).

"Verily, for the pious there lies a path to salvation:
Gardens and vineyards. And young full-breasted
maidens of equal age. And a cup overflowing. In it they
hear neither gossip nor falsehood."
                                        (Qur'an 78:31–35)

Some Muslims, unfortunately, think they can avoid Hellfire and enter
Allah's Gardens without a strong commitment to the Islamic
teachings. A careful reading of the Qur'an, nevertheless, helps realize
that Allah confines the admission to His Gardens of bliss to the
righteous—those who have taqwa. The previous ayahs from the
surahs of Al-Imran, Al-Zumar, and Al-Naba' represent evidence that
the admission to Allah's Gardens is usually explicitly associated with
taqwa.

Sometimes, however, Allah does not point directly to the issue of
taqwa in connection with the entrance of His Gardens. Instead, He
points to its effects in relation to this issue, such as in the following
ayahs from the surah of Al-Teen (The Fig), in which He says:

(لَقَدْ خَلَقْنَا الْإِنسَانَ فِي أَحْسَنِ تَقْوِيمِ .ثُمَّ رَدَدْنَاهُ أَسْفَلَ سَافِلِينَ . إِلَّا
الَّذِينَ ءَامَنُوا وَعَمِلُواْ الصَّالِحَاتِ فَلَهُمْ أَجْرٌ غَيْرُ مَمْنُونِ).[121]

"Verily, We created man in the best structure. Then We
brought him down to the lowest of the low. Save them

---

[121] According to the scholars of the exegesis of the Holy Qur'an, *"the lowest of the low,"*
in this ayah, refers to Hell (Al-Saadi 2011, p. 887; Ibn Kathir 2014, p. 528).

who believe and do righteous deeds. Then they shall have a reward without end."

(Qur'an 95:4–6)

Here the last ayah highlights the effects of taqwa that qualifies these people for the admission to the Gardens of Allah and for the enjoyment of a *"reward without end"* that the ayah proclaims. Again, they are involved in righteous deeds that are products of taqwa, which is the soul of eiman; without it, eiman is dead and has no effects on believers' lives.

Similarly, the ayah below, from surah Al-Shura (The Consultation), does not mention the issue of taqwa as a condition for the entrance of the Gardens of bliss. However, the influence of taqwa on those who will be admitted to those Gardens is clear: They have eiman and *tawakkul*. In reference to this, Allah announces the following:

(وَمَا عِندَ اللَّهِ خَيْرٌ وَأَبْقَى لِلَّذِينَ ءَامَنُواْ وَعَلَى رَبِّهِمْ يَتَوَكَّلُونَ).

"But that which is with Allah is better and more lasting for those who believe and put their trust in their Lord." (Qur'an 42:36)

Tawakkul that characterizes the believers in this ayah is a fruit of an advanced stage of eiman that requires action that requires taqwa. Also the glad tidings that this ayah carries to these believers suggest that Allah is pleased with them, for He doesn't approve of or praise believers who are careless about His teachings. Ibn Al-Qayyim (1997) argued that "Whoever denies the role of action in the issue of tawakkul his [her] tawakkul is incomplete" (p. 338).

Besides, the Holy Prophet's different hadiths emphasize the role of commitment and action underlying the message in this ayah and the one previous to it. In one of these hadiths, for example, he proclaimed:

"Belief isn't a wish, but it is that which is firm in the heart [a strong belief] and confirmed by deeds."

" ليس الإيمان بالتمني ، ولكن ما وقر في الصدر وصدقه العمل."[122]

Moreover, in both of the surahs of Al-Imran and Al-Tahreem (The Prohibition), Allah warns believers, in particular, against Hellfire. This warning, in fact, suggests that some believers may enter it due to their negligence of the Islamic teachings. First, in the surah of Al-Imran and with respect to this issue, Allah warns the believers—not the disbelievers—against Hellfire, and He advises them to observe taqwa so that they won't enter this extremely ugly place with disbelievers. He says:

(يَا أَيُّهَا الَّذِينَ آمَنُواْ لاَ تَأْكُلُواْ الرِّبَا أَضْعَافًا مُّضَاعَفَةً وَاتَّقُواْ اللّهَ لَعَلَّكُمْ تُفْلِحُون. وَاتَّقُواْ النَّارَ الَّتِي أُعِدَّتْ لِلْكَافِرِينَ).

"O you who believe! Do not consume usury, doubled and multiplied. And fear Allah so that you may prosper. And avoid the Fire made ready for the unbelievers."
(Qur'an 3:130–131)

Second, in the surah of Al-Tahreem and in reference to the same previous issue, Allah warns believers—again, not disbelievers—against Hellfire. He says to them:

(يَا أَيُّهَا الَّذِينَ آمَنُوا قُوا أَنفُسَكُمْ وَأَهْلِيكُمْ نَارًا وَقُودُهَا النَّاسُ وَالْحِجَارَةُ عَلَيْهَا مَلَائِكَةٌ غِلَاظٌ شِدَادٌ لَا يَعْصُونَ اللَّهَ مَا أَمَرَهُمْ وَيَفْعَلُونَ مَا يُؤْمَرُونَ).

"O you who believe! Ward off from yourselves and your families a Fire (Hell) whose fuel is humans and stones. Over which are angels stern and severe, who do not disobey Allah in what He Commands them, and carry what they are commanded."   *(Qur'an 66:6)*

---

[122] Al-Bayhaqi, Shu'ab Al-Eiman, p. 158, hadith no. 65

CHAPTER 6

——— — ———

Lessons of Taqwa
from
Ibad Al-Rahman

The Holy Qur'an includes descriptions of special groups of believers beloved of Allah, such as the *mukhbitun*,[123] the *mu'minun*, the *muhsinun*,[124] and the *slaves of Al-Rahman*. In His descriptions of these distinguished groups of believers, Allah highlights major attributes of taqwa they enjoy. Such descriptions, in fact, give these honourable believers glad tidings that He is pleased with them; they also motivate them to carry on. These descriptions, in addition, are supposed to call other believers' attention to the significance of the values they underscore and thus motivate them to acquire the same values so that they may reach the level of these special, honourable groups of believers that Allah celebrates. In connection with the question of taqwa, this section briefly discusses the slaves of Al-Rahman's characteristics that Allah highlights in surah Al-Furqan.

It is, indeed, a great honour that Allah has associated this group with His beautiful name Al-Rahman (the Most Gracious) by calling them Ibad Al-Rahman, meaning the slaves of the Most Gracious. The following is Allah's complete, beautiful description of these special and honourable believers:

(وَعِبَادُ الرَّحْمَنِ الَّذِينَ يَمْشُونَ عَلَى الأَرْضِ هَـوْناً وَإِذَا خَاطَبَهُمُ الْجَاهِلُونَ قَالُواْ سَـلاَماً . وَالَّذِينَ يَبِيتُونَ لِرَبِّهِمْ سُجَّداً وَقِيَاماً . وَالَّذِينَ يَقُولُونَ رَبَّنَا اصْرِفْ عَنَّا عَذَابَ جَهَنَّمَ إِنَّ عَذَابَهَا كَانَ غَرَاماً . إِنَّهَا سَآءَتْ مُسْتَقَرّاً وَمُقَاماً . وَالَّذِينَ إِذَآ

---

[123] Mukhbitoon means those who are humble and obedient to Allah.
[124] Ayahs 3 and 4 in surah Luqman

153

أَنفَقُوا لَمْ يُسْرِفُوا وَلَمْ يَقْتُرُوا وَكَانَ بَيْنَ ذَلِكَ قَوَاماً . وَالَّذِينَ لاَ يَدْعُونَ مَعَ اللّهِ إِلَهَا

ءَاخَرَ وَلا يَقْتُلُونَ النَّفْسَ الَّتِي حَرَّمَ اللّهُ إِلاَّ بِالْحَقِّ وَلاَ يَزْنُونَ وَمَن يَفْعَلْ ذَلِكَ يَلْقَ

أَثَاماً. يُضَاعَفْ لَهُ الْعَذَابُ يَوْمَ الْقِيَامَةِ وَيَخْلُدْ فِيهِ مُهَاناً . إِلاَّ مَن تَابَ وَءَامَنَ

وَعَمِلَ عَمَلاً صَالِحاً فَأُوْلَئِكَ يُبَدِّلُ اللّهُ سَيِّئَاتِهِمْ حَسَنَاتٍ وَكَانَ اللّهُ غَفُوراً رَّحِيماً.

وَمَن تَابَ وَعَمِلَ صَالِحاً فَإِنَّهُ يَتُوبُ إِلَى اللّهِ مَتَاباً . وَالَّذِينَ لاَ يَشْهَدُونَ الزُّورَ وَإِذَا

مَرُّوا بِاللَّغْوِ مَرُّوا كِرَاماً . وَالَّذِينَ إِذَا ذُكِّرُوا بِآيَاتِ رَبِّهِمْ لَمْ يَخِرُّوا عَلَيْهَا صُمّاً

وَعُمْيَاناً . وَالَّذِينَ يَقُولُونَ رَبَّنَا هَبْ لَنَا مِنْ أَزْوَاجِنَا وَذُرِّيَّاتِنَا قُرَّةَ أَعْيُنٍ وَاجْعَلْنَا

لِلْمُتَّقِينَ إِمَاماً).

"And the servants of the Most Gracious are those who walk on the earth in humility, and when the foolish address them they say: 'Peace!' They are those who spend the night in worship of their Lord, prostrating and standing. And they are those who say: 'Our Lord! Avert from us the torment of Hell. Verily, its torment is an eternal penalty. Wretched is it as a residence and abode!' And (they are) those who, when they spend, are neither extravagant nor stingy, but are in a just balance between them. And (they are) those who do not invoke any other god along with Allah, nor kill the soul that Allah has forbidden, except for just cause, nor commit illegal sexual intercourse, and whoever does this shall undergo punishment. The torment will be doubled for him on the Day of Resurrection, and he will abide therein in humiliation. Except those who repent and believe, and do righteous deeds. For those, Allah will change their sins into good deeds, and Allah is Oft-Forgiving, Most Merciful. And that who repents and does righteous deeds; then indeed he has repented to Allah in all sincerity. And (they are) those who do not bear witness to falsehood, and if they pass by some evil play or evil talk, they pass by it with dignity. And (they are) those who, when reminded of the verses of their Lord, they do not fall deaf and blind. And (they are) those who say: 'Our Lord! Grant us from*

*our wives and our offspring the comfort of our eyes, and
make us leaders of those who are pious.'"*

(Qur'an 25:63–74)

The slaves of Al-Rahman's longings, concerns, and excellent reactions
to different stimuli, shown in these ayahs, shed light on their ideal
Islamic character, mentality, psychology, attitude, and perception of
this life. First, the way they walk—in a humble manner—agrees with
the excellent attributes that characterize them. Al-Qurtubi (2014)
narrated that Zayd ibn Aslam said, "I used to ask about the meaning
of [Allah's description of Ibad Al-Rahman in which He says, those]
'who walk on the earth in humility,' [125] but I didn't receive a
satisfactory answer. Then I saw a dream in which someone told me
that these are people who do not involve themselves in mischief." Al-
Qurtubi added that "the way these people walk from place to another
is in full harmony with their manners [which are characterized by
humbleness, fear of Allah, His observance, and His obedience]" (pp.
47–48).

A Muslim's ideal reaction to the negative attitude of the ignorant
towards Islam is to ignore them. This is, actually, the second attribute
that decorates these honourable people—the slaves of Al-Rahman.
With respect to this, Allah describes them saying:

(...وَإِذَا خَاطَبَهُمُ الْجَاهِلُونَ قَالُوا سَلَامًا).

"...and when the foolish address them they say, peace."

The slaves of Al-Rahman highly value their time. Therefore, they
avoid all types of dispute that not only waste their time and energy but
also damage their decent Islamic character, for they believe that Allah
has created them to be involved in important and valuable issues, not
in trivialities.

The third characteristic of these special people, interestingly, helps
them handle the ignorant the way Allah describes in this surah.
Precisely, they spend their nights praying. Concerning this, Allah
states:

---

[125] (الَّذِينَ يَمْشُونَ عَلَى الْأَرْضِ هَوْنًا).

(وَالَّذِينَ يَبِيتُونَ لِرَبِّهِمْ سُجَّداً وَقِيَاماً).

"And those who spend the night in worship of their Lord, prostrating and standing."

Grammatically, here the present tense in the Arabic clause *yabeetoon*, meaning *"they spend the night"* suggests that Al-Rahman's slaves are regularly engaged in night prayer. So while others spend their night-time enjoying their sleep or spend it on worthless or even unethical activities, these distinguished people spend theirs enjoying the connection and communication with Allah. In fact, this unique type of worship in which Al-Rahman's slaves are engaged comprises major qualities of taqwa: fear of Allah, love for Him, great gratitude to Him, a strong desire to please Him, as well as the pleasure of connection and communication with Him.

Hence, their night comfort isn't the sleep in their comfortable bed, but it is their enjoyable connection with their Lord. Sleep is, certainly, an important human need, for it re-energizes the body, invigorates the brain, rejuvenates the heart, and refreshes the soul. These honourable people do sleep, of course, but only enough to enable them to perform their daily duties and establish their beloved night prayer.

A. Al-Ghazali (2004) narrated that the Holy Messenger of Allah said:

> "Be engaged in night prayer, for it is the way of the righteous previous to you. Verily, standing in the night [establishing night prayer] brings you closer to Allah, takes care of [your] sins, cures . . . [your] body of diseases, and deters [you] from committing sins." (p. 258)

"عليكم بقيام الليل فإنه دأب الصالحين قبلكم ، فإن قيام الليل قربة إلى الله عز وجل ،

وتكفير للذنوب ومطردة للداء عن الجسد ، ومنهاة عن الإثم."

The worship of *tahajjud*[126] (night prayer) is demanding, indeed, and because of its seemingly rough nature, it attracts only a small

---

[126] The issue of tahajjud (night prayer) can generate lot's of invaluable thoughts that require an elaborative treatment and discussion. This section, however, has touched upon it only lightly to call the readers' attention to its unique character and to the

percentage of believers: the exceptionally ambitious. Due to its unique nature and unparalleled effects, tahajjud was prescribed to the Holy Prophet early in his difficult mission to help him acquire important qualities necessary for its successful accomplishment. The effects of night prayer, in general, reflect on the worshiper's brain, heart, soul (*nafs*), eyes, tongue, hearing faculty, body, personality, and character. Its influence on the brain, for example, reflects on the way the worshiper perceives this life and relates to it. That is, it helps those engaged in it to look at this life as a piece of land to cultivate today and harvest its excellent fruits tomorrow, or as a means of public transportation, such as a bus or a train, that they take from one place to a specific destination.

In fact, this is how our Holy Prophet, Mohammad, dealt with this life, and this is what he has advised his followers to do. Imam Al-Bukhari narrated that Ibn Omar said:

> "The Messenger of Allah took me by my shoulders and said, 'Be in this life as if you were a stranger or a traveller.'"
> (Ibn Al-Uthaymeen, 1431, p. 454)

"عن ابن عمر رضي الله عنهما قال : أخذ رسول الله (ص) بمنكبيَّ فقال : "كن في الدنيا
كأنك غريب أو عابر سبيل."

The effect of tahajjud on the soul reflects on the believer's strong commitment and keenness to obey Allah and His Holy Prophet. When the soul reaches this level, it could be said it has started a journey to the best stage it could ever reach: the state of becoming a *mutma'innah*[127] soul. A believer with this type of righteous soul enjoys strong belief in the oneness of Allah, His wisdom, the wisdom of His decrees, and His promises. Also such a believer enjoys many other attributes of taqwa—for example, *inabah*, which briefly refers to devotion to Allah, love for Him, and complete submission to Him. Further, he or she reacts in an ideal manner to all types of stimuli, whether such stimuli are positive or negative.

---

exceptionally fundamental role it can play in believers' relationship with Allah and in their honourable journey to Him.

[127] مطمئنّة

The effect of tahajjud on believers' hearts reflects on their fear of Allah and on their love for Him. Such hearts, in addition, teem with other psychological feelings that are essential to the issue of taqwa and are, therefore, conducive to believers' successful journey to Allah. These psychological feelings, as mentioned before, are hope, happiness, longing, fear, worry, and sorrow. Further, tahajjud influences the heart's positive and negative attitudes towards different issues and various stimuli. More precisely, its love, hate, likes, dislikes, longings, concerns, and indifference spring from Allah's pleasure only. That is, such a heart loves what Allah loves and hates or dislikes what He also hates or dislikes.

The effect of tahajjud on the tongue reflects on its persistent occupation with whatever pleases Allah, such as His glorification, appreciation, recitation of the Holy Qur'an, istighfar, and advising others to do the good and avoid evil. It also reflects on the tongue's decent and pure verbal communication; precisely, it says only the right things and refrains from all the forbidden and worthless talk—laghw. And when it is silent, the tongue is continuously engaged in intense, passionate remembrance and glorification of Allah, which is a practice that reflects believer's keenness to follow the Holy Prophet's footprints in this matter. In this regard, Al-Qurtubi (2014) reported that the Holy Prophet stated that Allah commanded him to make all his speech remembrance of Him (p. 224).

In reference to the tongue's vital role in human life, Al-Tamimi cited Ibn Kathir to have narrated the following about Luqman,[128] the wise:

> One day his master told him [Luqman] to slaughter a goat and bring him its two best organs. Luqman slaughtered one and brought his master the tongue and the heart. Sometime thereafter, his master told him to slaughter another goat and to throw away the two worst organs of it. Luqman slaughtered a goat and threw away the same previous organs: the tongue and the heart. Then his master said to him, "When I told you to bring me the two best organs of the first goat, you brought me the tongue and the heart, and when I told you to throw away the

---

[128] No one knows exactly what Luqman used to do for a living; nevertheless, people who wrote about him reported different occupations that he used to have. For example, they claimed he worked as a judge, carpenter, shepherd, upholsterer, and tailor (Al-Tamimi, 2008, p. 26).

two worst organs of the second, you also threw away the tongue and the heart. Would you explain this?" Luqman answered, "When these two organs are well cultivated, they are the best; when they're neglected, however, they're the worst." (1417/2008, pp. 27–28)

The fourth characteristic of Al-Rahman's honourable slaves is highlighted in the following ayahs:

(وَالَّذِينَ يَقُولُونَ رَبَّنَا اصْرِفْ عَنَّا عَذَابَ جَهَنَّمَ إِنَّ عَذَابَهَا كَانَ غَرَامًا .

إِنَّهَا سَاءتْ مُسْتَقَرًّا وَمُقَامًا).

"And those who say: 'Our Lord! Avert from us the torment of Hell. Verily, its torment is an eternal penalty. Wretched is it as a residence and abode.'"

The threat of Allah's punishment in the Hereafter is supposed to influence every aspect of believers' lives. But such influence won't occur until they receive the required mental and psychological effects in reaction to the message in the above ayah and in reaction to other even more intimidating ones in the Holy Qur'an. Obviously, the first ayah above reveals that the slaves of Al-Rahman, in reaction to the threatening Qur'anic speech, have received the ideal dosage of the fear of Allah's punishment in Hellfire.

Grammatically, the present form of the verb "*yaqool*"[129] in the Arabic clause "*yaqooloon*,"[130] meaning, "they say," suggests that these distinguished servants of Allah are consistently engaged in this invaluable prayer. Even the Holy Prophet—though he is the farthest from Allah's torment—showed a perfect reaction to this threat of Allah's punishment. It is narrated that whenever he read a frightening ayah, he would implore Allah to save him and all Muslims from His punishment (A. Al-Ghazali, 2004, p. 364). In short, this ayah shows believers the ideal reaction to the threat of Allah's punishment in Hellfire, and such a reaction should, of course, translate into a strong commitment to the teachings of Islam.

يقول [129]

يقولون [130]

The slaves of Al-Rahman's fifth attribute highlights the way they handle financial issues. In the description of these distinguished believers and in reference to this important matter, Allah says:

$$(\text{وَالَّذِينَ إِذَآ أَنفَقُواْ لَمْ يُسْرِفُواْ وَلَمْ يَقْتُرُواْ وَكَانَ بَيْنَ ذَلِكَ قَوَاماً}).$$

"And those who, when they spend, are neither extravagant nor stingy, but are in a just balance between them."

According to Ibn Manthoor (2008), *israf*[131] refers to the act of going beyond the limits. He also argued that israf refers to everything spent in a way that doesn't reflect obedience to Allah. He narrated that in reference to this ayah, Sufian [Al-Thawri] said, "Al-Rahman's slaves neither spend their money on the wrong things, nor do they fail to spend it on matters that require expenditure" (p. 172). Ibn Kathir, in addition, reported Al-Hasan Al-Bassri to have said, "Expenditure in the cause of Allah [no matter how much it is] isn't israf" (2014, p.513).

The Holy Prophet himself, in fact, did many things that support Al-Bassri's position on this issue. Imam Muslim, for example, narrated that Anas said the Holy Prophet offered a man herds of sheep and goats that were filling the space between two mountains (A. Al-Ghazali, 2004, p. 478). Similarly, Imam Al-Bukhari reported that when the Holy Messenger of Allah received the amount of ninety thousand *dirhams* from Bahrain, he put it on the floor and started to give from it whoever asked him, until he spent the whole money (A. Al-Ghazali, 2004, p. 478). Ibn Al-Qayyim (2012), in addition, stated that as a result of his victory at the Battle of Hunaiyn, the Holy Messenger of Allah received plenty of wealth. He immediately started to dispense it among many people, until he had nothing left in his exceptionally generous hands (pp. 560–561).

An individual's strong economy can play a significant role in his or her autonomy, success, and happiness. A believer's extravagant, unwise expenditure, however, represents a misunderstanding of the role of wealth in life, and it may lead to a direct or an indirect deviation from the course of Islam. Wealthy people who have *wara*[132] (state of being

---

[131] إسراف

[132] ورع

extremely cautious not to violate Allah's rules) are fully aware of the huge responsibility of being rich. They look at their wealth as a test that if they don't handle wisely, it will harm their relationship with Allah and may cause them a lot of trouble on the Day of Judgment.[133] As a result, they manage their wealth wisely, and they distance themselves from all evil things and conduct associated with it. To such people, the best delight they derive from being wealthy is spending wisely on themselves, families, relatives, and in the cause of Allah.

Further, the slaves of Al-Rahman distance themselves from the worst sins: *shirk* (associating others with Allah), homicide, and adultery. In reference to this, Allah says:

$$\text{(وَالَّذِينَ لاَ يَدْعُـون مَعَ اللَّـهِ إِلَهَا ءَاخَـرَ وَلا يَقْتُلُونَ النَّفْسَ الَّتِي حَرَّمَ اللَّـهُ إِلاَّ}$$

$$\text{بِالْحَقِّ وَلاَ يَـزْنُـونَ ...)}$$

"And (they are) those who do not invoke any other god along with Allah, nor kill the soul that Allah has forbidden, except for just cause, nor commit illegal sexual intercourse..."

Freedom from *shirk*, which is Ibad Al-Rahman's sixth attributes, will be discussed later, in "Chapter 9: Lessons of Taqwa from Luqman's Advice."

Al-Rahman's slaves' seventh characteristic of taqwa is that they don't kill the innocent human soul, for Allah has strongly forbidden killing it unlawfully. To show how horrible a crime it is and to help humans distance themselves from it, Allah likens the killing of only one innocent human soul to the killing of the entire humanity! Precisely, in surah Al-Ma'idah, He says:

$$\text{(مِنْ أَجْلِ ذلِكَ كَتَبْنَا عَلَى بَنِي إِسْرَائِيلَ أَنَّهُ مَن قَتَلَ نَفْساً بِغَيْرِ نَفْسٍ أَوْ فَسَادٍ}$$

---

[133] Different governments in the Muslim world waste their countries' wealth on many unnecessary matters and activities, such as celebrations of their anniversaries, while many of their citizens die as a result of hunger or lack of medical care or both. Also a huge number of children in these countries cannot find shelter or education or even appropriate clothing.

فِى الأَرْضِ فَكَأَنَّمَا قَتَلَ النَّاسَ جَمِيعاً وَمَنْ أَحْيَاهَا فَكَأَنَّمَا أَحْيَا النَّاسَ جَمِيعاً...)

"Because of that, We ordained for the Children of Israel that if anyone killed a person not in retaliation of murder, or (and) to spread mischief in the land, it would be as if he killed all humankind, and if anyone saved a life, it would be as if he saved the lives of all humankind..."   *(Qur'an 5:32)*

Indeed, nothing can make the crime of killing an innocent human soul as ugly as this ayah; consequently, nothing can be as effective in deterring humans from committing such a terrible crime. Because of the evil consequences of killing an innocent human soul, Allah has repeatedly threatened—as in the ayah next to this one[134]—to throw in Hellfire whoever commits this hideous crime. He also threatens to make such a person suffer from Hellfire's horrible torment everlastingly. Today, in different Muslim and non-Muslim countries, a lot of innocent people are, regrettably, ruthlessly killed in the name of Islam, an issue that has, unfortunately, created an extremely negative image of this peaceful religion in the minds of those who don't know it.

Chastity is another invaluable attribute that decorates these ideal servants of Allah. Praising them, Allah says:

(...وَلاَ يَزْنُونَ).

"...nor commit illegal sexual intercourse."

The Creator has chosen sex as a way to keep and increase human race, but only through the tie of Islamic marriage. Hence, the unique pleasure associated with sex shouldn't cause people to decline to the animals' level. We can understand the ugliness of fornication and

---

[134] In this ayah, Allah threatens whoever kills an innocent soul saying:

(يُضَاعَفْ لهُ العَذَابُ يَوْمَ القِيَامَةِ وَيَخْلُدْ فِيهِ مُهَاناً).

"The torment will be doubled to him on the Day of Resurrection, and he will abide therein in disgrace."   *(Qur'an 25:69)*

adultery[135] better if we notice that Allah, in this ayah, has mentioned them immediately after the crime of killing an innocent human soul. The slaves of Al-Rahman are, of course, remote from fornication and adultery, for—as we saw earlier—they distance themselves from things that are even way less harmful.

The vice of illegal sex can find its way to the Muslim society through different channels. The lack of *hijab* and unnecessary integration of the two genders in one place, for example, may gradually cram Muslims in the dirty swamps of forbidden sex. In a moment of human weakness, the strong, natural desire for sex may overpower believers' determination to keep pure and cause them to fall blindly and helplessly in the bed of filthiness. Therefore, Muslims who live in places where adultery, fornication, and sexually-exciting conduct prevail should be extremely watchful. They should distance themselves from all stimuli of forbidden sex, including sexually arousing movies and unnecessary relationships with members of the other sex in the workplace or elsewhere.

The slaves of Al-Rahman's ninth characteristic is highlighted in the following ayah. Again, praising them, Allah says:

(...وَالَّذِينَ لاَ يَشْهَدُونَ الزُّورَ).

"...and those who do not bear witness to falsehood"

The Arabic word *zoor* means the following: falsification, fabrication, lying, and false accusation. People falsify information and fabricate things for many reasons—for example, to have something that they can't otherwise, to avoid responsibility for wrongdoing, and to harm others. In all cases of zoor, it is the innocent people who usually suffer—they get either deprived of their rights or punished for things they haven't done. Even worse, their reputation becomes badly damaged, and their self-esteem gets ruined; as a result, they undergo extremely painful psychological feelings that no one knows for how long.

---

[135] Adultery and fornication are called *zina* in Arabic and both are strongly forbidden in Islam, of course.

Qutb (1992) stated that the message in this ayah implies an indirect meaning, which is, therefore, more general and more significant. According to him, the slaves of Al-Rahman distance themselves from everything having to do with falsehood (p. 2580). The Holy Messenger of Allah emphasized the danger of zoor and strongly warned against it. According to Imams Muslim and Al-Bukhari, He addressed his companions saying:

> "May I tell you the worst [major] sins?" His companion answered, "Yes, indeed, O Messenger of Allah." Then the Holy Prophet said, "Shirk [association of others with Allah], being undutiful to one's parents, and the witness of zoor [falsification or fabrication of facts]. . . ." (Al-Bukhari, 1422, p. 172)

"ألا أنبئكم بأكبر الكبائر ؟ " قالوا : "بلى يا رسول الله . " قال: "الإشراك بالله، وعقوق الوالدين . " وكان متكئاً، ثم جلس فقال : "ألا وقول الزور . " فما زال يكررها حتى قلنا : "ليته سكت . "

The narrator of this hadith reported that the Holy Prophet kept warning his companions against zoor repeatedly until they became extremely worried. He also mentioned that the Holy Prophet was initially reclining, but when he was about to mention the "zoor," he sat up then he said it. His shift from a reclining to a sitting position may indicate the danger of zoor. Zoor, of course, wasn't more abhorrent or more alarming to the Holy Prophet than shirk; however, perhaps because people ignore the danger of zoor but not that of shirk, he changed his posture—from reclining to sitting—in order to show his companions how alarmed he felt about it. Also the changing of his posture was likely a natural reaction of his body to both his feeling and state of mind regarding the issue of zoor, as extremely dirty and harmful conduct.

The slaves of Al-Rahman's tenth attribute reflects their attitude towards trivialities. With respect to this issue, Allah praises them saying:

(...وَإِذَا مَرُّواْ بِاللَّغْوِ مَرُّواْ كِرَاماً).

"...and if they pass by some frivolity, they pass by it with dignity."

Originally, the Arabic word "laghw" means idle talk. But in this ayah, according to Al-Shawkani (2012), it stands for any talk or activity that has no importance (p.111). Since the slaves of Al-Rahman highly value themselves and their time, and since the book of Allah and His Prophet's Sunnah govern their entire lives, they don't spend their time on trifle issues. Therefore, when they come across people who are involved in laghw, they pass with honour. These servants of Allah are, in fact, fully aware of the danger of despicable matters, which not only waste their time and energy but also diminish their value in Allah's sight. The message in this ayah may also suggest the high level of solemnity, dignity, and honour that Allah wants all believers to enjoy by distancing themselves from all forms of laghw.

Allah has emphasized the virtue of the avoidance of laghw in two other surahs, namely Al-Mu'minoon (The Believers) and Al-Qassass (The Narration). In the former, the virtue of self-restraint from laghw comes second among Al-Mu'minoon's major attributes, which Allah favourably highlights at the beginning of this surah. In the latter, He also stresses this virtue as a chief characteristic of the people of the Book (Jews and Christians) who were contemporaneous with the Holy Prophet and believed in Him.

More explicitly, in the surah of Al-Mu'minoon, He states:

(وَالَّذِينَ هُمْ عَنِ اللَّغْوِ مُعْرِضُونَ).

"And those who turn away from idle chatter."
(Qur'an 23:3)

And in the surah of Al-Qassass, He declares:

(وَإِذَا سَمِعُوا اللَّغْوَ أَعْرَضُوا عَنْهُ...) [136]

---

[136] The full context in which this attribute of these people of the Book (Jews and Christians contemporary with the Holy Prophet) is mentioned in the same surah, ayahs 52–55.

"*And when they hear evil vain talk, they turn away from it...*"   *(Qur'an 28:55)*

To deter people not only from bad and seriously harmful speech but also from laghw, Allah emphatically declares that whatever a person may utter is recorded—either for or against him or her. With regard to this, He says:

$$(مَّا يَلْفِظُ مِن قَوْلٍ إِلاَّ لَدَيْهِ رَقِيبٌ عَتِيدٌ)!$$

"*Whatever he utters of a word but there is a vigilant watcher by him!*"   *(Qur'an 50:18)*

Obviously, this ayah carries a strong warning against being loose-tongued. It also helps people become well aware of their responsibility for their speech, and it motivates them to say only good things and to refrain from any speech they may regret on the Day of Judgment. To realize the ugliness of laghw, we should remember that Allah repeatedly describes His Gardens of bliss as free from it. He, actually, highlights this fact five times in the Holy Qur'an: in the surahs of Mariam, Al-Tur, Al-Waqi'ah,[137] Al-Naba', and Al-Ghashiyah.

In the surah of Al-Naba', for example, He says:

$$(لَا يَسْمَعُونَ فِيهَا لَغْوًا وَلَا كِذَّابًا).$$

"*No vanity shall they hear therein, nor untruth.*"
(Qur'an 78:35)

And in the surah Al-Ghashiyah, He declares:

$$(لَا تَسْمَعُ فِيهَا لَاغِيَةً).$$

"*You shall hear no (word) of vanity in it (the Garden).*"   *(Qur'an 88:11)*

The human tongue, obviously, has the largest share of laghw. Accordingly, the Holy Prophet has strongly warned of the danger of excessive and idle talk. For instance, in the famous hadith narrated by

---

[137] Ayahs 62, 23, and 25 respectively

Al-Tirmithi, the Holy Prophet informed his distinguished companion Mu'ath ibn Jabal that the major reason that throws people into Hellfire is what their tongues say.

Al-Tirmithi also narrated that Sufian ibn Abd Allah Al-Thaqqafi narrated:

> "I asked the Holy Messenger of Allah, 'O Messenger of Allah, what is something that you fear the most for me?' He [the Holy Prophet] held his tongue and said, 'Have full control over this!'"

It is narrated that Abu Bakr Al-Siddiq (whose position is next to the Holy Messengers of Allah)[138] used to hold his tongue with his fingers and say, "This has brought me lots of trouble!"[139] Also Ibn Al-Qayyim (2005) reported Ibn Mas'ud to have said, "Nothing requires firmer control than the tongue!" (p. 145).[140] In addition, according to Al-Tirmithi, Jabir reported that the Holy Messenger of Allah said:

> "The most beloved of me and the closest to me amongst you on the Day of Judgment are the best in morals. And the most abhorrent to me and the farthest from me amongst you are the talkative, those who condescend, and those who speak with pride." (Ibn Al-Uthaymeen, 1431, p. 570)

"إن من أحبكم إلي، وأقربكم مني مجلساً يوم القيامة، أحاسنكم أخلاقاً. وإن أبغضكم

إلي، وأبعدكم مني مجلساً يوم القيامة الثرثارون والمتشدقون والمتفيهقون . "[141]

Interestingly, A. Al-Ghazali (2004) identified twenty issues in which the tongue can be negatively involved. They are summarized as follows:

(1) Talking about issues that are none of the speaker's business, (2) redundancy in speech, (3) evil talk, (4) argumentativeness, (5) hostile dispute, (6) condescension, (7) obscenity, (8) cursing, (9) singing and

---

[138] This is based on an authenticated hadith, narrated by Al-Tabarani.

[139] "هذا أوردني الموارد!"

[140] "ما على وجه الأرض شيئ أحوج إلى طول حبس من لسان!"

[141] Sunan Al-Tirthimi, p. 370, hadith no. 2018

[some types of] poetry, (10) excessive humour, (11) mockery and sarcasm, (12) secret disclosure, (13) unfulfilled promises, (14) lying, (15) defamation, (16) backbiting, (17) hypocrisy, (18) flattery or undue praise, (19) inaccuracy of speech, (20) and speaking about issues beyond one's knowledge (pp. 145–209).

Also according to him, an awful problem that laghw may cause those involved in it—and who isn't?—is that it afflicts the heart with incurable diseases. Such diseases include *ghaflah* (heedlessness), *qaswah* (hardness of the heart), *iradh* (lack of interest in connection with Allah and whatever pleases Him), and *nifaq* (hypocrisy)[142] (pp. 145–209).

Today laghw has, unfortunately, become a social epidemic that has inflicted a wide sector of the Muslim community. Every day, Muslims around the world spend plenty of time on different forms of laghw, such as watching TV programs and surfing the Internet to view and/or to read things that are more harmful than helpful. Smartphones, in addition, have become a social phenomenon—more and more people possess them and excessively talk on them, through Tango, Skype, FaceTime, etc., and a lot—if not most—of their talk is idle, not to mention the millions of text messages that most of the time are, at least, time wasters. Further, social media—such as Facebook, Twitter, and Instagram—represents channels of communication through which many people get engaged in not only idle talk but also disgraceful activities. By and large, it seems that people are either unaware of their huge responsibility for their communication activities—verbal and nonverbal—or they simply don't care.

The slaves of Al-Rahman's eleventh characteristic reveals their ideal reaction to the ayahs of Allah when they are reminded of them. Concerning this, Allah says:

(وَالَّذِينَ إِذَا ذُكِّرُواْ بِآيَاتِ رَبِّهِمْ لَمْ يَخِرُّواْ عَلَيْهَا صُمّاً وَعُمْيَاناً).

"And those who, when they are reminded of the verses of their Lord, they do not fall deaf and blind."

In reference to this ayah, Qutb (1992) said:

This ayah condemns polytheists, who are strongly attached to false gods and creeds, like a deaf and blind person who can't hear or see. Hence, they don't look forwards to receiving guidance from Allah. In fact, the way Allah depicts the reaction of disbelievers to His ayahs reflects their heedlessness and prejudice against the truth. The slaves of Al-Rahman, however, are fully aware of the truth that their faith represents. They are also aware of the truthfulness in the ayahs of Allah; therefore, they consciously believe in them. In other words, their belief is based on a [well-thought] decision, not on prejudice and blindness. (p. 2580)

The underlying message of this ayah is that the slaves of Al-Rahman aren't angels; they are humans who may err, and when they do and are reminded of Allah's teachings, they instantaneously acknowledge their mistakes and correct them. Being the harshest event in the Islamic history, the death of the Holy Prophet, for instance, took most of his companions by surprise. The horrible shock of this extremely painful incident rendered them confused and unable to think.

Even Omar ibn Al-Khattab—whom, as mentioned earlier, the Qur'an supported in different occasions—was badly shocked by the Holy Prophet's death, and as a result, he said:

"The Messenger of Allah hasn't died, but he has left to his Lord, the way Musa ibn Imran did. . . . By the name of Allah, he will come back and will cut the hands and feet of men who think he has died." (Al-Mubarakpuri, 2007, p. 431)

Nevertheless, when Abu-Bakr Al-Siddiq reminded him of an ayah in the Holy Qur'an that informs Muslims that the Holy Prophet Mohammad would also die,[143] Omar immediately accepted the Holy Messenger's death and changed his position.

The final attribute of this ideal group of believers sheds light on an important aspect of their heavenly longings. It is this invaluable,

---

[143] Al-Imran, ayah 144

heartfelt supplication in which they humbly, eagerly, sincerely, and hopefully approach their Merciful, Most Generous Lord saying:

(رَبَّنَا هَبْ لَنَا مِنْ أَزْوَاجِنَا وَذُرِّيَّاتِنَا قُرَّةَ أَعْيُنٍ...) [144]

"Our Lord! Bestow on us from our wives and our offspring the comfort of our eyes..."'

In surah Mariam, we learn that Prophet Zakariyya (Zechariah) prayed Allah to offer him a son. He also articulately explained his honourable objective of this invaluable wish saying:

(وَإِنِّي خِفْتُ الْمَوَالِيَ مِن وَرَائِي وَكَانَتِ امْرَأَتِي عَاقِرًا فَهَبْ لِي مِن لَّدُنكَ وَلِيًّا.
يَرِثُنِي وَيَرِثُ مِنْ آلِ يَعْقُوبَ وَاجْعَلْهُ رَبِّ رَضِيًّا).

"And verily, I fear my relatives after me, and my wife is barren. So give me from Yourself an heir. Who shall inherit me, and inherit (also) the posterity of Ya'qub (Jacob) (inheritance of the religious knowledge and my Prophethood, not of wealth). And make him, my Lord, one with whom You are Well-pleased!"
                                                        (Qur'an 19: 5–6)

Scholars of the Qur'anic exegesis, such as Al-Shawkani (2012), claimed that Prophet Zakariyya was afraid his faith would be neglected and gradually lost after his death. He, therefore, prayed Allah to grant him a son who would keep the torch of his faith burning and thus guide

---

[144] This invaluable supplication, interestingly, reflects on Prophets Ibrahim and Ismail's prayer when they asked Allah saying:

(رَبَّنَا وَاجْعَلْنَا مُسْلِمَيْنِ لَكَ وَمِن ذُرِّيَّتِنَا أُمَّةً مُّسْلِمَةً لَّكَ وَأَرِنَا مَنَاسِكَنَا وَتُبْ عَلَيْنَا إِنَّكَ أَنتَ التَّوَّابُ الرَّحِيمُ).

"Our Lord! And make us submissive unto You and of our offspring a nation submissive unto You, and show us our holy rituals, and accept our repentance. Truly, You are the One Who accepts repentance, the Most Merciful"   *(Qur'an 2:128)*

people to His path (p. 400). Ibad Al-Rahman have the same honourable concern—they want to make sure their children will be righteous and will stand for righteousness.

Responsible, conscientious farmers won't expect Allah to fill their farms with different crops while they spend their days and nights sleeping on their farms. They first work hard on their farms; then they wait for Allah to handle the rest. Likewise, Al-Rahman's slaves don't pray Allah to make their wives and children good Muslims without doing their own part in the accomplishment of such a demanding, honourable goal.

Also one important underlying message in this part of the ayah is that young Muslims, men and women, should verify that those they are going to marry will aid—not hinder—them to live a good Islamic life in ideal Islamic home environments, where their children—the future Muslim generations—will learn and earn Islamic morals and values that help them become good servants of Allah and good Muslim citizens of their own countries and of the world they share with billions of others.

In fact, the way that Ibad Al-Rahman have expressed their desired spouses and children suggests that their expectations of them are at the highest level ever: They want these people to be *"quratu aiun"* for them, meaning a source of ultimate happiness. More specifically, Ibad Al-Rahman hope their spouses and children will enjoy perfect awareness of their Islamic identity and a firm commitment to their Islamic "aqeedah," morals, ethics, values, and responsibilities.

In reaction to this part of Ibad Al-Rahman's prayer, A. Y. Ali has the following insight:

> We must also pray for the maintenance of God's law after us, through our wives and descendants: in our eyes they should not be mere accidents or playthings, but a real comfort and fulfilment of our spiritual longings. Perhaps, through them, as well through ourselves, we may, by God's grace, be able to give a lead for truth and righteousness. (2008, p. 943)

The second part of this heartily and invaluable supplication sheds light on another aspect of these people's honourable concerns and aspirations. Precisely, they pray Allah to make them leaders of the righteous. According to Al-Saadi, Ibad Al-Rahman aspire to be among the *siddiqeen* (the sincere) and to become role models for the righteous (2011, p.529). So they pray Allah saying:

$$(...وَاجْعَلْنَا لِلْمُتَّقِينَ إِمَامًا).^{145}$$

"...and make us leaders of those who are pious."

Allah's love for the slaves of Al-Rahman—which is, again, the underlying message of His extensive description of them in this surah—should motivate all believers to work diligently so that they may join them. But, of course, they won't reach these people's exceptionally high level of taqwa without the acquisition of these attributes that Allah highlights in this surah. In other words, this intensive, beautiful description of Al-Rahman's slaves is supposed to elicit the element of taqwa in believers' hearts by inspiring them to acquire these ideal attributes that Allah Himself celebrates.

Finally, it is worth mentioning that this exceptionally beautiful and inviting description of Al-Rahman's slaves comes in the shadow of two extremely significant messages, expressed in the following two articulate, heart-capturing ayahs, in which Allah says:

$$(تَبَارَكَ الَّذِي جَعَلَ فِي السَّمَاءِ بُرُوجاً وَجَعَلَ فِيهَا سِرَاجاً وَقَمَراً مُّنِيراً . وَهُوَ$$
$$الَّذِي جَعَلَ الَّيْلَ وَالنَّهَارَ خِلْفَةً لِّمَنْ أَرَادَ أَن يَذَّكَّرَ أَوْ أَرَادَ شُكُوراً).$$

"Blessed is He Who has set up constellations in the sky, and has placed therein a great lamp and a resplendent moon. And He it is Who has put the night and the day in succession for such who desires to remember or desires to show his gratitude."   *(Qur'an 25:61–62)*

As an introduction to this issue, interestingly, Allah calls people's attention to His miraculous and astonishing creation in the sky,

---

[145] The assumption of such an honourable role, in fact, requires important qualities—such as good Islamic knowledge, self-denial, high level of taqwa, commitment, perseverance, and patience.

signified by three amazing entities: the constellations, the sun, and the moon. He also calls people's attention to the recurrence of the day and night as an excellent opportunity for them to establish a strong, heartfelt link with Him. But, as the second ayah explicitly indicates,[146] the establishment of this honourable link is left to the human ambition. Al-Rahman's slaves have, evidently, proven to be ideally aspirant, for they invest their day and night on the glorification of their Lord.

Indeed, everyone has a similar chance to be one of Al-Rahman's honourable slaves; yet, again, as the second ayah above suggests, the launching pad to reach that extremely high level of taqwa is the individual's heavenly aspirations and strong commitment.

---

[146] (...لِمَنْ أَرَادَ أَن يَذَّكَّرَ أَوْ أَرَادَ شُكُورًا).

"...for such who desires to remember or desires to show his gratitude." (Qur'an 25:62)

CHAPTER 7

——— —— ———

The Qur'anic Question

Asking the right question has a vital role in the generation and the acquisition of knowledge. A good question sparks the fire of critical thinking and leads to better understanding and wise decisions, for it functions like a flashlight in the hand of a person entering an utterly dark room. With this flashlight, such a person can easily see the things in that room; without it, nevertheless, he or she won't see anything. Knowing the significant role of the element of the question in critical thinking, understanding, learning, and decision-making, Allah often uses it in the Holy Qur'an.

According to the scholars of the Qur'anic exegesis, Allah employs the Qur'anic question to motivate, disapprove, condemn, reprimand, warn, threaten, and elicit reflection. He also uses it to help people free themselves from their unjustifiable social conformity and from the chains of their inherited and deep-rooted cultural biases that blind them from seeing or accepting the truth.[147]

---

[147] Social conformity is a human crisis that seems to affect a huge portion of human society. It refers to people's lack of courage to question socially accepted values and practices, even when such values and practices are wrong. An example of this was the Makkans' strong determination to adhere to their old faith just because it was their fathers', not because of its validity or merits. In surah Al-Zukhruf (Gold Adornments), Allah sheds light on this human crisis of intellectual autonomy saying:

(بَلْ قَالُوا إِنَّا وَجَدْنَا آبَاءَنَا عَلَىٰ أُمَّةٍ وَإِنَّا عَلَىٰ آثَارِهِم مُّهْتَدُونَ).

"Nay! They say: 'We found our fathers following a certain religion, and we do guide ourselves by their footsteps.'"   *(Qur'an 43:22)*

Examples of Qur'anic questions that aim at freeing people from the chains of their wrong, inherited faiths are represented in the series of questions that Allah poses in surah Al-Naml, specifically ayahs 59–64.

Obviously, Allah's employment of the element of the question to communicate specific Qur'anic messages indicates that it is the best linguistic device to express and deliver such messages. And, hence, it is the most effective strategy to generate the required human response to these Qur'anic messages.

On a surah's level, the Qur'anic question occurs in different places. It sometimes comes at the beginning, such as in the surahs of Al-Ghashiyah and Al-Insan. It also takes place at the end of the surah—as a conclusion or closure—such as in the surahs of Al-Qiyamah and Al-Mursalat (Those Sent Forth). Other times, it occurs between the beginning and the end of the surah, such as in the surahs of Hud and Al-Waqi'ah. Occasionally, however, the Qur'anic question recurs frequently and consistently throughout the body of the surah, such as in the surahs of Al-Qamar (The Moon) and Al-Rahman. The following throws some light on the role of this Qur'anic phenomenon in the issue of taqwa.

The Rhetorical Question in Surah Al-Rahman

Like other Qur'anic surahs, Al-Rahman has a specific type of question, namely the rhetorical question. According to Al-Rumi (2011), the rhetorical question is meant to make the audience members agree with the communicator regarding common-sense issues that they can't deny (p. 588). Also Quirk and Greenbaum (1973) argued, "The rhetorical question is one which functions as a forceful statement" (p. 200). In other words, this type of question can be used to invite critical thinking and to modify a negative human attitude and behaviour. If a father, for instance, says to his young son, "How many times did I tell you to use your cell phone constructively?" he, of course, doesn't expect an answer from his son; rather, he wants to tell him he is not listening.

Surah Overview

Because the rhetorical question we will discuss in this surah recurs consistently and in a regular pattern in it (thirty-one times), it is important to provide the readers with a general overview of the surah so that they can see the context in which this question occurs. The audience of this surah are humankind and the jinns; it initially highlights different favours that Allah bestows on them. It begins with the most valuable one: the teaching of the Holy Qur'an. Then it sheds light on a couple of other favours that the Creator has honoured humans with, namely their creation and their learning of *al bayan*, which refers to the power of verbal expression that Allah has taught them (Al-Saadi, 2011, p. 772).[148] After this, Allah declares that both the sun and the moon are accurately computed [149] and that both *al najm*[150] and the trees prostrate to Him. Then He sheds light on the miracle of the creation of the heavens in general, and He points to the scale of justice that He has established in them.

In the light of this, He enjoins on all humans and jinns not to transgress the scale of justice and to be fair in all dealings and in all transactions. He says:

(وَالسَّمَآءَ رَفَعَهَا وَوَضَعَ الْمِيزَانَ . أَلَّا تَطْغَوْا۟ فِي الْمِيزَانِ). [151]

"And the heaven He has raised high, and He has set up the balance. In order that you may not transgress (due) balance."   *(Qur'an 55:7–8)*

Inspired by the message in this ayah, A. Y. Ali (2008) wrote the following comment:

---

[148] Al-Saadi claimed that *albayan* includes the ability of self-expression in both verbal and written forms (2011, p.772). Al-Tabari (2010), however, argued that *albayan* refers to the ability of expressing and explaining all that people need to know about issues in this life and in the one thereafter, such as *halal* and *haram* issues (lawful and unlawful things) (p. 532).

[149] Maybe this issue refers to different facts: the accuracy of the creation of the sun and the moon, their relation to each other, their functions, and their relation to the earth. And all of these, of course, signify Allah's amazing power and His mercy on humankind.

[150] Some exegetes of the Holy Qur'an, such as Al-Shawkani, claimed that in this surah the word *alnajm*, which is translated as "stars," refers to plants that don't have stems [vines]" (2012, p. 164). Other exegetes, such as Al-Saadi (2011), argued that this word refers to the actual stars (p. 772).

[151] Ibn Ashoor claimed that humans, not the jinns, are the addressee of the second ayah above (1984, p. 243).

To be taken both literally and figuratively, a man should be honest and straight in every daily matter, such as weighing out things which he is selling, and he should be straight, just and honest, in all the highest dealings, not only with other people, but with himself and in his obedience to God's Law. Not many do either the one or the other when they have an opportunity of deceit. Justice is the central virtue, and the avoidance of both excess and defect in conduct keeps the human world balanced just as the heavenly world is kept balanced by mathematical order. (p. 1473)

Then the surah brings its audience back to earth, and of the endless favours that Allah bestows on humankind, it highlights only four: fruits, date-palms, grains, and sweet-smelling plants. Next, the surah informs humans and jinns about their origins: the former from dry clay and the latter from fire, a matter that indicates the Creator's amazing, infinite power.

Then the rhetorical question takes the surah's audience by surprise. It says:

$$(\text{فَبِأَيِّ ءَالَاءِ رَبِّكُمَا تُكَذِّبَانِ})^{152}؟$$

"Then which of the blessings of your Lord will you both deny?" 　　　　　*(Qur'an 55:13)*

This question comes after the audience has, in fact, been mentally and psychologically prepared to provide the right response to it. It is their expected full acknowledgment of all Allah's favours—the ones that He has mentioned in this surah and countless others. In other words, this question helps humans acknowledge and appreciate their infinitely Powerful, Merciful, Generous, and Gracious Lord.

Then the surah reminds its audience that Allah is the Lord of the two easts and the two wests.[153] After that, it reminds the same addressees

---

[152] Ibn Ashoor (1984) argued that the addresses of this ayah are the human believers and disbelievers only; that is, the jinns are not addressed by this ayah, for the Hoy Qur'an was revealed to address humankind, not the jinns (pp. 243–244).

(رَبُّ الْمَشْرِقَيْنِ وَرَبُّ الْمَغْرِبَيْنِ).[153]

of some more favours that Allah bestows on them, such as the two seas[154] along with the pearls and the corals that they obtain from them.

Next, the surah draws its audience's attention to an inevitable and indisputable fact—everything will perish but Allah, a matter that is supposed to ignite and intensify His glorification deep in the heart. Another significantly important message that this surah communicates is that everything in this vast universe seeks Allah's support to exist and to function, which is also supposed to help the human heart experience a profound, overwhelming sense of glorification of Allah and a deep, genuine sense of gratitude to Him. With respect to this and in reference to Himself, Allah says:

(يَسْأَلُهُ مَن فِي السَّمَاوَاتِ وَالْأَرْضِ كُلَّ يَوْمٍ هُوَ فِي شَأْنٍ)!

"Everyone in heaven and earth entreats Him; every day
He manifests Himself in yet another (wondrous) way!"
(Qur'an 55:29)

Then the surah goes on to mention additional favours of Allah and to highlight other different issues, including the end of the world and the commencement of the Day of Judgment. The latter event is represented by the occurrence of a dreadful universal phenomenon expressed in the following message, in which Allah states:

"(He is) Lord of the two Easts and the Lord of the two Wests."
(Qur'an 55:17)

Generally, scholars of the exegesis of the Holy Qur'an argued that the two easts and the two wests refer to the sun's rising and setting and to the moon's appearance and absence. They also argued that these two expressions refer to the locations of these phenomena. Ibn Kathir, however, claimed that the two easts and the two wests refer to the sunrise and the sunset in the summer and in the winter (2014, p. 337).

[154] According to Al-Qurtubi (2014), "Ibn Abbas said, '*Albahrain* [the two seas]' refers to the sea of the sky and that of the earth." He also said that Ibn Jarir claimed that albahrain refers "to the seas, [which have salty water] and the rivers, [which have fresh water]" (p 105)

(فَإِذَا انشَقَّتِ السَّمَاءُ فَكَانَتْ وَرْدَةً كَالدِّهَانِ)!

"When the sky is rent asunder, and it becomes red like ointment!" *(Qur'an 55:37)*

The second half of the surah speaks exclusively about the Day of Judgment, with a special focus on the element of reward than on the issue of punishment. These two opposite topics of punishment and reward are, of course, effective stimuli that Allah uses to help humans and jinns become thankful today and successful on the Day of Judgment. With respect to this issue, the surah starts with throwing light on the disbelievers' miserable situation on that day, represented by the extremely ruthless and humiliating manner in which they will be treated. In reference to this matter, Allah says:

(يُعْرَفُ الْمُجْرِمُونَ بِسِيمَاهُمْ فَيُؤْخَذُ بِالنَّوَاصِي وَالْأَقْدَامِ)!

"The sinners will be known by their marks: and they will be seized by their forelocks and their feet!" *(Qur'an 55:41)*

In this context, Allah points to Hellfire as a major threat so that disbelievers may give up their negative attitude and correct their hostile or apathetic position on His message to them. In a threatening tone, He points to Hellfire saying:

(هَذِهِ جَهَنَّمُ الَّتِي يُكَذِّبُ بِهَا الْمُجْرِمُونَ)!

"This is Hell that the criminals deny!" *(Qur'an 55:43)*

Then He follows this threat with another even more intimidating message that sheds light on a particular horrible situation that disbelievers will experience. Precisely, they will alternate between burning in Hellfire and drinking from an extremely hot, boiling liquid! With respect to this, Allah declares:

(يَطُوفُونَ بَيْنَهَا وَبَيْنَ حَمِيمٍ ءان)!

*"In its midst and in the midst of boiling water will they
wander round!"*   *(Qur'an 55: 44)*

Next, the surah shifts from talking about the element of punishment
to speaking—extensively—about the element of reward in Allah's
Gardens, and it highlights different, lavish forms of bliss that Allah
has prepared for His obedient, honourable servants.

The Surah's Rhetorical Question

This surah has two rhetorical questions;[155] our discussion, however,
casts light on the major one, which, again, addresses both humans and
jinns. It says to them:

(فَبِأَيِّ ءَالَآءِ رَبِّكُمَا تُكَذِّبَانِ)؟

*"Then which of the blessings of your Lord will you both
deny?"*   *(Qur'an 55:13)*

As mentioned earlier, this rhetorical question recurs throughout the
surah, and it comes between messages that highlight different issues,
such as Allah's countless blessings in this life, His infinite power, the
end of the world, and the element of punishment and reward on the
Day of Judgment. The recurrence of this question, in fact, has three
different lengths of intervals. Initially, it comes after twelve ayahs.
After that, this gap reduces dramatically to include either one or two
ayahs, but for only a short while. Then in the last two-thirds of the
surah—with the exception of only one case—it recurs every other
ayah, until the end.

This quick, consistent recurrence of this compelling rhetorical
question increases its momentum; accordingly, it becomes
overwhelmingly challenging to the ungrateful humans and jinns. It also

---

155 The other ayah that carries a rhetorical question is this one:

(هَلْ جَزَاءُ الْإِحْسَانِ إِلَّا الْإِحْسَانُ)؟

"Is there any reward for good other than good?"

(Qur'an 55:60)

leaves them no reason to deny any of Allah's infinite favours. Thus, it helps them realize that they had better acknowledge their Lord and be thankful to Him before they find themselves in big trouble on the Day of Judgment before and after which, He—in this surah—poses this question saying:

(فَبِأَيِّ ءَالَآءِ رَبِّكُمَا تُكَذِّبَانِ . فَإِذَا انشَقَّتِ السَّمَاءُ فَكَانَتْ وَرْدَةً كَالدِّهَانِ. فَبِأَيِّ ءَالَآءِ رَبِّكُمَا تُكَذِّبَانِ)؟

"Then which of the blessings of your Lord will you deny? Then when the heaven is rent asunder and it becomes rosy or red like red-oil, or hide. Then which of the blessings of your Lord will you deny?"

(Qur'an 55:36–38)

Further, though directed to the human and jinn disbelievers, this rhetorical question has special mental and psychological effects on believers. Specifically, when they approach it mindfully, it raises the level of their awareness of Allah's greatness, His mercy, and His generosity. As a result, it intensifies their appreciation of His countless favours and endless blessings that they enjoy every fraction of a second. It also transforms their thankfulness to Him from being dry and coming from the mouth to being heartfelt and mixed with the sweetness of cordial appreciation and genuine gratitude.

Al-Tabari (2010) narrated that Ibn Omar said:

> The Holy Messenger of Allah read surah of Al-Rahman to his companions, but they kept silent. Then he said, "Why do I hear the jinns give a better answer to their Lord than you do?" They said, 'What is that, O Messenger of Allah?' He answered, "Whenever I read *'Then which of the blessings of your Lord will you both deny?'* the jinns answered, 'Nothing of your blessings we deny, O our Lord. Praise be to You.'" (p. 544)

قرأ رسول الله (ص) سورة الرحمن على أصحابه فسكتوا . فقال : "مالي أسمع الجن أحسن جواباً لربها منكم ؟ " قالوا : "وما ذاك يا رسول الله ؟" قال :"ما أتيت على قول الله عزَّ

وجل : (فَبِأَيِّ ءالآءِ رَبِّكُمَا تُكَذِّبَانِ ؟) إلا قالت الجن : "لا بشيئ من نعمك ربنا نكذب ،
فلك الحمد ."

In conclusion, the consistent, frequent recurrence of this rhetorical question in this surah should lead to the following important question: Why does Allah pose it this intensively and this frequently? The answer, in this case, is obvious: The majority of humans and jinns are ungrateful to Him. That is, the humans' and jinns' negative attitude is so extreme that Allah has reacted to it this intensively.

People, for example, have a serious ethical problem: When someone does them a small favour, they usually immediately and profusely express their appreciation of that person. Yet when Allah showers them with all the blessings they enjoy, He is overlooked! Even worse, they sometimes—if not usually—express their unhappiness with what He grants them.

Allah often points out to this human ingratitude, such as in the surahs of Saba' and Al-Mulk. In the former, He states:

(...وَقَلِيلٌ مِنْ عِبَادِيَ الشَّكُورُ)!

"...but few of My servants are grateful!"

(Qur'an 34:13)

In the latter, He says:

(...قَلِيلًا مَّا تَشْكُرُونَ)!

"...little thanks you give..."

(Qur'an 67:23)

The Element of the Question in Surah Al-Qamar

Surah Al-Qamar has four different questions;[156] our discussion, however, confines itself to the two major ones. The first of them comes in reference to the dreadful end of the disbelievers of Prophets

---

[156] Other Qur'anic questions in this surah are in ayahs 43 and 44. Ayah 25 also carries a question, but it doesn't belong to the type of questions under discussion.

Noah, Hud, and Salih. The second occurs in connection with the obliteration of these same communities in addition to that of Prophet Lut's.

The First Question

The first question in this surah has a warning, threatening tone, and it emphasizes the significance of the lesson underlying the horrible end of each community of the previously mentioned disbelievers. It says:

(فَكَيْفَ كَانَ عَذَابِى وَنُذُرِ)؟

"Then, how was My torment and My warnings?"
(Qur'an 54:30)

This question, in fact, occurs four times in this surah. Its first occurrence takes place after the eradication of Prophet Noah's disbelieving community. Its second and third come in reference to Ad, the people of Prophet Hud; it occurs immediately before and after their obliteration. Its fourth appearance, however, takes place in reference to Thamud, the people of Prophet Salih. It comes directly before their merciless punishment, but not after it.

Now let's examine the effects of this question in the context of the people of Thamud's punishment after they had committed their awful and unpardonable crime of killing Allah's she-camel. With respect to this, Allah says:

(فَنَادَوْاْ صَاحِبَهُمْ فَتَعَاطَى فَعَقَرَ).

"But they called their comrade, and he took (a sword) and killed (the she-camel of Allah)."
(Qur'an 54:29)

In the light of this awful crime, Allah introduces the question, which creates special mental effects. He says:

(فَكَيْفَ كَانَ عَذَابِى وَنُذُرِ)؟

"Then, how was My torment and My warnings?"
(Qur'an 54:30)

The occurrence of this question before the demonstration of Thamud's punishment helps the surah's addressees realize the extremely awful nature of the crime that this community had committed. It also makes the surah's audience wonder, "How might the All-Mighty's retaliation have been?" It seems that the underlying message of this question in this context is that: "Can you imagine how dreadfully Allah punished these people, as a result of this unforgivable crime?" Or "No matter how hard you try, you will never be able to imagine how mercilessly Allah punished them."

Then, after giving the audience a chance to imagine the magnitude of these people's awful, merciless punishment, the All-Mighty—in the subsequent ayah—explains how He punished them. Using the royal pronoun, "We," He emphatically declares:

(إِنَّا أَرْسَلْنَا عَلَيْهِمْ صَيْحَةً وَاحِدَةً فَكَانُواْ كَهَشِيمِ الْمُحْتَظِرِ)!

"Verily, We sent against them a single mighty blast, and they became like the dry stubble used by one who pens cattle."   *(Qur'an 54:31)*

Obviously, this question carries a strong warning to all disbelievers who are hostile to Islam, regardless of who or where they are.[157] The context of continuous, merciless, obliterative punishment in which this question recurs makes it remarkably effective in the creation of special mental and psychological effects essential to the modification of the human negative attitude toward Allah, His message, and His Holy Messenger. The mental effect is the realization that such hostility may lead to the withdrawal of Allah's mercy and the arrival of His punishment. The psychological effects, however, can be a mixture of feelings that include fear, worry, and insecurity.

The Second Question

Whereas the previous question occurs four times in this surah, this one recurs six times in it. In four of these recurrences, it is linked with a statement that highlights the facilitation of the Qur'an so that people

---

[157] This ayah will be looked at again in chapter 10, under "Lessons of Taqwa from Disbelievers' Ends."

may recite it, understand it, live according to it, and glorify Allah. The two other occurrences of this question, however, are connected with other topics.[158] Here our discussion is confined to the context in which this question is connected with the facilitation of the Qur'an.

First, the statement linked with this question declares:

(... وَلَقَدْ يَسَّرْنَا الْقُرْآنَ لِلذِّكْرِ)

"And certainly We have made the Qur'an easy for remembrance..."   *(Qur'an 54:17)*

Then the question connected to this statement says:

(فَهَلْ مِن مُّدَّكِرٍ؟...)

"...then is there anyone who will remember?"

Now look at the question in the whole context of the ayah—that is, in connection with its statement:

(وَلَقَدْ يَسَّرْنَا الْقُرْآنَ لِلذِّكْرِ فَهَلْ مِنْ مُدَّكِرٍ؟)

"And certainly We have made the Qur'an easy for remembrance; then is there anyone who will remember?"   *(Qur'an 54:17)*

Unlike the previous question, this one always comes after—not before—the severe punishment of the disbelieving communities of Prophets Noah, Hud, Salih, and Lut. Therefore, the effect of its message on the surah's audience depends substantially on the mental and the psychological impact they experience in reaction to the nature of each community's obliteration: the stronger the mental and psychological impact of each community's punishment, the stronger the mental and psychological effects of this question.

Further, the occurrence of this question in the context of continuous, merciless extermination of these disbelievers transforms it into a

---

[158] The other two ayahs where this question occurs are 15 and 51.

threatening advice that has two underlying messages. The first is that people should learn a good lesson from the punishment of the foolish communities of Noah, Hud, Salih, and Lut. The second threatening advice underlying this question is that people—including uncommitted Muslims—had better reconsider their negative position on the Qur'anic message before it is too late.

Looking at it from a different perspective, however, one can realize that this question carries a challenging message that addresses all humankind saying, "Believe in the Qur'an, live according to it, then see how honourable you will be in the Hereafter." To make sense of this, consider the following:

Suppose a young man asks a helpful business owner to offer him a job. Assume the business owner's answer is this: "I will, certainly, give you one, but would you see me in my office so that we can speak about the job that matches your qualifications and experience?" Similarly, Allah has made the Qur'an easy and available to everyone wishing to establish a strong bond with Him, but humans are free to choose. If they decide to connect with Him, they will, indeed, find Him committed to His beautiful promise.

With this in mind, you may now examine this Qur'anic question once again:

$$(وَلَقَدْ يَسَّرْنَا الْقُرْآنَ لِلذِّكْرِ فَهَلْ مِنْ مُدَّكِرٍ)؟$$

"And certainly We have made the Qur'an easy for remembrance; then is there anyone who will remember?" *(Qur'an 54:17)*

The Rhetorical Question in Surah Al-Qiyamah

An enormous percentage of people, surprisingly, disbelieve in the Day of Judgment. In the early Makkan Qur'an, therefore, Allah recurrently assures such people that the issue of resurrection is inevitable, for—as He expresses it in different surahs[159]—the One Who created them the first time can recreate them after death. Amongst the many Makkan

---

[159] Al-Isra', ayah 51 and Ya-Sin , ayah 79

surahs that address this issue are Al-Naba', Al-Nazi'at (Those Who Pull Out), Al-Infitar (The Cleaving), and Al-Qiyamah.

At the beginning of the surah of Al-Qiyamah, Allah points to the Day of Judgment and guarantees disbelievers He will bring them back to life after death. He also concludes this surah with the same issue using a series of forceful, compelling rhetorical questions. This is how He concludes it:

(أَيَحْسَبُ الإنسَانُ أَن يُتْرَكَ سُدى . أَلَمْ يَكُ نُطْفَةً مِّن مَّنِيٍّ يُمْنَى .ثُمَّ كَانَ عَلَقَةً فَخَلَقَ فَسَوَّى . فَجَعَلَ مِنْهُ الزَّوْجَيْنِ الذَّكَرَ وَالأُنثَى . أَلَيْسَ ذَلِكَ بِقَادِرٍ عَلَى أَن يُحْيِيَ الْمَوْتَى)؟

"Does man think he will be abandoned to futility? Was he not a drop of sperm emitted? Then became a blood clot, which He created and fashioned? And made from it a pair, male and female? Is such a Being not capable of reviving the dead?" (Qur'an 75:36–40)

As you can see, the last powerful rhetorical question comes as a conclusion of a logical, persuasive argument that makes the issue of resurrection common sense. Thus, it leaves the disbelievers no chance to deny the Creator's ability to bring them back to life after death, for, again—logically speaking—since He has created them the first time from this despised matter in this amazing, sequential manner, He is, indeed, capable of recreating them. Therefore, if these people use common sense, the question of resurrection won't be an issue anymore. The issue, nevertheless, will be their destiny on that day and their preparation for it, which should be their biggest concern, as a result.

The Rhetorical Question in Surah Al-Insan

Here it is worth mentioning that the previous surah and this one are adjacent in the Holy Book of Allah: Al-Qiyamah comes first and Al-Insan next. Interestingly, whereas the former ends with a rhetorical question, the latter begins with it saying:

(هَلْ أَتَى عَلَى الإنسَانِ حِينٌ مِّنَ الدَّهْرِ لَمْ يَكُن شَيْئاً مَّذْكُوراً)؟

"Has there not been a period of time, when the human was not a thing worth mentioning?"

(Qur'an 76:1)

This rhetorical question signifies Allah's reaction to a nasty human attitude—precisely, arrogance, insolence, and ingratitude. The disapproving tone in it, in addition, offers the surah a dynamic introduction that can positively influence the audience's reaction to its whole message. It also calls the attention of the arrogant to a fact they seem to have forgotten or they pretend to ignore: They have just come into existence. Being expressed in this manner, the message in this rhetorical question is supposed to sting the ungrateful people's conscience and ignite an intense sense of shame deep in their hearts. As if it says to them, "Don't forget who you are, have a low profile, and be grateful to your Lord."

Certainly, humans aren't original on Earth, let alone their originality in this endless universe. According to Mayell (2005), a recent study claimed that the oldest human fossils—represented by two skulls found in Ethiopia—are 195,000 years old. The age of the earth is thought to be around 4.5 billion years, and according to the geological column, life started to appear on this planet around 3.8 billion years ago. Based on this, imagine the novelty of the human race on the earth in particular and in the solar system in general. Then imagine—if you can—the human race's novelty in relation to the commencement of the entire universe.

Further, the Arabic word *insan*,[160] meaning human, in this context carries an important underlying message. Precisely, most of the time, Allah uses it in association with negative human attributes, such as disbelief in Him, hostility to Him,[161] ignorance, arrogance,[162] insolence,

---

[160] إنسان

[161] (خَلَقَ الإِنسَانَ مِن نُّطْفَةٍ فَإِذَا هُوَ خَصِيمٌ مُّبِينٌ)!

"He has created man from a sperm-drop; and behold this same (man) becomes an open disputer!"   *(Qur'an 16:4)*

[162] (كَلَّا إِنَّ الْإِنسَانَ لَيَطْغَى).

"Nay, but man does transgress all bounds."   *(Qur'an 96:6)"*

ingratitude,[163] haste,[164] and argumentativeness,[165] to mention only a few. Its usage in this ayah, therefore, suggests that humans—with the exception of a small percentage, of course—are arrogant, insolent, and ungrateful to Allah. These extremely negative meanings should increase the previously mentioned sense of shame in the ungrateful heart and create a strong sense of guilt in it.

Based on all of this, consider—once again—the deterring nature of this powerful rhetorical question:

(هَلْ أَتَى عَلَى الإِنْسَانِ حِينٌ مِّنَ الدَّهْرِ لَمْ يَكُن شَيْئاً مَّذْكُوراً)؟

"Has there not been a period of time, when the human was not a thing worth mentioning?"

(Qur'an 76:1)

---

163 (إِنَّ الْإِنسَانَ لِرَبِّهِ لَكَنُودٌ)!

"Truly man is, to his Lord, ungrateful!"   *(Qur'an 100:6)*

164 (...وَكَانَ الإِنسَانُ عَجُولاً).

"Man is given to haste."   *(Qur'an 17:11)*

165 (...وَكَانَ الْإِنسَانُ أَكْثَرَ شَيْءٍ جَدَلًا)!

"But, man is ever more quarrelsome than anything!" *(Qur'an 18:54)*

CHAPTER 8

The Qur'anic Analogies

According to Dodd (2004), people use "analogy or a comparison of two things—usually, one known and one unknown—to show how they are alike. . . . a good analogy can make an abstract concept more concrete" (p. 385). Because of their effectiveness, analogies are common in education. Textbooks and teachers of different subjects, in all levels of education, for example, use various kinds of analogies to help students understand new concepts and lessons. Acknowledging the role of analogies in human education, Allah recurrently employs different types of them in the Qur'an to teach invaluable lessons.

According to Al-Rumi (2011), the Qur'anic analogies are three categories: the explicit, the implicit, and the proverb-like ones. First, the explicit[166] analogy includes the Arabic word *mathal*,[167] meaning "likeness," as in the following ayah, from surah Al-Baqarah:

(مَثَلُهُمْ كَمَثَلِ الَّذِي اسْتَوْقَدَ نَاراً فَلَمَّا أَضَاءَتْ مَا حَوْلَهُ ذَهَبَ اللّـهُ بِنُورِهِمْ وَتَرَكَهُمْ فِي ظُلُمَاتٍ لاَّ يُبْصِرُونَ).

"Their likeness is as the likeness of one who kindled a fire; then, when it lighted all around him, Allah took away their light and left them in darkness. (So) they could not see."   *(Qur'an 2:17)*

---

[166] المُصَرِّحة

[167] مثل

Second, unlike the explicit analogy, the implicit[168] one does not include the Arabic word "mathal," such as the following one from the same previous surah—Al-Baqarah:

$$(...لاَّ فَارِضٌ وَلاَ بِكْرٌ عَوَانٌ بَيْنَ ذَلِكَ...)$$

"...verily, it is a cow neither too old nor too young, but (it is) between the two conditions..."

(Qur'an 2:68)

Finally, like the implicit one, the proverb-like analogy[169] doesn't have the Arabic word "mathal." Ayahs from this type of the Qur'anic analogies are used like proverbs, for they are distinguished by their meaning, not by their words (pp. 595–598). An example of this kind of analogy is the following one from surah Al-Ma'idah:

$$(...لَا يَسْتَوِي الْخَبِيثُ والطَّيِّبُ...)$$

"...bad cannot be likened to good..."

(Qur'an 5:100)

This chapter, however, sheds light on the explicit analogy. Using three examples, it explores the role of this analogy in taqwa.

The First Analogy

The surah of Yunus provides the first Qur'anic analogy in this discussion. In a kind, merciful manner, Allah communicates to all humankind this important message about this life. He states:

$$(إِنَّمَا مَثَلُ الْحَيَاةِ الدُّنْيَا كَمَاءٍ أَنْزَلْنَاهُ مِنَ السَّمَاءِ فَاخْتَلَطَ بِهِ نَبَاتُ الْأَرْضِ مِمَّا يَأْكُلُ$$
$$النَّاسُ والْأَنْعَامُ حَتَّى إِذَآ أَخَذَتِ الْأَرْضُ زُخْرُفَهَا وَازَّيَّنَتْ وَظَنَّ أَهْلُهَآ أَنَّهُمْ قَادِرُونَ$$
$$عَلَيْهَآ أَتَاهَآ أَمْرُنَا لَيْلاً أَوْ نَهَارًا فَجَعَلْنَاهَا حَصِيْدًا كَأَن لَّمْ تَغْنَ بِالْأَمْسِ ، كَذَلِكَ$$
$$نُفَصِّلُ الْآيَاتِ لِقَوْمٍ يَتَفَكَّرُونَ).$$

---

168 الكامنة

169 المرسلة

"Verily, the parable of the life of the world is as the water which We send down from the sky; so by it arises the intermingled produce of the earth of which men and cattle eat: until when the earth is clad in its adornments and is beautified, and its people think that they have all the powers of disposal over it, Our command reaches it by night or by day and We make it like a clean-mown harvest, as if it did not flourish yesterday! Thus do We explain the signs in detail for people who reflect."

(Qur'an 10:24)

This analogy explains the real essence of this life, and it reveals the unpleasant reality it hides behind its false charm. It starts to look beautiful, friendly, loving, and promising. The majority of people—especially disbelievers—fall in love with it, trust it, and rely solely on it. They sow all their aspirations on its soil, hoping it will offer them all their dreams: various and countless possessions, wealth, health, joy, happiness, and security. Allah may grant them all they want and even more, but—no matter how long they live or how much of this limited life's fruits they enjoy—they will finally die. Then they will discover they had spent their entire lives running after nothing but a mirage! They will also realize that they were blind, ignorant, foolish, and that it is too late to do anything to avoid their ugly, eternal destiny in Hellfire!

Therefore, Allah—Who usually lets people learn about life themselves—has decided to warn them Himself against its deceptive nature. In this analogy, He depicts it as rainwater falling on a piece of land and causing it to grow abundant promising plants. When the harvest season arrives, nevertheless, a natural disaster hits them, and it ruins everything! The beautiful, charming place—just a short while ago—has now become not only empty of life but full of destruction and desolation.

Imagine the falling of the rain and the process in which its water mingles with the plants. Then imagine the full growth of these plants and their gorgeous, delightful view. At this point, their owners think they are in full control; they also take it for granted that they will gather and enjoy abundant amounts of different crops. Paradoxically, at this moment—when these owners' beautiful dreams have almost become a reality—the irresistible disaster arrives and obliterates everything!

The comment that Allah makes on the way these plants look after their destruction emphasizes these people's tragic situation. He says:

$$(\text{...كَأَن لَّمْ تَغْنَ بِالْأَمْسِ...})!$$

"...as if it did not flourish only the day before..."

This comment, in addition, has an important message to convey. More precisely, it warns people against focusing on this unreliable, short, and rapidly ending life on the account of the other everlasting one. It also helps increase the addressee's chance to internalize this invaluable lesson better.

Finally, Allah concludes this analogy with a recommendation to people to reflect on the reality of this life so that they may deal with it wisely—in a way that makes them victorious in the Hereafter. He declares:

$$(\text{...كَذلِكَ نُفَصِّلُ الآيَاتِ لِقَوْمٍ يَتَفَكَّرُونَ}).$$

"...thus do We explain the signs in detail for those who reflect."

It is narrated that Omar Ibn Al-Khattab said:

If everything in this life—from its beginning to its end—were given to only one man then death came to him, he would be like a person who saw a beautiful dream. When he woke up, however, he found nothing in his hand!

لو أنَّ الدنيا من أولها لآخرها أُعْطِيت لرجل واحد ، ثم أدركه الموت ، لكان بمثابة من رأى حلماً جميلاً ثم استيقظ فلم يجد في يده شيئاً!

The Second Analogy

The surah of Al-Kahf offers the second analogy to help people understand the reality of this life and deal with it accordingly. Out of mercy, the Creator of this life Himself advises humankind not to be victims of its false charm. He says:

(وَاضْرِبْ لَهُم مَّثَلَ الْحَيَاةِ الدُّنْيَا كَمَاءٍ أَنْزَلْنَاهُ مِنَ السَّمَاءِ فَاخْتَلَطَ بِهِ نَبَاتُ الْأَرْضِ فَأَصْبَحَ هَشِيمًا تَذْرُوهُ الرِّيَاحُ ، وَكَانَ اللَّهُ عَلَى كُلِّ شَيْءٍ مُّقْتَدِرًا).

"And mention the parable of the worldly life: It is like the water which We send down from the sky, and the vegetation of the earth mingles with it, and becomes fresh and green. But it soon becomes dry and broken pieces, which the winds scatter. And Allah is able to do everything."   *(Qur'an 18: 45)*

This analogy, in fact, teaches the same previous lesson but—to some extent—from a different perspective. Precisely, the preceding analogy sheds light on the concept of time that the plants need to grow and flourish, but this one doesn't. The element of time in the first analogy is expressed by the Arabic word *hatta*,[170] the equivalent of the English word "until," which signifies the notion of time between the rainfall and the full growth of the vegetation. In addition, the usage of this word in the previous analogy allows the brain to imagine the highlighted beauty of that vegetation before its destruction. In this regard, Allah says:

(...حَتَّى إِذَا أَخَذَتِ الْأَرْضُ زُخْرُفَهَا وَازَّيَّنَت...)

"...until when the earth is clad in its adornments and is beautified..."

This analogy, nevertheless, doesn't offer the brain a chance to imagine the view of the vegetation before its destruction. As if the falling of the rain, its mixing with the plants, the destruction of these plants, and the work of the winds all happened simultaneously. Amazing! Further, this example is shorter than the previous one, and the way Allah portrays the scene of the place after the destruction is more dramatic and more depressing. Specifically, the element of the winds in this analogy adds another tragic dimension to this saddening, mental picture. With respect to this and in reference to the destroyed vegetation, Allah says:

(...فَأَصْبَحَ هَشِيمًا تَذْرُوهُ الرِّيَاح...)!

---

170 حَتَّى

"...but it soon becomes dry and broken pieces, which the winds scatter...!"

Here the Qur'an provides a vivid, dramatic, mental picture in which the wind dominates the whole scene of destruction. It blows the weightless and helpless wreckage of the destroyed plants here, there, and everywhere! Such a dramatic representation of this life implies its sad reality, lack of weight, and lack of value, which are all suggested by the work of the wind. Thus, in reaction to this remarkably effective Qur'anic message, the living heart—not the dead one, of course—is apt to hear the sound of the winds filling and dominating the whole place of emptiness, destruction, and desolation.

So the lesson to learn from this Qur'anic analogy is that no matter how beautiful or vigorous or powerful or exciting or promising this life may look, it always has the same sad reality—perishment! Thus, people should take advantage of every second in this unguaranteed, fast-moving life to prepare a better place for themselves in the next eternal one.

The Third Analogy

The third analogy in this chapter comes from surah Al-Hadid (Iron). Allah says:

(اعْلَمُوا أَنَّمَا الْحَيَاةُ الدُّنْيَا لَعِبٌ وَلَهْوٌ وَزِينَةٌ وَتَفَاخُرٌ بَيْنَكُمْ وَتَكَاثُرٌ فِى الأَمْوَالِ وَالأَوْلَادِ كَمَثَلِ غَيْثٍ أَعْجَبَ الْكُفَّارَ نَبَاتُهُ ثُمَّ يَهِيجُ فَتَرَاهُ مُصْفَرّاً ثُمَّ يَكُونُ حُطَامًا وَفِى الآخِرَةِ عَذَابٌ شَدِيدٌ وَمَغْفِرَةٌ مِّنَ اللَّهِ وَرِضْوَانٌ وَمَا الْحَيَاةُ الدُّنْيَآ إِلاَّ مَتَاعُ الْغُرُورِ)!

"(O humankind!) Know that the life of this world is only play and amusement, pomp and mutual boasting among you, and rivalry in respect of wealth and children. (It is) as the likeness of vegetation after rain, thereof the growth is pleasing to the tiller; afterwards it dries up and you see it turning yellow; then it becomes straw. But in the Hereafter (there is) a severe torment (for the disbelievers), and (there is) forgiveness from Allah and

*(His) Good Pleasure (for the committed believers). And
the life of this world is only a deceiving enjoyment!"*
(Qur'an 57:20)

First, this amazing analogy begins with an imperative, specifically
ilamu,[171] which means *"O humankind, know."* This Arabic expression
is, actually, a whole clause—it includes a subject and a predicate.[172]
The verb of this predicate is derived from the root *a-l-m;*[173] one of the
different present forms derived from it is *yalam,*[174] meaning "to know."
Obviously, "to know" doesn't mean "to learn," for people learn in
order to know. Learning, in other words, is a demanding, complicated
process that finally leads to knowing. In this ayah, nevertheless, Allah
wants humans to know the reality of this life without spending any
time or effort on the long phase of learning.

Thus, being the Most Knowledgeable, the All-Knowing, and the
Highest Authority, He addresses all humanity in this regard, saying:

$$(اعْلَمُوا ...)^{175}$$

"(O humankind) know…"

Second, in this analogy, Allah depicts people spending their lives in
different, worthless issues.[176] The first of them is *la'ib,*[177] and it denotes
activities in which a person is engaged, but without significant benefits.
Therefore, only the idle, who don't value their time, will involve
themselves in it. The second worthless matter in which people are

---

[171] اعلموا

[172] According to Pence and Emery, the "predicate" is whatever has been declared
about the subject of the sentence (1963, pp. 8–9).

[173] علم

[174] يعلم

[175] Ibn Ashoor (1984) argued that the opening of a statement with *"ilam,"* meaning
"know," indicates that what will be mentioned is extremely important; thus, the
addressee should pay special attention to it (p. 393).

[176] Ibn Ashoor claimed that in this analogy, Allah mentions the most predominant
issues in people's lives (1984, p. 401).

[177] لعب

engaged, according to this ayah, is *lahw*,[178] which refers to whatever diverts from important issues. It is, therefore, worse than "la'ib." According to some exegetes of the Holy Qur'an, such as Al-Shawkani (2012), "lahw" refers to everything that distracts people from getting ready for the Day of Judgment (p. 217). The third worthless issue in which people are busy in this life is *zeenah*.[179] It stands for items that people use to adorn themselves; it also refers to articles they use to beautify things. The fourth and fifth trivial issues in which people are engaged are not only worthless but also despicable and disgraceful: competition in piling of wealth, in number of one's own children, and boasting.

In reference to all of this, Qutb (1992) said:

> When this life is judged by the standards that we create, it seems to have magnificent value, but when it is evaluated by the Hereafter's scale, it becomes despicable and worthless. Here in this depiction, this life looks like a child's toy, in comparison with whatever is in the Hereafter, where people's destinies will be decided. (p. 3491)

Like the two previous analogies, this one likens this whole life to vegetation that starts to look beautiful. After a short period of time, however, it ends in total destruction. Here Allah escorts the human heart through the process of this vegetation's perishment slower than He does in the previous couple of analogies. Precisely, He presents this perishment as a process that takes place gradually. This graduality is suggested by the Arabic word *thumma*,[180] meaning "then," which indicates a gap between the different stages that these plants go through before they are entirely destroyed.

Initially, Allah depicts the beginning of this life as beautiful, promising plants that have fully grown as a result of rainwater. He also projects the farmers who own them delighted. He says:

$$(... كَمَثَلِ غَيْثٍ أَعْجَبَ الْكُفَّارَ نَبَاتُهُ ...)$$

---

[178] لهو

[179] زينة

[180] ثُمَّ

"...(It is) as the likeness of vegetation after rain, thereof the growth is pleasing to the tiller..."

Next, He sheds light on the subsequent stage in the life of these plants in which they start to wither gradually. This gradual withering is suggested by, again, the Arabic word "thumma," which implies that the withering process begins later, after a considerable amount of time in which the plants maintain their strength and beauty. With regard to this and in reference to the plants, Allah says:

(...يَهِيجُ ثُمَّ...)

"...afterwards, it dries up..."

After that, these plants look completely different. They turn yellow, which suggests they are dying. Here Allah indicates this phase in this withering process saying:

(...مُصْفَرّاً فَتَرَاهُ...)

"...and you see it turning yellow..."

Finally, Allah demonstrates the final phase in the destruction of these plants as a process that takes place gradually, again, using the word "thumma" to indicate that this destruction takes time before it is complete. He says:

(...حُطَاماً يَكُونُ ثُمَّ...)

"...then it becomes straws..."

The destruction of this vegetation, of course, represents the destiny of everything in this life. So the place that was full of life, beauty, and hope has now turned into a gloomy one, similar to that of the graveyard. Liveliness becomes death; beauty ugliness; delight despondency; hope despair; and happiness grief! Further, the conclusion of this analogy confirms that this life, with which humans are unjustifiably preoccupied, is nothing but a mere delusion. In other words, Allah ends this analogy in a way that reflects His own view of this life. He declares:

(الْغُرُورِ مَتَاعُ إِلاَّ الدُّنْيَا الْحَيَاةُ وَمَا ...)!

"...and the life of this world is only a deceiving enjoyment!"

This delusion, unfortunately, wraps up the majority of humankind in its darkness, including a considerable percentage of Muslims. Being concerned with only earthly matters and desires, the human brain and heart usually fail—dramatically—to take people beyond the very close boundaries of this short, limited life—even with the aid of the Holy Qur'an!

In all these three analogies, as it is the case in other Qur'anic messages, Allah describes this life as "of a lower level"—*dunia*, in Arabic. So being provided by the Creator Himself, such a description of this life should inspire people to deal with it as a piece of land to cultivate today in order to reap its fruits tomorrow. Yet this doesn't mean Islam encourages withdrawal from the theatre of life, a misunderstanding over which many Muslims have stumbled, unfortunately.

CHAPTER 9

Lessons of Taqwa
from
Luqman's Advice

To realize its great value, Luqman's advice for his son requires an excellent quality of critical thinking. Its inclusion in the Qur'an suggests its preciousness in Allah's sight and indicates the significance of the lessons it teaches. First, you are invited to a careful reading of the whole text of this advice that Allah, out of mercy, narrates to humankind. He says:

(وَإِذْ قَالَ لُقْمَانُ لِابْنِهِ وَهُوَ يَعِظُهُ يَا بُنَيَّ لَاتُشْرِكْ بِاللَّهِ إِنَّ الشِّـرْكَ لَظُلْمٌ عَظِيــمٌ. وَوَصَّيْنَا الْإِنْسَـانَ بِوَالِدَيْهِ حَمَلَتْهُ أُمُّهُ وَهْنـاً عَلَى وَهْـنٍ وَفِصَالُـهُ فِى عَامَـيْنِ أَنِ اشْكُرْ لِى وَلِوَالِدَيْكَ إِلَيَّ الْمَصِيــرُ. وَإِن جَاهَدَاكَ عَلَى أَن تُشْرِكَ بِي مَا لَيْسَ لَكَ بِهِ عِلْمٌ فَلاَ تُطِعْهُمَـا، وَصَاحِبْهُمَـا فِى الدُّنْيَـا مَعْرُوفاً، وَاتَّبِعْ سَبِيلَ مَنْ أَنَابَ إِلَيَّ، ثُمَّ إِلَيَّ مَرْجِعُكُمْ فَأُنَبِّئُكُمْ بِمَا كُنتُمْ تَعْمَلُون. يَا بُنَيَّ إِنَّهَآ إِن تَكُ مِثْقَالَ حَبَّةٍ مِّنْ خَـرْدَلٍ فَتَكُنْ فِى صَخْـرَةٍ أَوْ فِى السَّمَاوَاتِ أَوْ فِى الأَرْضِ يَأْتِ بِهَا اللَّهُ، إِنَّ اللَّـهَ لَطِيفٌ خَبِيرٌ. يَا بُنَيَّ أَقِمِ الصَّلاَةَ وَأْمُرْ بِالْمَعْرُوفِ وَانْهَ عَنِ الْمُنْكَرِ وَاصْبِرْ عَلَى مَآ أَصَابَكَ، إِنَّ ذَلِكَ مِنْ عَزْمِ الأُمُورِ. وَلاَ تُصَعِّـرْ خَـدَّكَ لِلنَّاسِ وَلاَ تَمْـشِ فِى الأَرْضِ مَرَحاً، إِنَّ اللَّهَ لاَ يُحِبُّ كُلَّ مُخْتَالٍ فَخُورٍ . وَاقْصِـدْ فِى مَشْيِكَ اغْضُضْ مِـن صَوْتِكَ، إِنَّ أَنكَرَ الأَصْوَاتِ لَصَوْتُ الْحَمِيرِ).

"And (remember) when Luqman said to his son when he was advising him: 'O my son! Join not in worship others with Allah. Verily, joining others in worship with Allah is a

200

terrible sin.' And We have enjoined on man to be dutiful and good to his parents. His mother bore him in weakness and hardship upon weakness and hardship, and his weaning is in two years; give thanks to Me and to your parents. Unto Me is the final destination. And if they strive with you to make you join in worship with Me others that of which you have no knowledge, then do not obey them; but behave with them in the world kindly, and follow the path of those who turn to Me in repentance and in obedience. Then to Me will be your return, and I shall tell you what you used to do. 'O my son! If it be (anything) equal to the weight of a grain of mustard-seed, and though it be in a rock, or in the heavens or on the earth, Allah will bring it forth. Verily, Allah is Subtle, Well-Aware. O, my son! Perform the salah, enjoin the good, and forbid the evil, and bear with patience whatever befalls you. Verily, these are some of the important commandments. And do not turn your face away from people with pride, nor walk in insolence through the earth. Verily, Allah likes not any arrogant boaster. And be moderate in your walking, and lower your voice. Verily, the harshest of all voices is the braying of the asses.'"

(Qur'an 31: 13—19)

In its opening, Allah quotes Luqman addressing his son using the word *bunaiyya*,[181] which is a whole phrase consisting of the diminutive form of the Arabic word *ibn*, meaning son, and the Arabic first person, singular, possessive case—the equivalent of the English one "my." Thus, this whole Arabic phrase, "bunaiyya," means my "dear son." In Arabic, the diminutive is used to express a positive feeling and/or a positive attitude—such as endearment, affection, and appreciation. It is also used to express a negative feeling and/or a negative attitude, for example, belittling the value of things, ideas, or people (Al-Ghaini, 2015, p. 231).

In the context of this advice, the phrase "bunaiyya" expresses endearment, love, and care. Therefore, its underlying meaning is that: "O my dear, beloved son, please pay special attention to this important advice." Al-Daqas (1977) argued that Luqman uses this

---

[181] بُنَيَّ

phrase three times in this advice "in order to encourage him [his son] to do righteousness" (Al-Tamimi, 2008, p. 39).

Belief in the oneness of Allah is the foundation of eiman and Islam.[182] Thus, Luqman commences his advice for his son with a strong warning against shirk, which refers to the association of others with Allah. He tells him:

(يَا بُنَيَّ لاَ تُشْرِكْ بِاللَّهِ إِنَّ الشِّرْكَ لَظُلْمٌ عَظِيمٌ).

"...O my son! Join not in worship others with Allah. Verily, joining others in worship with Allah is a terrible sin, indeed."

With regard to the ugliness of associating others with Allah, Ibn Al-Qayyim said, "A person who associates others with Allah is the most ignorant of Him, for he [she] comes up with [an imaginary] partner of Allah equal to Him, and this is the worst kind of wrongdoing" (Al-Tamimi, 2008, p. 46).

It is expected that Allah continue narrating Luqman's advice, which He has just started. Surprisingly, however, He shifts to another topic, namely being dutiful to one's own parents. He states:

(وَوَصَّيْنَا الْإِنْسَانَ بِوَالِدَيْهِ حَمَلَتْهُ أُمُّهُ وَهْناً عَلَى وَهْنٍ وَفِصَالُهُ فِي عَامَيْنِ أَنِ اشْكُرْ لِي وَلِوَالِدَيْكَ إِلَيَّ الْمَصِيرُ . وَإِنْ جَاهَدَاكَ عَلَى أَنْ تُشْرِكَ بِي مَا لَيْسَ لَكَ بِهِ عِلْمٌ فَلَا تُطِعْهُمَا وَصَاحِبْهُمَا فِي الدُّنْيَا مَعْرُوفًا وَاتَّبِعْ سَبِيلَ مَنْ أَنَابَ إِلَيَّ ثُمَّ إِلَيَّ مَرْجِعُكُمْ فَأُنَبِّئُكُمْ بِمَا كُنْتُمْ تَعْمَلُونَ).

"And We have enjoined on man to be dutiful and good to his parents. His mother bore him in weakness and hardship upon weakness and hardship, and his weaning is in two years; give thanks to Me and to your parents. Unto Me is the final destination. And if they strive with you to make you join in worship with Me others that of which you

---

[182] The Islamic creed begins with the belief in Allah and in His oneness, and the first pillar of Islam is the belief in Allah's Oneness and the belief in Prophet Mohammad as His final Messenger.

have no knowledge, then do not obey them; but behave
with them in the world kindly, and follow the path of those
who turn to Me in repentance and in obedience. Then to
Me will be your return, and I shall tell you what you used
to do."

This apparent interruption may lead to the following question: What's the relationship between the message in these two ayahs and Luqman's advice? Since the speaker is Allah Himself, then this seemingly interrupting message must have a good reason to occur in this context. More precisely, it comes immediately after Luqman's warning for his son against the association of others with Allah. It also stresses the importance of being dutiful to one's parents, especially the mother, whose role Allah has emphasized. In addition, the significance of being obedient to one's parents is more emphasized by the link that Allah has established between being thankful to Him and being thankful to them. With respect to this, He says:

$$\text{(...أَنِ اشْكُرْ لِي وَلِوَالِدَيْكَ...)}$$

"...give thanks to Me and to your parents..."

But, notwithstanding His firm command that children be dutiful to their parents, Allah strongly forbids their obedience if they—knowingly or unknowingly—want their child to associate others with Him. Thus, this apparent interruption is in full harmony with this advice, and it emphasizes the first element in it, specifically no one should associate anyone or anything with Allah, even if it is the very parents who are pushing in that direction.

Then Luqman teaches his son an amazing attribute of Allah: His infinite knowledge and infinite power. He tells him that no matter how minute a thing is, and no matter where it exists—be it in the texture of a rock, or anywhere on earth, or wherever in the heavens—Allah will, indeed, bring it! He says:

$$\text{(يَا بُنَيَّ إِنَّهَا إِن تَكُ مِثْقَالَ حَبَّةٍ مِّنْ خَرْدَلٍ فَتَكُنْ فِي صَخْرَةٍ أَوْ فِي السَّمَاوَاتِ}$$
$$\text{أَوْ فِي الأَرْضِ يَأْتِ بِهَا اللَّهُ ، إِنَّ اللَّهَ لَطِيفٌ خَبِيرٌ)!}$$

*"O my son! If it be (anything) equal to the weight of a
grain of mustard-seed, and though it be in a rock, or in
the heavens or on the earth, Allah will bring it forth (to
light). Verily, Allah is Subtle, Well-Aware!"*

Here, in fact, Luqman's wisdom reflects not only on the value of this
lesson he teaches his son but also on the remarkably eloquent way he
has articulated it. Examine the effective way he has chosen to express
this fundamental issue of the Islamic *aqeedah;*[183] it is, namely, Allah's
unlimited knowledge and infinite power that this beautiful ayah
communicates. Further, consider the mental image that Luqman
creates by this extremely powerful exemplification, and consider the
psychological effects that such an exemplification generates.

If approached thoughtfully, this message will overwhelm the
addressees' hearts with a deep feeling of the Majesty of Allah, and it
will, consequently, radically revolutionize their lives in a way that
makes it in full accordance with His teachings. The underlying
message of this ayah is that humans are fully accountable for whatever
they do, say, or even think of. Thus, they had better observe Allah in a
way that corresponds with His infinite knowledge and power that this
ayah highlights.

Then Luqman advises his son to establish salah saying:

(... يا بُنَيَّ أَقِمِ الصَّلَاةَ)

"O my son establish salah…"

Because of its highly significant position in Islam, and because of its
dynamic role in the question of taqwa, the issue of salah requires a
special treatment in this discussion. Therefore, we will shed light on
different aspects of it. According to Al-Basyuni (2005), salah is the
most extensive and inclusive form of *ibadah* (worship) in Islam. It
includes, for example, *duwa'* (supplication), *thikr* (glorification of Allah),

---

[183] Islamic creed refers to the belief in the following: Allah's existence and His
Oneness, His angels, His Books, His Holy Messengers, the Day of Judgment, and
qada' and *qadar*—that is, all preordained matters and their actual occurrence in life
(Ba Jabir & Ba Dahdah, 2012, p. 79).

fear of Allah, *qunoot* (invocation), recitation of the Qur'an, gratitude to Allah, and *zakah* of the body (p. 399).

In the Qur'an, Allah usually uses the Arabic root *q-w-m*[184] in association with salah. Also in reference to it, He employs this root in different grammatical forms. Commanding the Holy Prophet and Muslims to establish salah, for instance, He uses this root in the imperative form saying:

$$ \text{(وَأَقِمِ الصَّلَاةَ طَرَفِي النَّهَارِ وَزُلَفًا مِنَ اللَّيْلِ ، إِنَّ الْحَسَنَاتِ يُذْهِبْنَ السَّيِّئَاتِ ،} $$
$$ \text{ذَٰلِكَ ذِكْرَىٰ لِلذَّاكِرِينَ).} $$

> *"And establish regular prayers at the two ends of the day and at the approaches of the night. Verily, the good deeds remove the evil deeds. That is a reminder for the mindful."* (Qur'an 11:114)

In addition, in surah Al-Anfal, Allah mentions the establishment of salah as one of the major qualities of the Mu'minun (true believers). He employs the above-mentioned root as a verb in the present form to indicate that these Mu'minun establish salah regularly. He states:

$$ \text{(الَّذِينَ يُقِيمُونَ الصَّلَاةَ...)} $$

> *"Who establish regular prayers..."* (Qur'an 8:3)

Further, He stresses the establishment of salah as one of the main characteristics of a distinguished group of men He honours. In this case, He uses the root q-w-m as a noun saying:

$$ \text{(رِجَالٌ لَا تُلْهِيهِمْ تِجَارَةٌ وَلَا بَيْعٌ عَنْ ذِكْرِ اللَّهِ وَإِقَامِ الصَّلَاةِ...)} $$

> *"By men whom neither trade nor sale can divert from remembrance of Allah nor from (the establishment of) regular prayer ..."* (Qur'an 24: 37)

---

[184] قَوَّم

But why is this continuous and consistent usage of this Arabic root in association with salah? Of course, there must be a good reason behind this Qur'anic phenomenon, for, again, the speaker is Allah Himself. According to Ibn Manthoor (2008), this root bears the following meanings and concepts: "reform, safeguarding, firmness, steadfastness, consistency, determination, dedication, commitment, and persistence" (pp. 224–226). Thus, one can conclude that these excellent values—which are, again, derived from the root q-w-m—apply directly to salah. More precisely, the usage of this root in connection with salah suggests that Muslims should establish it in a way that generates all these excellent values in both the individual's life and the community's at large.

To understand the role of salah from this perspective, one may compare it to the role of an important company established in a specific community. The benefits of the foundation of such a company in that community will not be confined to its owner or owners. The whole community will, of course, profit from it in different ways. Many people, for example, will enjoy the products it produces or the services it provides, and many others will find jobs at it. In addition, the money that these people earn helps the whole community's economy, when, for instance, they buy different things and pay for various local services. Similarly, when salah is established—not performed—it creates excellent effects on the individuals', the families', and the entire society's lives.

Grammatically, adjectives/adjectivals and adverbs/adverbials modify or describe nouns and verbs consecutively. Consider the following example: Our neighbours have a nice house. The word "nice" in this sentence has a specific grammatical function; namely, it modifies (describes) the noun "house." Also in the sentence "Ahmed recites the Holy Qur'an in an engaging manner," the phrase "in an engaging manner" modifies the verb "recites;" that is, it explains how Ahmed recites the Holy Qur'an.

With the exception of only three cases in the entire Holy Qur'an,[185]

---

[185] The first case in which Allah uses the root *q-w-m* reference to salah and with a modifier that describes how salah should be established is the following one from surah Al-Baqarah. Here, according to Al-Qurtubi (2014), Allah commands believers to pray with *khushua* (p. 140). He says:

when Allah employs the root *q-w-m* in reference to salah, He doesn't use these grammatical elements (adjectives/adjectivals and adverbs/adverbials) to describe the salah or to explain how believers pray or how they should pray. This is because the different concepts and meanings embedded in the derivations of this root, which were mentioned previously, render the usage of such grammatical elements redundant.

Instead of the root q-w-m, in fact, Allah could've used another Arabic root in reference to salah, namely *w-d-i,*[186] from which the Arabic noun *ada',*[187] meaning performance, is derived. But the derivations from this root won't imply the positive meanings suggested by those from the root q-w-m unless they are modified by adjectives/adjectivals and adverbs/adverbials. In other words, if the root w-d-i had been used in association with salah, then different modifiers (adjectivals and

---

(حَافِظُوا عَلَى الصَّلَوَاتِ وَالصَّلَاةِ الْوُسْطَى وَقُومُوا لِلَّهِ قَانِتِينَ).

"Guard strictly your (habit of) prayers, especially the Middle Prayer; and stand before Allah in a devout (frame of mind)."

(Qur'an 2:238)

The second comes in surah Hud, and it prescribes the time at which the five, daily prayers are supposed to be established. With respect to this, Allah says:

(وَأَقِمِ الصَّلَاةَ طَرَفِيِ النَّهَارِ وَزُلَفًا مِنَ اللَّيْلِ إِنَّ الْحَسَنَاتِ يُذْهِبْنَ السَّيِّئَاتِ ، ذَلِكَ ذِكْرَى لِلذَّاكِرِينَ) .

"And establish regular prayers at the two ends of the day and at the approaches of the night: For those things, that are good remove those that are evil: Be that the word of remembrance to those who remember (their Lord)."   *(Qur'an 11:114)*

The third occurs in surah Al-Isra'. It addresses the same issue addressed in the previous ayah. Here Allah says:

(أَقِمِ الصَّلَاةَ لِدُلُوكِ الشَّمْسِ إِلَى غَسَقِ الْلَّيْلِ وَقُرْآنَ الْفَجْرِ ، إِنَّ قُرْآنَ الْفَجْرِ كَانَ مَشْهُودًا).

"Establish regular prayers from mid-day till the darkness of the night, and recite the Qur'an in the early dawn (the Morning Prayer). Verily, the recitation of the Qur'an in the early dawn is ever witnessed."   *(Qur'an 17:78)*

[186] ودي

[187] أداء

adverbials) would've been needed, again, to suggest the concepts that are already embedded in the derivations of the root q-w-m. For example, adverbs of manner—such as accurately, excellently, mindfully, and effectively—would've been needed to show, for instance, the way in which salah is done or that in which it should be done. But, to reiterate, the derivations from the root q-w-m don't need any of these adverbials.

As previously stated, the journey to Allah is long, challenging, and difficult. Hence, it requires an excellent quality of provision so that believers may not collapse in the middle of the road. Fortunately, Allah has made most of this provision available in the establishment of salah; therefore, He has prescribed it five times a day. This frequent recurrence of salah, however, will not provide believers with the quality of the provision they need unless they accomplish a high level of *khushua*[188] in it, for khushua is the soul of salah; without it, salah is dead and will not offer its excellent fruits.

To show the significance of "khushua" during salah and to encourage Muslims to accomplish it, Allah has mentioned it as one of the major requirements they need to meet in their salah so that they may be successful on the Day of Judgment. He says:

(قَدْ أَفْلَحَ الْمُؤْمِنُونَ . الَّذِينَ هُمْ فِي صَلَاتِهِمْ خَاشِعُونَ).

> *"Successful indeed are the believers. Those who humble themselves in their prayer."*[189]
>
> *(Qur'an 23:1–2)*

As mentioned earlier, "khushua" originates in the heart, the actual vehicle that carries believers in their honourable journey to Allah. But what is it and how may one develop it? This word—which comes from the Arabic root *kh-sh-a*[190]—represents a mental and a psychological state in which a believer becomes submissive to Allah as

---

[188] خُشُوع

[189] Abdel Haleem, A. Ali, A. Y. Ali, Asad, Khalidi, and Pickthall translated the word *khashi'oon* in this ayah as "humble." Al-Hilali and Khan, however, provided a somewhat different translation of it, specifically "solemnity and full submissiveness."

[190] خَشَعَ

a result of both the realization of His Greatness and the experience of His Majesty. In reference to it, Ibn Al-Qayyim stated the following:

> It is said that "khushua" is used to indicate submission and succumbing of the heart to Allah. It also refers to both the extinguishment of the evil fire in the heart and the rise of the sun of Allah's glorification in it. (1997, p. 270)

Further, the recurrent establishment of salah throughout the day and the close proximity between each couple of salahs help believers observe Allah better. Such a quality of observance of Allah leaves Muslims no chance to involve themselves in anything that may harm their Islamic identity, damage their integrity, or undermine the quality of their connection with Allah. In other words, salah functions as a loyal, vigilant guard that protects believers' Islamic identity and character from all kinds of evil.

The following story of a young Muslim man demonstrates this significant role that salah plays in believers' protection from the Satan's enticement:

He went to the U.S. as a student, and he lived in the dormitory for a short while. A young woman, who was a student at the same university, met him; soon thereafter, she started to visit him in his room. One night after he went to bed, he heard someone knock on his door, so he went to answer it. To his surprise, it was the young woman. She told him she couldn't sleep and that she thought she could stop by for a while. He let her in, and he soon realized what brought her that late to his room: sex. Though he was very religious and had determined to never have illegal sex, that night he became weak and experienced a strong desire to sleep with her.

Everything went in that direction—a young man and a young woman, alone in one room, in the middle of the night, dying for sex. But when they were about to start, he asked himself: "Am I going to pray the *fajr* (dawn) prayer, a few hours from now or am I not?" Then he answered himself, "Since I pray to Allah, and since He watches me, I either sleep with this woman and stop praying, or I let her go and keep my prayer."

He got rid of her!

Among the daily prayers, the dawn (*fajr*) salah, for example, is the most disciplinary one. This disciplinary aspect of this specific salah, in fact, stems from its unique nature. Muslims are called upon at the very beginning of dawn to interrupt their sleep and leave their comfortable beds and homes to the mosques in response to the call of Allah: "Come to the prayer. Come to success. Salah is better than sleep!" At dawn, the brain, the heart, the soul, the nervous system, and the whole body are usually in their best conditions. Also at this time of the day, people aren't preoccupied with their daily duties and routine yet. The establishment of this salah at this time of the day, therefore, re-energizes the brain, rejuvenates the soul, and invigorates the heart. This huge spiritual energy that this specific salah instils into believers' hearts early in the morning governs their concerns, longings, desires, speech, priorities, decisions, activities, behaviours, and all interactions throughout the day.

The fact that Allah has entrusted Muslims with His final message to humankind requires them to be responsible and dynamic in playing their role in guiding humanity to Allah—*dawah*.[191] Being fully aware of this huge responsibility, Luqman advises his son to be involved in the work of dawah. He says to him:

(... وَأْمُرْ بِالْمَعْرُوفِ وَانْهَ عَنِ الْمُنْكَرِ ...)

"...and enjoin the good and forbid the evil..."

In this part of his advice, in fact, Luqman highlights two of the believers' three major characteristics that Allah highlights in surah Al-Imran. Addressing the Muslim nation in this regard, He says:

(كُنْتُمْ خَيْرَ أُمَّةٍ أُخْرِجَتْ لِلنَّاسِ تَأْمُرُونَ بِالْمَعْرُوفِ وَتَنْهَوْنَ عَنِ الْمُنْكَرِ وَتُؤْمِنُونَ بِاللَّهِ ...)

"You are the best of peoples, evolved for mankind, enjoining what is right, forbidding what is wrong, and believing in Allah..."   (Qur'an 3:110)

---

[191] Propagation of Islam

Ibn-Taymiyyah (2006) stated that "enjoining the good and forbidding evil is why Allah has revealed His books and sent His messengers, and they [enjoining the good and forbidding evil] are part of the Islamic faith" (p. 51).

Further, being aware that the mission of dawah can be expensive and troublesome, Luqman warns his son that exposure to hardship in this field is inevitable; therefore, he should bear all the adversities that he may encounter with patience and fortitude. He advises him saying:

$$ (...وَاصْبِرْ عَلَى مَآ أَصَابَكَ...) $$

"...and bear with patience whatever befalls you..."

Hardship isn't confined to the issue of dawah, of course. Life, in general, exposes all people to different forms of adversity, which require different levels of endurance and patience. Exposure to hardship is, actually, fundamental to human development and preparation for the future, and this is why it is purposefully embedded in different walks of life. Besides their natural gifts, many athletes, for example, stand out as a result of continuous, demanding, and extremely rigorous exercises that require high levels of patience, endurance, and fortitude. Also at times of epidemics, people receive vaccinations that contain the same viruses they want to avoid. The objective of this is to help their bodies develop a strong defence system that can immediately fight against the expected disease and beat it if it attacks.

Likewise, Allah employs the element of hardship to test believers' level of belief and to equip them with the experience that is necessary for their success in this life and in the Hereafter. In an emphatic tone, for instance, He warns believers that He will test them with different forms of adversity. He confirms this issue saying:

$$ (وَلَنَبْلُوَنَّكُم بِشَيْءٍ مِّنَ الْخَوفْ وَالْجُوعِ وَنَقْصٍ مِّنَ الْأُمَوَالِ وَالْأَنْفُسِ وَالثَّمَـرَاتِ $$
$$ وَبَشِّرِ الصَّابِرِينَ). $$

"And certainly, We shall test you with something of fear, hunger, loss of wealth, lives and fruits, but give glad tidings to the patient."   *(Qur'an 2:155)*

The warning of affliction with hardship, in fact, recurs many times in the Qur'an, and it may occur more than once in the same surah, such as in the surahs of Al-Imran and Mohammad. In surah Al-Imran and in reference to issues pertinent to the Battle of Uhud, for example, Allah states:

(ثُمَّ أَنزَلَ عَلَيْكُم مِّن بَعْدِ الْغَمِّ أَمَنَةً نُّعَاسًا يَغْشَى طَآئِفَةً مِّنكُمْ ، وَطَآئِفَةٌ قَدْ أَهَمَّتْهُمْ أَنفُسُهُمْ يَظُنُّونَ بِاللّهِ غَيْرَ الْحَقِّ ظَنَّ الْجَاهِلِيَّةِ ، يَقُولُونَ هَل لَّنَا مِنَ الأَمْرِ مِن شَيْءٍ قُلْ إِنَّ الأَمْرَ كُلَّهُ لِلّهِ ، يُخْفُونَ فِي أَنفُسِهِم مَّا لاَ يُبْدُونَ لَكَ ، يَقُولُونَ لَوْ كَانَ لَنَا مِنَ الأَمْرِ شَيْءٌ مَّا قُتِلْنَا هَاهُنَا ، قُل لَّوْ كُنتُمْ فِي بُيُوتِكُمْ لَبَرَزَ الَّذِينَ كُتِبَ عَلَيْهِمُ الْقَتْلُ إِلَى مَضَاجِعِهِمْ ، وَلِيَبْتَلِيَ اللّهُ مَا فِي صُدُورِكُمْ وَلِيُمَحِّصَ مَا فِي قُلُوبِكُمْ ، وَاللّهُ عَلِيمٌ بِذَاتِ الصُّدُورِ).

"Then after the distress, He sent down security for you. Slumber overtook a party of you, while another party was thinking about themselves and thought wrongly of Allah— the thought of ignorance. They said: 'Do we have any part in the affair?' Say (O Mohammad): 'Indeed the affair belongs wholly to Allah.' They hide within themselves what they dare not reveal to you, saying: 'If we had anything to do with the affair, none of us would have been killed here.' Say (O Mohammad): 'Even if you had remained in your homes, those for whom death was decreed would certainly have gone forth to the place of their death,' but (all this was) that Allah might test what is in your breasts; and to purify that which was in your hearts. And Allah is All-Knower of what is in (your) breasts." (Qur'an 3:154)

Later in the same surah and with regard to the same issue—affliction with hardship—Allah, in an emphatic manner, addresses all believers saying:

(لَتُبْلَوُنَّ فِي أَمْوَالِكُمْ وَأَنفُسِكُمْ وَلَتَسْمَعُنَّ مِنَ الَّذِينَ أُوتُواْ الْكِتَابَ مِن قَبْلِكُمْ وَمِنَ الَّذِينَ أَشْرَكُواْ أَذًى كَثِيرًا ، وَإِن تَصْبِرُواْ وَتَتَّقُواْ فَإِنَّ ذَلِكَ مِنْ عَزْمِ الأُمُورِ).

"You shall certainly be tried and tested in your possessions and in your personal selves; and you shall certainly hear much that will grieve you, from those who received the Book before you and from those who ascribe partners to Allah. But if you persevere patiently, and guard against evil, then that will be a determining factor in all affairs."   *(Qur'an 3:186)*

In surah Mohammad and in reference to this matter, He also says:

(فَإِذَا لَقِيتُمُ الَّذِينَ كَفَرُوا فَضَرْبَ الرِّقَابِ حَتَّى إِذَا أَثْخَنْتُمُوهُمْ فَشُدُّوا الْوَثَاقَ فَإِمَّا مَنًّا بَعْدُ وَإِمَّا فِدَاءً حَتَّى تَضَعَ الْحَرْبُ أَوْزَارَهَا ، ذَلِكَ ، وَلَوْ يَشَاءُ اللَّهُ لَانتَصَرَ مِنْهُمْ وَلَكِن لِّيَبْلُوَ بَعْضَكُم بِبَعْضٍ ، وَالَّذِينَ قُتِلُوا فِي سَبِيلِ اللَّهِ فَلَن يُضِلَّ أَعْمَالَهُمْ).

"So when you meet those who disbelieve, smite (their) necks till when you have killed and wounded many of them, bind and bond firmly. Thereafter (is the time) either for generosity or ransom, until the war lays down its burden. But if it had been Allah's will He Himself could certainly have punished them. But (He lets you fight) in order to test some of you with others. But those who are killed in the way of Allah, He will never let their deeds be lost."   *(Qur'an 47:4)*

Also later in the same surah, He emphatically assures believers that He will test them with hardship. He warns:

(وَلَنَبْلُوَنَّكُمْ حَتَّى نَعْلَمَ الْمُجَاهِدِينَ مِنكُمْ وَالصَّابِرِينَ وَنَبْلُوَ أَخْبَارَكُمْ).

"We shall try you until We test those among you who strive their utmost and persevere in patience; and We shall try your reported (mettle)."   *(Qur'an 47:31)*

In their explanation of the message in this ayah, Al-Saadi and Al-Shawkani argued that here the issue of testing refers to *jihad*, whereas Al-Qurtubi and Ibn Ashoor claimed that it refers to all the do-and-don't issues in order to prove who will and who will not obey Allah's commands (2011, p. 732; 2012, p. 50; 2014, p. 409; 1984, p. 123).

According to Al-Tirmithi, the Holy Prophet said:

> "The messengers of Allah incurred more hardship than anyone else." (Al-Basyuni, 2005, p. 211)

The sufferings that each of Allah's messengers endured were, in fact, applicable to his own challenges. That is, Allah made each of His messengers suffer in a way that would qualify him to handle the different obstacles and challenges of dawah in the very social environment where he worked. Being the seal of all prophets and being honoured with the final and best revelation (The Holy Qur'an), the Holy Prophet Mohammad suffered the most.

Luqman goes on to equip his son with some more Islamic values to help him become beautiful in Allah's sight and beloved of Him. So he enjoins on him to be humble, not arrogant or insolent. He says:

$$ (\text{وَلاَ تُصَعِّرْ خَدَّكَ لِلنَّاسِ}...) $$

"And turn not your face away from people with pride..."

To help his son realize the ugliness of insolence and arrogance, Luqman uses the clause *tusa'ir.*[192] The verb in this Qur'anic clause is derived from *su'ar,*[193] which is a disease that afflicts camels and screws their necks. The Arabs' environment in which the Holy Qur'an was revealed used to teem with this animal, and the Arabs of that time were familiar with the ugly view of camels suffering from this particular disease. The camel's remarkably long neck, in fact, makes such a view even uglier. A camel in this case would be going in a specific direction, whereas its head would be facing another—a very odd and unpleasant view, indeed.

So as if this part of the ayah warns humans saying, "If you turn your cheek in arrogance or insolence to others, you will look as ugly as a camel afflicted with su'ar!" The usage of this metaphor, in this ayah, can be dramatically deterrent and, thus, significantly effective in the generation of the positive response that Allah wants to see—being

---

[192] تُصَعِّرْ

[193] صُعَار

humble, no matter how successful, prestigious, or powerful a person might be.

The way a person walks is—to some extent—a window into his or her feelings, attitude, state of mind, personality, and character. Islam requires that a Muslim be beautiful in all aspects—physically, morally, and behaviourally. Thus, Luqman forbids his son from walking proudly and enjoins on him to walk in a decent, humble manner. He addresses him in this concern saying:

$$ (...\text{وَلاَ تَمْشِ فِي الأَرْضِ مَرَحاً إِنَّ اللَّهَ لاَ يُحِبُّ كُلَّ مُخْتَالٍ فَخُورٍ . وَاقْصِدْ فِي مَشْيِكَ}...)^{194} $$

"...nor walk in insolence through the earth. Verily, Allah likes not any arrogant boaster. And be moderate (or show no insolence) in your walking ..."

Insolence represents a nasty attitude that grows on the soil of a sick mind and a morally ill heart. Had humans—these little, helpless creatures—realized the Greatness and the Majesty of their Lord and experienced any level of awe as a result, pride wouldn't have found its way to their hearts.

In addition, people's decency of speech isn't confined to the words they use; it also includes their tones and the volume of their voices. In this priceless advice, therefore, Luqman goes on to enjoin on his son to speak moderately. He tells him:

$$ (...\text{وَاغْضُضْ مِن صَوْتِكَ إِنَّ أَنكَرَ الأَصْوَاتِ لَصَوْتُ الْحَمِيرِ}) . $$

---

[194]In a remarkably beautiful, powerful, and deterring expression, Allah issues the same command in surah Al-Isra' saying:

$$ (\text{وَلا تَمْشِ فِي الأَرْضِ مَرَحًا ، إِنَّكَ لَن تَخْرِقَ الأَرْضَ وَلَن تَبْلُغَ الْجِبَالَ طُولاً}) ! $$

"And walk not on earth with conceit and arrogance. Verily, you can neither rend nor penetrate the earth, nor can you reach the mountains in height!"   *(Qur'an 17:37)*

"...and be moderate in your walking, and lower your voice. Verily, the harshest of all voices is the braying of the asses."

To show his son the ugliness of speaking loudly, Luqman likens it to the donkey's braying, for, indeed, no one wants to sound like a donkey. People, in general, hate noise, and when talking loudly becomes a person's typical trait, people perceive such a person rude. So they dislike him or her, and they may do their best to avoid interactions with this person. Based on this, it should be noted that Allah's keenness to see believers enjoy an ideal Islamic character extends to include even the proper volume at which they should speak.

Luqman died a long time ago; nonetheless, his invaluable advice hasn't—and it, certainly, never will!—for Allah has included it in His best and final Book to humanity, the Holy Qur'an. Its inclusion in it indicates the fundamental role of guidance Muslim parents should play in their children's lives. More precisely, it suggests that the most important thing Muslim parents can offer their children is the creed of *tawheed* and the adherence to its teachings and values. Perhaps this is why the relationship between Luqman and his addressee—a father and his son—is made clear in this invaluable advice.

The inclusion of this advice in the Holy Qur'an, in addition, proves that Allah appreciates all the good deeds that believers do, even the minutest. Muslims should, therefore, take advantage of every opportunity to do something good, for—no matter how small it might be—Allah appreciates it[195] and rewards for it, if it is done solely for His sake, of course.

---

[195] Allah has expressed His appreciation of His servants' good deeds more than once in the Holy Qur'an. In surahs Al-Nisa', for instance, He says:

(...وَكَانَ اللّٰهُ شَاكِرًا عَلِيمًا).

"And Allah is Ever All-Appreciative (of good) and All-Knowing."
(Qur'an 4:147)

Allah's Holy Messenger, in addition, has strongly recommended that Muslims be involved in doing the good—any good. According to Imam Muslim, the Holy Prophet said:

CHAPTER 10

The Qur'anic Stories

The art of storytelling and story-writing has two major purposes: entertainment and education. A story usually provides—in a dramatic sense—a general idea about the community it projects. It reflects, for example, different cultural aspects of that community—faith, values, ethics, traditions, arts, lifestyle, dreams, challenges, and problems. If employed wisely, this special genre of art can be considerably effective in social reform. In the Muslim world, the art of fiction should, therefore, derive its principles, objectives, and general framework from the Islamic creed (aqeedah) so that it serves the cause of Islam and plays its indispensable role in the renaissance—not the decline—of the Muslim nation. The Qur'anic stories represent a perfect model for Muslim fictionists who should benefit from the way Allah employs this form of art to address the issue of the Islamic creed and to form the Islamic mentality, morality, psychology, character, and society.

M. Al-Ghazali claimed that the story element is predominant in the Holy Qur'an (2006, p. 83). According to him, Allah communicates most of the Qur'anic message in a narrative form. Thus, it is necessary to understand why Allah—the best to communicate—has chosen this particular style to be the main pattern of communication to deliver His message and to teach important lessons.

Generally, the element of the story has many characteristics that make it effective in teaching important lessons. Besides its entertaining

---

"Belittle no good deed [if you get a chance to do it, no matter how insignificant it might seem], even meeting your brother [in Islam] with a smile in your face."

"لا تحقرنَّ من المعروف شيئاً ، ولو تلقى أخاك بوجه طليق ".

nature, a story has the ability to inflame the audience's eagerness to follow its different events with strong curiosity and an intense passion. A good story, in addition, involves its audience members in critical thinking and makes them experience different emotions helpful in the creation of a particular psychological atmosphere in which the story's lessons can be learned indirectly yet effectively. More precisely, in reaction to different factors in a story—such as the characters of the story, their personalities, motives, values, ethics, attitudes, and behaviours—the audience likes some of the characters and dislikes others or even hates them. The audience, in addition, becomes hopeful, hopeless, relaxed, worried, happy, sad, or even angry due to different events in the story.

The Qur'anic stories are real: They narrate authentic, human experiences from which people can learn many excellent lessons of taqwa. The story of Prophet Yusuf, for instance, represents a perfect model that demonstrates the fundamental role of the Qur'anic stories in the heart's spiritual and moral cultivation, through the creation of a special mental and psychological atmosphere that leads to specific mental and psychological effects conducive to the internalization of this story's lessons.

From its onset, this story, for instance, surprises its audience and excites their curiosity in reaction to Yusuf's unusual dream when he addresses his father saying:

(...يَا أَبَتِ إِنِّي رَأَيْتُ أَحَدَ عَشَرَ كَوْكَبًا وَالشَّمْسَ وَالْقَمَرَ رَأَيْتُهُمْ لِي سَاجِدِينَ).

"O my father I did see eleven stars and the sun and the moon: I saw them prostrate themselves to me!"
(Qur'an 12:4)

His father's warning to him in response to this strange dream makes the story's audience more surprised, more interested, and more engaged. He cautions him saying:

(...يَا بُنَيَّ لاَ تَقْصُصْ رُؤْيَاكَ عَلَى إِخْوَتِكَ فَيَكِيدُواْ لَكَ كَيْدًا إِنَّ الشَّيْطَانَ لِلإِنسَانِ عَدُوٌّ مُّبِينٌ).

"...my dear little son! Relate not your vision to your brothers, lest they should arrange a plot against you. Verily, Satan is to man an avowed enemy."

(Qur'an 12:5)

Thus, the audience asks, "Does this mean the Satan may entice Yusuf's brothers to plot against him?" The story quickly introduces another more dramatic element. In their secret, evil conference, Yusuf's elder brothers—believe it or not—plan to either murder or throw him away. They want to get rid of him at any price! In that sinful meeting, they secretly tell each other:

$$(اقْتُلُواْ يُوسُفَ أَوِ اطْرَحُوهُ أَرْضًا...)!$$

"Kill Yusuf or cast him out to some (other) land...!"

(Qur'an 12:9)

"But why?" the audience may ask. Then Yusuf's brothers answer:

$$(...لَيُوسُفُ وَأَخُوهُ أَحَبُّ إِلَى أَبِينَا مِنَّا وَنَحْنُ عُصْبَةٌ إِنَّ أَبَانَا لَفِي ضَلَالٍ مُّبِينٍ).$$

"...Yusuf and his brother are loved more by our father than we, while we are a group. Really, our father is in a plain error."

(Qur'an 12:8)

"But should this make them murder their own little brother?" the audience may wonder. Accordingly, the audience intuitively takes the side of Yusuf—the innocent child, who is unaware of his brothers' horrible criminal plot against him.

Fortunately, however, the brothers have finally decided not to murder Yusuf, but to throw him away. They say:

$$(...لاَ تَقْتُلُواْ يُوسُفَ وَأَلْقُوهُ فِي غَيَابَتِ الْجُبِّ يَلْتَقِطْهُ بَعْضُ السَّيَّارَةِ...)$$

"...murder not Joseph, but if you must do something, throw him down to the bottom of the well: he will be picked up by some caravan of travellers..."

(Qur'an 12:10)

Now here is Yusuf—the innocent, little boy—accompanying his elder brothers to the scene of the crime. Perhaps this is one of his happiest moments ever, for—as it occurs to him—he will enjoy himself and have a wonderful time, there in the beautiful countryside. But, regrettably, his brothers will soon ruthlessly throw him into the darkness of the unknown, the gate to which is the bottom of the well. Then they will return home, but never will he. His brothers' jealousy has made them this blind, this malicious, this heartless, this ugly, and this evil!

The beginning, the middle, and the conclusion of this amazing story teem with lively, stirring events. It is a real story of a real, wonderful man: a Holy Prophet of Allah. The Creator narrates it in an exciting, unprecedented manner that makes its audience deeply engrossed in its various, dramatic events—from the start to the end. Almost every event in it is arousing and leads to another even more thrilling one. As mentioned earlier, these different, dramatic incidents immerse the brain, the soul, and the heart in an ideal psychological atmosphere fundamental to the learning and the internalization of this story's invaluable lessons.

Gradually and smoothly, the story arrives at its conclusion. The audience sees how things start, how they end, who wins, who loses and why. The audience, as a result, learns many invaluable lessons: falsehood withdraws, truthfulness prevails; wickedness fails, morality overcomes; evilness loses and righteousness triumphs.

The Purpose of the Qur'anic Stories

Scholars of the exegesis of the Holy Qur'an have identified several objectives of the Qur'anic stories. According to them, these stories are meant to achieve the following: (1) to confirm that the Holy Qur'an is the Book of Allah and Mohammad is His final Messenger, (2) to firm the Holy Prophet's heart, (3) to assure him and his followers that Allah grants victory to His messengers and their followers, (4) to show the unity of all Allah's messages, (5) to teach important lessons of taqwa, and (6) to warn disbelievers so that they may repent.

Here the discussion of this issue, however, is confined to only two of these objectives: the learning of important lessons of taqwa and the strengthening of the Holy Prophet's heart. These two objectives are, in fact, mentioned in three surahs: Al-A'raf, Hud, and Yusuf.

The Learning of Taqwa Lessons

The surah of Al-A'raf suggests that the purpose of the Qur'anic stories is the internalization of important lessons of taqwa. In this surah, Allah points to this matter implicitly, using the concept of reflection. He says:

(فَاقْصُصِ الْقَصَصَ لَعَلَّهُمْ يَتَفَكَّرُونَ). (Qur'an 7:176)

"Therefore relate the narrative that they may reflect."
(Qur'an 7:176)

Obviously, the issue of reflection that this ayah invites people to isn't a goal per se. The goal is, of course, the development of taqwa through the internalization of the lessons in the stories of previous individuals and communities narrated in the Holy Qur'an. Ibn Ashoor (1984) claimed that the message in this ayah instructed Allah's Holy Messenger to narrate this story[196] and the other Qur'anic ones so that people may reflect on them, for reflection is crucial to learning their lessons and to guiding people to the path of Allah (p. 179). Also according to "Al-Tafsir Al-Muyassar," this Qur'anic message means "So narrate, O Messenger of Allah, the stories of previous communities . . . so that your people may reflect on what you have come with and believe [as a result]" (2009, p173).

The surah of Yusuf confirms the purpose of the Qur'anic stories mentioned in the surah of Al-A'raf. It declares that the stories of previous individuals and communities teach lessons of *ibrah*—that is, lessons of taqwa (Al-Tabari, 2010, p. 750; Ibn Kathir, 2014, p. 211). With respect to this, Allah declares:

(لَقَدْ كَانَ فِي قَصَصِهِمْ عِبْرَةٌ لِأُولِي الْأَلْبَابِ مَا كَانَ حَدِيثًا يُفْتَرَىٰ وَلَٰكِنْ تَصْدِيقَ

---

[196] You may refer to Ibn Kathir who cited two different narrations regarding this story (2014, pp. 50–51).

الَّذِي بَيْنَ يَدَيْهِ وَتَفْصِيلَ كُلِّ شَيْءٍ وَهُدًى وَرَحْمَةً لِقَوْمٍ يُؤْمِنُونَ).

"Indeed in their stories, there is a lesson for men of understanding. It (the Qur'an) is not a forged statement but a confirmation of what went before it, a detailed exposition of all things, and a guide and a mercy for people who believe."   *(Qur'an 12:111)*

The Firming of the Holy Prophet's Heart

The surah of Hud almost concludes with an ayah that explains the Qur'anic stories' second objective in this discussion. Specifically, it is the strengthening of the Holy Prophet's heart, by learning good examples from his previous brothers—the messengers of Allah (Ibn Kathir, 2014, p. 189).

Speaking to His Holy Messenger in this regard, Allah says:

(وَكُلاًّ نَّقُصُّ عَلَيْكَ مِنْ أَنْبَاءِ الرُّسُلِ مَا نُثَبِّتُ بِهِ فُؤَادَكَ...)

"All that We relate to you of the stories of the messengers is in order that We may make strong and firm your heart thereby..."   *(Qur'an 11:120)*

To have an idea about the Holy Prophet's psychological feeling in that phase of his mission and to realize the role of the Qur'anic stories in addressing that feeling, we can refer to the surah of Al-Hijr. In this surah, Allah addressed him concerning this psychological feeling, which he was, in fact, experiencing as a result of the Makkan disbelievers' hostile attitude. He said to him:

(وَلَقَدْ نَعْلَمُ أَنَّكَ يَضِيقُ صَدْرُكَ بِمَا يَقُولُون).

"Indeed, We know that your heart becomes tight because of what they say."   *(Qur'an 15:97)*

According to Qutb (1992), this surah was revealed to the Holy Prophet in the critical phase of his dawah, between the Year of Grief and his immigration to Al-Madinah (p. 2121).

Also being one of the earliest surahs revealed from the Holy Qur'an, Al-Muzzammil warned him that he was going to receive a weighty or—literally speaking—a heavy talk. In this surah, Allah said to him:

(إِنَّا سَنُلْقِي عَلَيْكَ قَوْلًا ثَقِيلًا)!

"Verily, We shall send down to you a weighty word!"
(Qur'an 73:5)

Allah describes the Holy Qur'an thus because of the nature of its teachings, which wouldn't appeal to the Holy Prophet's local and regional Arab communities; thus, they would strongly reject it and fiercely fight against it. The Holy Messenger of Allah and his companions would, therefore, incur sufferings of different nature, and they would pay an extremely heavy price for their new faith. For example, they would sustain the loss of almost everything—including their family members, their friends, and their whole community. They would also experience all kinds of persecution, and they would be forced to leave their own homes, property, and beloved city of Makkah, in which they were born and brought up.

Obviously, the Holy Prophet's mission in that extremely hostile social and political environment—both in Makkah and in the whole region—required that his heart receive special preparation. Allah had, accordingly, decided to favour the Qur'anic stories with this preparation.[197]

Hud, for instance, represents a major story surah that Allah revealed to the Holy Prophet in an extremely critical phase of his prophetic

---

[197] As it is the case with his reaction to the entire Holy Qur'an, the Holy Prophet's mental and psychological reaction to the Qur'anic stories was perfect. Al-Tabarani cited Sahl ibn Al-Sa'idi to have reported that the Holy Prophet said:

"It is Hud and its sisters [surahs similar in their messages to that of surah Hud] turned my hair into grey!"

This indicates that the Holy Prophet's hair turned grey as a result of the significant psychological impact of these surahs on him; obviously, the psychological impact of Hud, as a story surah, on him was remarkable, for he chose it to label the whole group of the surahs that turned some of his hair into grey.

mission. He revealed it to him after the death of his uncle Abu Talib and the death of his wife Khadijah who were then the most supportive people to him. The name that he gave to that year reflects the extremely high level of sadness and distress he experienced as a result of their death. According to Qutb (1992), Al-Maqrizi reported that the Holy Messenger of Allah called it "The Year of Grief" (p. 1840).

In fact, due to his uncle's death in that critical phase of dawah, the Holy Prophet's sufferings from Quraysh intensified dramatically, and his need for the Qur'anic psychological support multiplied.[198] So the context in which this surah was revealed as well as the stories it narrates indicate the fundamental role it played in the firming of his heart and in the success of his mission, for it summarizes the tremendously difficult experiences of a galaxy of holy messengers who preceded him: Noah, Hud, Salih, Ibrahim, Lut, Shu'ayb, and Mosa.

The firming of the Holy Prophet's heart with this surah took place as a result of his realization that he was not the only messenger of Allah who suffered at the hand of the very community he was trying to guide and save. The previous messengers of Allah had also incurred the same from their own communities. The firming of his heart with this surah, in addition, was a result of his realization that no matter how long his sufferings might persist, Allah's victory would inevitably come to his side, the way it did with respect to those previous

---

[198] The Prophet's hideous experience at Alta'if, for example, was unique in its nature. The great, articulate, and transparent supplication he made to Allah in reaction to this extremely difficult and humiliating experience reflects the severe, unprecedented psychological pain he went through. Here is most of the text of that amazing, heartfelt, touching supplication:

"O Allah! To You I complain of my helplessness, the paucity of my resources and my insignificance before humankind. O the most Merciful! You are the Lord of the weak and the Lord of the helpless, and You are my Lord. [O my Lord!] To whom do You leave me? To a distant, unfriendly one who sullenly frowns at me (in rejection), or to an enemy whom You have given full control over my affairs? But if You are not angry with me, then I certainly won't worry [no matter what happens to me]. But Your Kindness is indeed vast enough to include me. I seek refuge in the light of Your Face, which has dispelled all (sources of) darkness and brought goodness to this life and to the life in the Hereafter, to let me incur Your wrath, or that You become wrathful to me. . . ."

messengers that the surah narrates their stories. However, he had to follow their footprints and hold firmly to Allah's rope, the very way they did. In this regard, Allah addressed him saying:

$$(\ldots \text{اقْتَدِهِ} \text{ فَبِهُدَاهُمُ} ، \text{أُولَئِكَ الَّذِينَ هَدَى اللهُ})$$

"They are those whom Allah had guided. So follow their guidance..."   (Qur'an 6:90)

Lessons of Taqwa from the Story of Adam and Eve

The story of Adam and Eve contributes considerably to the provision of taqwa that people need in their long journey to Allah. It occurs in different surahs, namely Al-Baqarah, Al-A'raf, Al-Hijr, Al-Isra', Al-Kahf, Taha, and Sad. Such a frequent recurrence of this story not only suggests the significance of the lessons it teaches, but it also reinforces their understanding and their internalization. In its narration, Allah uses different, effective techniques helpful in learning its invaluable lessons. For example, He projects the Satan's negative attitude towards humankind as an answer to a question He poses to him.[199] This style (presentation of information in a question-answer format) helps grab the addressees' attention and triggers their eagerness to know the answer; thus, it increases their chance of benefiting from it.

Specifically, the question that Allah asks Iblis in the context of this story occurs three times, and it is expressed in almost two different ways. Its first occurrence takes place in surah Al-A'raf, and it is almost similar to that in surah Al-Hijr. In both surahs, Allah asks Iblis about

---

[199] The following is an example of the question-answer style that reveals Iblis's nasty attitude towards humankind:

$$(\text{قَالَ يَا إِبْلِيسُ مَا لَكَ أَلَّا تَكُونَ مَعَ السَّاجِدِينَ . قَالَ لَمْ أَكُنْ لِأَسْجُدَ لِبَشَرٍ خَلَقْتَهُ مِنْ صَلْصَالٍ مِنْ حَمَإٍ مَسْنُونٍ}).$$

"He (Allah) said: 'O Iblis! What is your reason for not being among those who prostrated themselves?' He (Iblis) said: 'I am not one to prostrate myself to man, whom You have created from sounding clay, from mud molded into shape.'"

(Qur'an 15:32–33)

the reason for not prostrating himself to Adam. In surah Sad, however, this question includes new important information; namely, it reveals that Allah created Adam with His own Hands, which, according to Al-Qurtubi (2014), "signifies an honour to Adam" (p. 149). Here is how Allah has expressed this question in surah Sad:

$$(...\text{يَا إِبْلِيسُ مَا مَنَعَكَ أَنْ تَسْجُدَ لِمَا خَلَقْتُ بِيَدَيَّ})?^{200}$$

"...O Iblis! What prevents you from prostrating to one whom I have created with My Hands?"

(Qur'an 38: 75)

Another effective technique that Allah uses in the narration of this story is the dialogue—such as in the surahs of Al-A'raf, Al-Hijr, Al-Isra', and Sad, where He presents the information in an engaging discourse between Him and Iblis. This dialogue, in fact, offers the story vividness and makes its audience more interested and thus more involved. It also offers the members of the audience an opportunity to observe, analyse, evaluate, conclude, and see—for themselves—how the Satan thinks and feels about the human race. Further, Allah introduces the subject matter of this story in a fashion that generates special mental and psychological effects. The mental effects, for example, take place in cause-and-effect contexts, such as that in which Allah expelled Iblis from the Garden as a result of his refusal to prostrate to Adam. Another similar cause-and-effect situation is Adam and Eve's eviction from the same Garden, due to their disobedience to Allah, which reflects on their listening to Iblis and eating from the forbidden tree.[201]

---

[200] Commenting on this issue A. Y. Ali said:

> With My hands: i.e., by My power and creative skill. This is the point. Man, as typified by Adam, is in himself nothing but frail clay. But as fashioned by God's creative power into something with God's spirit breathed into him, his dignity is raised above that of the highest creatures. (2008, p. 1232)

[201] With respect to this incident, Allah says:

$$(\text{قَالَ اهْبِطُوا بَعْضُكُم لِبَعْضٍ عَدُوٌّ ، ولَكُم في الأَرْضِ مُسْتَقَرٌّ ومَتَاعٌ إلى حِينٍ}).$$

"He said, 'All of you get out! You are each other's enemies. On earth you will have a place to stay and livelihood—for a time.'"

(Qur'an 7:24)

The psychological effects, however, occur in situations that excite specific emotions in the audience of the story, such as surprise, disappointment, and resentment. For instance, the audience may feel surprised and disappointed in reaction to Adam and Eve's irresponsible and unjustifiable behaviour—precisely, their believing Iblis and eating from the forbidden tree. The audience may also feel resentful owing to Iblis's extremely rude answer to the All-Mighty Himself and due to his nasty attitude towards humankind.

Another strategy that Allah employs in the narration of this story is the recurrence of the same issues, but in a fashion that allows each narration to shed light on a different aspect of each issue. For example, in surah Al-Baqarah—where this story occurs for the first time in the Holy Qur'an—we learn that because of his arrogance, Iblis refused to prostrate to Adam. However, in surah Al-A'raf, where this story has its second occurrence in the Holy Qur'an, Iblis's arrogance becomes more specific: He argued his origin was better than Adam's. Further, in surah Al-Baqarah, Iblis, Adam, and Eve seem to have been evicted from the Garden together,[202] while in the surah of Al-A'raf, we

---

[202] Surah Al-Baqarah speaks about Iblis's refusal to prostrate to Adam, but it doesn't talk about his eviction from the Garden until Adam and Eve ate from the forbidden tree. The following ayahs demonstrate the sequence of these events: Iblis's refusal to prostrate to Adam, Allah's permission of Adam and Eve to dwell in the Garden and enjoy whatever they please—with exception of one tree—and their eviction from the Garden:

(وَإِذْ قُلْنَا لِلْمَلَائِكَةِ اسْجُدُواْ لآدَمَ فَسَجَدُواْ إِلاَّ إِبْلِيسَ أَبَى وَاسْتَكْبَرَ وَكَانَ مِنَ الْكَافِرِينَ. وَقُلْنَا يَا آدَمُ اسْكُنْ أَنتَ وَزَوْجُكَ الْجَنَّةَ وَكُلاَ مِنْهَا رَغَداً حَيْثُ شِئْتُمَا وَلاَ تَقْرَبَا هَذِهِ الشَّجَرَةَ فَتَكُونَا مِنَ الظَّالِمِينَ. فَأَزَلَّهُمَا الشَّيْطَانُ عَنْهَا فَأَخْرَجَهُمَا مِمَّا كَانَا فِيهِ وَقُلْنَا اهْبِطُواْ بَعْضُكُمْ لِبَعْضٍ عَدُوٌّ وَلَكُمْ فِي الأَرْضِ مُسْتَقَرٌّ وَمَتَاعٌ إِلَى حِينٍ).

"And (remember) when We said to the angels: 'Prostrate yourselves before Adam.' And they prostrated except Iblis (Satan), he refused and was proud and was one of the disbelievers (disobedient to Allah). And We said: "O Adam! Dwell you and your wife in Paradise and eat both of you freely with pleasure and delight of the things therein as wherever you will, but come not near this tree or you both will be of the Zalimeen (wrongdoers).' Then the Shaitan (Satan) made them slip therefrom (Paradise), and got them out from that in which they were. We said: 'Get you down, all, with enmity between yourselves. On earth will be a dwelling-place for you and an enjoyment for a time.'"
(Qur'an 2:34–36)

learn that Iblis was expelled first; then, sometime thereafter, Adam and
Eve followed him. The surah of Taha, in addition, reveals that Allah
warned Adam not to let Iblis throw him and his wife out of the
Garden, but the surahs of Al-Baqarah, Al-Hijr, Al-Isra', Al-Kahf, and
Sad don't mention this issue. Also in different surahs, Allah expresses
Iblis's refusal to prostrate to Adam differently. This way, He casts light
on different aspects of Iblis's bad attitude towards the human race, an
issue that helps people become more vigilant of him.

Lessons 1, 2, and 3

As previously mentioned, the first occurrence of this story takes place
in surah Al-Baqarah. In this surah, Allah mentions two issues that He
doesn't in the other surahs where this story occurs. Specifically, He
mentions Adam's both vicegerency and knowledge acquisition. First,
the assignment of Adam as a vicegerent on earth represents an honour
to him and to his children—the human race. It also suggests the high
level of responsibility that Allah has placed on him and on his
children. To achieve his demanding mission as a vicegerent, Adam
needed to have special qualifications, without which the
accomplishment of his mission was impossible. Some of these
qualifications were the observance of Allah, knowledge, allegiance,
honesty, commitment, diligence, persistence, far-sightedness, patience,
and justice.

Second, Adam's learning of the names of all things suggests the
significance of knowledge in the achievement of his mission as a
vicegerent on earth.[203] Perhaps this is why, immediately after this
assignment, Allah mentions that He taught Adam the names of all
things. With respect to these two issues—Adam's vicegerency and
knowledge acquisition—Allah says:

(وَإِذْ قَالَ رَبُّكَ لِلْمَلَائِكَةِ إِنِّي جَاعِلٌ فِي الْأَرْضِ خَلِيفَةً ، قَالُوا أَتَجْعَلُ فِيهَا مَنْ يُفْسِدُ
فِيهَا وَيَسْفِكُ الدِّمَاءَ وَنَحْنُ نُسَبِّحُ بِحَمْدِكَ وَنُقَدِّسُ لَكَ ، قَالَ إِنِّي أَعْلَمُ مَا لَا تَعْلَمُونَ.
وَعَلَّمَ آدَمَ الْأَسْمَاءَ كُلَّهَا ثُمَّ عَرَضَهُمْ عَلَى الْمَلَائِكَةِ فَقَالَ أَنْبِئُونِي بِأَسْمَاءِ هَؤُلَاءِ إِنْ كُنْتُمْ
صَادِقِينَ).

---

[203] Unfortunately, humans have, most of the time, failed to fulfill their vicegerency
role.

"Behold, your Lord said to the angels: 'I will create a vicegerent on earth.' They said: 'Will You place therein one who will make mischief therein and shed blood, whilst we glorify You with praises and thanks and sanctify You?' He said: 'I know that which you do not know.' And He taught Adam the names of all things; then He placed them before the angels, and said: 'Tell me the names of these if you are right.'"

(Qur'an 2:30–31)

Knowledge acquisition requires a language in which humans can express, record, communicate, and share ideas, facts, as well as feelings. Humans, in fact, started to communicate through a spoken language since the day Adam had learned the names of all things, as the second ayah above indicates. Allah has repeatedly emphasized the significance of knowledge in the Holy Qur'an.[204] In the first five ayahs ever revealed, for example, He points to this issue six times—directly and indirectly—using different words. More precisely, the first of these ayahs commanded the Holy Prophet to read; the third one repeated the same command to him. In addition, the root *a-l-m*[205]— from which the word *ilm*,[206] meaning knowledge, is derived—occurs three times in these five ayahs. Further, the word *qalam*, which means pen, comes once. From this, one can infer that the Holy Qur'an directed Muslims—from the onset—to the significance of knowledge acquisition and knowledge creation, by highlighting these three aspects of intellectuality: reading, writing,[207] and learning.

After revealing these five ayahs, interestingly, Allah stopped the revelation of the Holy Qur'an for a number of days or perhaps for

---

[204] An example of this is the message in the following ayah from surah Al-Zumar:

(... ‏قُلْ هَلْ يَسْتَوِي الَّذِينَ يَعْلَمُونَ وَالَّذِينَ لَا يَعْلَمُونَ ...)؟

"...Say: 'Are those who know equal to those who know not...?'"

(Qur'an 39:9)

عَلِمَ [205]

عِلْم [206]

[207] The concept of writing in these ayahs is suggested by the Arabic word *qalam*, which means pen.

years, as some scholars argued (Al-Mubarakpuri, 2007, p. 58). Maybe this interval, be it short or long, was meant to invite reflection on the underlying message in these five ayahs. Evidently, the significance of knowledge acquisition and knowledge creation in Islam represents a major element in this contemplation. In other words, since Muslims are assigned the vicegerent's mission on Earth, they are required to be profoundly knowledgeable, in a way that qualifies them to fulfil their spiritual leadership role on this planet.

Third, the story of Adam and Eve in surah Al-Baqarah highlights the supremacy of the knowledgeable. This is suggested by Allah's command to the angels and Iblis to prostrate themselves before Adam, who had already learned the names of all things and was able to tell them to the angels, who—previous to this incident—had confessed that they didn't know those names. With respect to this Allah says:

$$\text{(وَإِذْ قُلْنَا لِلْمَلاَئِكَةِ اسْجُدُواْ لآدَمَ...)}$$

"When We told the angels: Prostrate yourselves before Adam..."   *(Qur'an 2:34)*

In short, the first three lessons in this story are as follows. First, the delegation of Adam as a vicegerent on earth implies the significant and honourable role that Adam and his children should play on this planet's well-being. Second, Adam's learning of the names of all things implies the significance of knowledge in the achievement of his mission as a vicegerent on earth. Third, Allah's command to the angels and Iblis to prostrate to Adam suggests the supremacy of the knowledgeable.

Lesson 4

When Allah commanded the angels and Iblis to prostrate to Adam, the latter openly refused.[208]Allah mentions this fact in all the previously

---

[208] In this regard, Allah says:

$$\text{(وَإِذْ قُلْنَا لِلْمَلاَئِكَةِ اسْجُدُواْ لآدَمَ فَسَجَدُواْ إِلاَّ إِبْلِيسَ أَبَى وَاسْتَكْبَرَ وَكَانَ مِنَ الْكَافِرِينَ).}$$

mentioned surahs, a matter that emphasizes Iblis's strong hostility towards humankind and the threat he poses to the members of this race. Allah, in addition, warned Adam and Eve that Iblis was their enemy and that they had to beware of him. With regard to this, Ibn Al-Qayyim (1988) said, "Allah has repeatedly and consistently emphasized the Satan's enmity towards humans, and this indicates that they should be extremely careful of him" (p. 134).

Although this warning occurs four times in the context of this story, only the surah of Taha implies that Allah issued it to Adam immediately after the Satan's refusal to prostrate before him. This is suggested by the Arabic prefix *fa,*[209] in the clause *faqulna,* meaning "Then We said." Further, only this surah reveals that Allah warned Adam not to let Iblis drive him and his wife out of the Garden and subject him to misery, as a result. With respect to this, Allah states:

(فَقُلْنَا يَا آدَمُ إِنَّ هَٰذَا عَدُوٌّ لَّكَ وَلِزَوْجِكَ فَلَا يُخْرِجَنَّكُمَا مِنَ الْجَنَّةِ فَتَشْقَىٰ).

> *"Then We said: 'O Adam! Verily, this is an enemy to you and to your wife. So let him not get you both out of the Garden, so that you will be distressed.'"*
>
> *(Qur'an 20: 117)*

In surah Al-A'raf—after showing the Satan's negative attitude towards humankind, his enticement and deception of Adam and Eve, as well as his role in their expulsion from the Garden—Allah advises all humans not to let the Satan lure them into violating His rules—as he previously did to their parents—and thus expose them to misery. In a merciful tone,[210] He tells them:

(يَا بَنِي آدَمَ لَا يَفْتِنَنَّكُمُ الشَّيْطَانُ كَمَا أَخْرَجَ أَبَوَيْكُم مِّنَ الْجَنَّةِ يَنزِعُ عَنْهُمَا

> *"And when We said to the angels: 'Prostrate yourselves before Adam.' And they prostrated except Iblis (Satan), he refused and was proud and was one of the disbelievers."* *(Qur'an 2:34)*

[210] This merciful tone is suggested by the recurrence of the phrase *"O children of Adam!"* at the beginning of both this ayah and the one before it.

لِبَاسَهُمَا لِيُرِيَهُمَا سَوْءَاتِهِمَا ، إِنَّهُ يَرَاكُمْ هُوَ وَقَبِيلُهُ مِنْ حَيْثُ لاَ تَرَوْنَهُمْ ، إِنَّا

جَعَلْنَا الشَّيَاطِينَ أَوْلِيَاء لِلَّذِينَ لاَ يُؤْمِنُونَ).

*"O children of Adam! Let not the Satan deceive you, as
he got your parents out of the Garden, stripping them of
their raiments, to show them their private parts. Verily,
he as well as his soldiers see you from whence you
cannot see them; surely We have made the satans to be
the guardians of those who do not believe."*

(Qur'an 7:27)

Also in surah Fatir, Allah warns people that the Satan is their enemy
and that they should deal with him accordingly. He says to them:

(إِنَّ الشَّيْطَانَ لَكُمْ عَدُوٌّ فَاتَّخِذُوه عَدُوّاً...)

*"Surely, Satan is an enemy to you, so take him as an
enemy..."*　　　　　　　　　　　　*(Qur'an 35:6)*

Allah, in fact, repeats the same merciful warning in surah Al-Zukhruf
saying:

(وَلَا يَصُدَّنَّكُمُ الشَّيْطَانُ إِنَّهُ لَكُم عَدُوٌّ مُبِينٌ).

*"And let not the Satan hinder you (from the right
path); surely, he is your open enemy."*

(Qur'an 43:62)

Further, in surah Al-Kahf, Allah expresses this warning in a question
form that carries a disapproving tone, which suggests that disbelievers
favour the Satan—their enemy—over Him, their Creator, Merciful
Lord. He says:

(وَإِذْ قُلْنَا لِلْمَلَائِكَةِ اسْجُدُوا لِآدَمَ فَسَجَدُوا إِلَّا إِبْلِيسَ كَانَ مِنَ الْجِنِّ فَفَسَقَ عَنْ

أَمْرِ رَبِّهِ ، أَفَتَتَّخِذُونَهُ وَذُرِّيَّتَهُ أَوْلِيَاء مِن دُونِي وَهُمْ لَكُمْ عَدُوٌّ ، بِئْسَ لِلظَّالِمِينَ

بَدَلًا).

*"And remember when We said to the angels: 'Prostrate
yourselves before Adam.' So they all did except Iblis,*

who was from the jinn. He disobeyed the Command of his Lord. Will you then take him and his offspring as protectors and helpers rather than Me while they are enemies to you? What an evil is the exchange for the wrong-doers."   *(Qur'an 18:50)*

Lesson 5

Another important lesson that this story teaches is that jealousy, arrogance, and superiority complex were the source of the first sin ever. Particularly, Iblis refused to prostrate to Adam because he was jealous and because he considered his origin superior to Adam's. Due to the significance of its lesson, Iblis's contempt for the human origin is highlighted four times in the context of this story. Precisely, it occurs in the surahs of Al-A'raf, Al-Hijr, Al-Isra', and Sad. Surah Sad, for instance, shows how proud Iblis feels about his origin and how contemptuous he is of the humans'. When Allah asked him why he didn't prostrate to Adam, he replied:

(...أَنَاْ خَيْرٌ مِّنْه خَلَقْتَنِي مِن نَّارٍ وَخَلَقْتَهُ مِن طِينٍ).[211]

"...I am better than he. You created me from fire, and You created him from clay."   *(Qur'an 38:76)*

Surah Al-Hijr draws our attention to Iblis's same nasty attitude, which reflects on his contempt for the humankind's origin.[212] It also shows how rude he was in answering Allah's previous question to him. He responded to Allah saying:

(... لَمْ أَكُن لِّأَسْجُدَ لِبَشَرٍ خَلَقْتَهُ مِن صَلْصَالٍ مِّنْ حَمَإٍ مَّسْنُونٍ)!

---

[211] The same response occurs in surah Al-A'raf, ayah12.

[212] Superiority complex, unfortunately, has badly afflicted the Muslims society today. The issues of origin, nationality, colour, economic status, level of education, and linguistic background have undermined the harmony and unity of Muslim communities in different parts of the world. Instead of being a sword that cuts the Muslim body into pieces, such differences—if employed wisely—can be significantly empowering. It is also outrageous to hear Muslims using slurs against others because of their ethnicity, colour, origin, or any other worldly element. The Holy Prophet has warned against this saying that all people "are from Adam and Adam was from dirt."

> *"...I am not to prostrate myself to a human, whom You created from dried (sounding) clay of altered mud!"*
> *(Qur'an 15:33)*

In surah Al-Isra', Iblis's disdain for the human origin, his refusal to prostrate to Adam, and his rudeness to Allah are more emphasized. Also the interrogative form he used in answering Allah's question to him not only suggests his objection to Allah's command, but it also implies that he considered the command itself completely wrong and unacceptable! He said to the All-Mighty Himself:

$$(...أَأَسْجُدُ لِمَنْ خَلَقْتَ طِينًا)؟$$

> *"...Shall I prostrate myself to one whom You created from clay?"*   *(Qur'an 17:61)*

The messages in these three ayahs (from surahs Sad, Al-Hijr, and Al-Isra'), which, again, reflect Iblis's hostile and contemptuous attitude towards humankind, should elicit people's hatred for Iblis, as a natural human reaction. They should also motivate people to deal with him as an enemy. In addition, people should avoid these three evil attributes—jealousy, arrogance, and superiority complex—for their evilness caused Iblis to be the worst enemy of Allah.

In this context, it is worth mentioning that the humans' low origin,[213] which is clay, and Iblis's contempt for them—due to their dirt origin—should be a strong motivator for people to build a significantly great fortune that helps them improve their value. Fortunately, Allah has made the achievement of this fortune possible through eiman and taqwa. That is, when people believe in Allah and observe Him closely, throughout their lives, they become more honourable in His sight than the angels themselves, a fact that Allah has emphatically highlighted in surah Al-Baiyinah (The Clear Evidence) to inform humans and, most importantly, to motivate them

---

[213] Allah could've created humans from one of the most precious substances He has, but it seems that the wisdom behind their creation from dirt—a matter that they walk and even spit on—is to help them in, at least, two ways: to be humble and to, again, motivate them to elevate themselves from the low level of their origin, through eiman and taqwa, which link them directly with Him.

to seek this honour earnestly and relentlessly. With respect to this issue, He says:

$$(إِنَّ الَّذِينَ آمَنُوا وَعَمِلُوا الصَّالِحَاتِ أُولَٰئِكَ هُمْ خَيْرُ الْبَرِيَّةِ).$$

"Verily, those who believe [in the Oneness of Allah and in His Messenger Mohammad] and do righteous good deeds, they are the best of creatures."

(Qur'an 98:7)

Ibn Kathir reported Abu Hurairah and other scholars to have considered the message in this ayah as evidence for the superiority of the righteous over the angels (2014, p. 537).

Motivated by his extreme hostility towards Adam and his children, Iblis declared he would ruin their relationship with Allah. This is clear in the emphatic form he repeatedly used in this respect, as the following ayahs from the surahs of Sad, Al-Hijr, Al-Isra', and Al-A'raf demonstrate.

First, surah Sad shows Iblis's strong determination to take humans astray. Addressing Allah in this respect, He said:

$$(...فَبِعِزَّتِكَ لَأُغْوِيَنَّهُمْ أَجْمَعِينَ . إِلَّا عِبَادَكَ مِنْهُمُ الْمُخْلَصِينَ).$$

"...I swear by Your Might! I will surely make them live an evil life, all. Except Your true servants, the purified ones."   *(Qur'an 38:82–83)*

Second, surah Al-Hijr demonstrates that Iblis has decided to make evil deeds look attractive to humans so that he will take them astray. In reference to all humankind, He emphatically said to Allah:

$$(...رَبِّ بِمَا أَغْوَيْتَنِي لَأُزَيِّنَنَّ لَهُمْ فِي الْأَرْضِ وَلَأُغْوِيَنَّهُمْ أَجْمَعِينَ . إِلاَّ عِبَادَكَ مِنْهُمُ الْمُخْلَصِينَ).$$

"...My Lord! Because you misled me, I shall indeed adorn the path of error for them (humankind) on earth,

*and I shall mislead them all. Except Your servants from
among them, the devoted ones."*

(Qur'an 15:39–40)

Third, in surah Al-Isra', Iblis's determination to take humans astray is
even stronger. This is clear in his strong threatening expression *"I will
surely seize and mislead his offspring."* [214] According to the scholars
of the Qur'anic exegesis, this expression suggests that Iblis has
determined to do whatever in order to subjugate humans and make
them do whatsoever he wishes. In an extremely rude manner, He
addressed Allah in this regard saying:

$$(...أَرَأَيْتَكَ هَذَا الَّذِي كَرَّمْتَ عَلَيَّ لَئِنْ أَخَّرْتَنِ إِلَى يَوْمِ الْقِيَامَةِ لَأَحْتَنِكَنَّ ذُرِّيَّتَهُ إِلاَّ قَلِيلاً).$$

*"...see this one whom You have honoured above me, if
You give me respite to the Day of Resurrection, I will
surely seize and mislead his offspring all but a few."*

(Qur'an 17:62)

Fourth, the surah of Al-A'raf reveals that Iblis has decided to block off
Allah's right path to prevent humankind from taking it. Talking to the
All-Mighty in the same previous rude manner, he said:

$$(...فَبِمَا أَغْوَيْتَنِي لَأَقْعُدَنَّ لَهُمْ صِرَاطَكَ الْمُسْتَقِيمَ . ثُمَّ لَآتِيَنَّهُمْ مِنْ بَيْنِ أَيْدِيهِمْ وَمِنْ خَلْفِهِمْ وَعَنْ أَيْمَانِهِمْ وَعَنْ شَمَائِلِهِمْ وَلَا تَجِدُ أَكْثَرَهُمْ شَاكِرِينَ).$$

*"...because You have sent me astray, I will certainly sit
in wait for them in Your straight path. Then I will
certainly come to them from before them and from
behind them, and from their right-hand side and from
their left-hand side; and You will not find most of them
thankful."* (Qur'an 7:16–17)

Iblis's threat in the above ayah is extremely alarming. The four
fronts—mentioned in the second ayah—that he uses to attack his

---

[214] (لَأَحْتَنِكَنَّ ذُرِّيَّتَهُ)

human victims may include human nature and countless situations that people experience in their daily lives, which can be in his favour to set his trap and prey on them. For example, if a believer desperately needs something that is difficult or impossible to have in an honest way, the Satan may take advantage of this believer's situation and gradually coax him or her into having it the wrong way. In addition, these different fronts, which he has determined to utilize in order to attack his human victims, suggest the subtle ways through which he seduces. They may also refer to humans' vulnerability to enticement.

To help humans avoid being an easy prey for the Satan's deception, Allah recurrently threatens to punish whoever obeys him. Such a threat, of course, is meant to generate fear of Allah, which, again, represents a major ingredient of taqwa—the fort that protects them from the Satan's attacks and the power that keeps them moving steadily in Allah's direction.

One of the threats that Allah has issued to prevent people from obeying the Satan is this:

(... لَّمَن تَبِعَكَ مِنْهُمْ لأَمْلأنَّ جَهَنَّمَ مِنكُمْ أَجْمَعِينَ).

"...whoever of them follows you, I will certainly fill Hell with you all."   (Qur'an 7:18)

Another similar threat that Allah has issued to help humans keep vigilant of the Satan's extensive, hidden trap is the following one from surah Al-Isra'. Talking to Iblis, He says:

(فَمَن تَبِعَكَ مِنْهُمْ فَإِنَّ جَهَنَّمَ جَزَآؤُكُمْ جَزَاءً مَّوْفُورًا) .

"If any of them follows you, verily Hell will be the recompense of you, an ample recompense."
                                    (Qur'an 17:63)

Lessons 6 and 7

In surah Al-Baqarah, Allah mentions that He admitted Adam and Eve to the Garden and allowed them to eat whatever they liked. Nevertheless, He forbade them from getting close to a specific tree, let alone eating its fruit. Addressing Adam and Eve in this regard, He said:

$$(...يَا آدَمُ اسْكُنْ أَنتَ وَزَوْجُكَ الْجَنَّةَ وَكُلَا مِنْهَا رَغَداً حَيْثُ شِئْتُمَا وَلَا تَقْرَبَا هَذِهِ الشَّجَرَةَ فَتَكُونَا مِنَ الظَّالِمِينَ).$$

"...O Adam! Dwell you and your wife in Paradise and eat both of you freely with pleasure and delight, of things therein as wherever you will, but come not near this tree or you both will be of the wrong-doers."
                                        (Qur'an 2:35)

The same strong prohibition occurs again in surah Al-A'raf, where in reference to Adam and Eve, Allah says:

$$(...فَكُلَا مِنْ حَيْثُ شِئْتُمَا وَلَا تَقْرَبَا هَٰذِهِ الشَّجَرَةَ فَتَكُونَا مِنَ الظَّالِمِينَ).$$

"And enjoy (its good things) as you wish: but come not near this tree or you both will be of the wrong-doers."
                                        (Qur'an 7:19)

In each of these ayahs, the warning *"come not near this tree,"* which Allah issued to Adam and Eve, suggests that human nature is fragile, and it can easily give in to temptation. Perhaps this prohibition is meant to teach Adam and Eve as well as their children values fundamental to a successful vicegerency—such as observance of Allah, compliance with His rules, honesty, responsibility, and self-restraint. So Adam and Eve found themselves in the middle of a challenging triangle-situation whose sides represent the human desires, the Satan's enticement, and the command of Allah.

It seems the Satan knew the human natural desire for survival and ownership, so he took advantage of this and decided to lure Adam and Eve into eating from that forbidden tree. He told them eating from it would allow them to be angels, become immortal, and/or enjoy an everlasting kingdom. He even swore by Allah that he was honest.[215]

---

[215] (وَقَاسَمَهُمَا إِنِّي لَكُمَا لَمِنَ النَّاصِحِينَ).

Allah highlights this incident twice in the context of this story, namely in the surahs of Al-A'raf and Taha. In the former, He states:

$$(\text{...وقال ما نَهَاكُمَا رَبُّكُمَا عَنْ هَذِهِ الشَّجَرَةِ إِلاَّ أَن تَكُونَا مَلَكَيْنِ أَوْ تَكُونَا مِنَ الْخَالِدِينَ}).$$

"...and he said: 'Your Lord did not forbid you this tree save that you should become angels or become of the immortals.'"   *(Qur'an 7:20)*

In the latter, He narrates:

$$(\text{...قال يَا آدَمُ هَلْ أَدُلُّكَ عَلَى شَجَرَةِ الْخُلْدِ وَمُلْكٍ لَّا يَبْلَى})\text{؟}$$

"...he said: 'O Adam! Shall I guide you to the tree of immortality and a kingdom which decays not?'"
(Qur'an 20:120)

Being influenced by their deep-rooted, intuitive human desire to live perpetually and to enjoy an everlasting kingdom, Adam and Eve, unfortunately, succumbed to Iblis's enticement and ate from the forbidden tree. Thus, they failed their first and only test and committed the first human sin ever. Concerning this issue, Allah says:

$$(\text{... فَأَكَلَا مِنْهَا}).$$

"And they both ate from it..."   *(Qur'an 20:121)*

But—one can't believe!—how did Adam and Eve forget that nothing could happen without Allah's will? In other words, how did they expect to achieve their goal—whether by eating from the forbidden tree or by whatever they might have done—without Allah's permission? Another lesson to learn from this incident is that believers shouldn't get close to forbidden areas, where they may—willingly or unwillingly—fall into the Satan's subtle trap, the way Adam and Eve,

---

"And he (Satan) swore by Allah to them both (saying): Verily, I am one of the sincere well-wishers for you both."   *(Qur'an 7:21)*

unfortunately, did. Believers are, certainly, safer away from forbidden areas and sources of sins than they are close to them.

Lessons 8 and 9

Unlike Iblis, who insisted he was right, Adam and Eve immediately realized their mistake, regretted it, and—assumingly—from the bottom of their hearts, they prayed Allah to forgive them. They also acknowledged that if Allah hadn't pardoned them, they would've certainly become losers. Hence, they proved to Iblis another aspect of the human's superiority over him and over his offspring. Here we also learn an important fact and a significant lesson of taqwa: Humans are apt to violate Allah's rules, but if they repent, Allah will forgive them.[216]

The following ayah, from surah Al-A'raf, shows Adam and Eve regretting their sin. It also reveals their sincere prayer to Allah to pardon them and to bestow His mercy upon them. The subsequent ayah, from surah Al-Baqarah, shows Allah's acceptance of Adam's and Eve's repentance.

First, here are Adam and Eve expressing their repentance to Allah and praying Him to pardon them. They said:

(... رَبَّنَا ظَلَمْنَا أَنفُسَنَا وَإِن لَّمْ تَغْفِرْ لَنَا وَتَرْحَمْنَا لَنَكُونَنَّ مِنَ الْخَاسِرِينَ).

"...Our Lord! We have wronged ourselves. If You don't forgive us and bestow Your mercy upon us, we shall certainly be of the losers."   *(Qur'an 7:23)*

Second, here is Allah's mercy showering them, in response to their sincere prayer:

(فَتَلَقَّى ءَادَمُ مِن رَّبِّهِ كَلِمَاتٍ فَتَابَ عَلَيْهِ إِنَّهُ هُوَ التَّوَّابُ الرَّحِيمُ).

---

[216] This issue recurs three times: in the surahs of Al-Baqarah, Al-A'raf, and Taha.

"Then Adam received from his Lord Words. And his Lord pardoned him. Verily, He is the One Who forgives, the Most Merciful." *(Qur'an 2:37)*

Lesson 10

Another important lesson of taqwa to learn from this story is the association of the revelation of Adam's and Eve's parts of shame with their disobedience to Allah. As soon as they ate from the forbidden tree, their genitals revealed themselves. So violations of Allah's rules subject humans to disgrace and shame,[217] and the more they violate His rules, the more disgraceful they become. This issue, in fact, recurs twice in the context of this story: in the surahs of Al-A'raf and Taha. Its recurrence, of course, indicates the significance of the lesson it teaches. In surah Al-A'raf and in reference to this issue, for example, Allah says:

(...فَلَمَّا ذَاقَا الشَّجَرَةَ بَدَت لَهُمَا سَوْءَاتُهُمَا...)

"...then when they tasted of the tree, that which was hidden from them of their shame (private parts) became manifest to them..." *(Qur'an 7:22)*

Lesson 11

Adam and Eve's story teaches another invaluable lesson of taqwa. It

---

[217] Surah Al-A'raf has another ayah that substantiates this inference; that is, violation of Allah's rules subjects humans to disgrace. The ayah says:

(يَا بَنِي آدَمَ لاَ يَفْتِنَنَّكُمُ الشَّيْطَانُ كَمَا أَخْرَجَ أَبَوَيْكُم مِّنَ الْجَنَّةِ يَنزِعُ عَنْهُمَا لِبَاسَهُمَا لِيُرِيَهُمَا سَوْءَاتِهِمَا إِنَّهُ يَرَاكُمْ هُوَ وَقَبِيلُهُ مِنْ حَيْثُ لاَ تَرَوْنَهُمْ إِنَّا جَعَلْنَا الشَّيَاطِينَ أَوْلِيَاء لِلَّذِينَ لاَ يُؤْمِنُونَ).

"O children of Adam! let not the Satan cause you to fall into affliction as he expelled your parents from the Garden, pulling off from them their clothing that he might show them their evil inclinations, he surely sees you, he as well as his host, from where you cannot see them; surely We have made the Satans to be the guardians of those who do not believe."

(Qur'an 7:27)

stems from the instantaneous, intuitive reaction they made when their genitals revealed themselves. They quickly covered them with the Garden's leaves. Allah highlights this incident twice in the context of this story, precisely in the surahs of Al-A'raf and Taha, where in each of these surahs, He says:

$$(\text{...وَطَفِقَا يَخْصِفَانِ عَلَيْهِمَا مِن وَرَقِ الْجَنَّةِ...})$$

"...they began to cover them with the leaves of the Garden..."   *(Qur'an 7:22)*

Generally, the human instinct of covering body parts is stronger in females than it is in males, for most of a woman's body can be sexually arousing to men than most of a man's body to women. This is why Muslim women, unlike Muslim men, are required to cover their entire body. But being uneducated in their religion, many Muslim women today, unfortunately, consider the western woman a role model, so they deserted their *hijab* and started to look and behave like her. It is regrettable, indeed, to see Muslim women reject the crown of modesty that Allah has honoured them with and abandon the attire of decency He has—figuratively speaking—sent Gabriel to deliver to them.

Lesson 12

Finally, Allah has employed the Arabic root *h-b-t*[218] eight times in the Holy Qur'an. With respect to Adam and Eve's eviction from the Garden, however, He has used it four times;[219] in each of them, He has employed it in the imperative form to say, "Descend!" Thus, the continuous usage of this root with this denotation in reference to this matter underscores the tragedy that Adam and Eve incurred, as a result of their disobedience to Allah. Their sin was extremely costly, for it threw them from the high Garden down to Earth. This moment, in fact, represents an awful tragedy in human history, yet it isn't

---

[218] In reference to this issue, Allah repeats the same above message in surah Taha, ayah 121.

[219] As mentioned, Allah has employed this root "h-b-t" four times in reference to this incident: twice in surah Al-Baqarah and once in each of the surahs of Al-A'raf and Taha. In these surahs, the number of the ayahs concerning this issue are 36, 38, 24, and 123 respectively.

recognized as an important milestone in it. Even worse, it isn't highlighted in the exegeses of the Holy Qur'an.

So Adam and Eve had just arrived on Earth. Adam felt extremely guilty, regretful, sad, depressed, and overwhelmed. His tearful wife beside him felt helpless, confused, insecure, and bitter. The moment of their arrival on Earth must have overwhelmed their broken hearts with painful feelings of desolation, for the earth was an entirely new environment—a whole planet—that they had never seen before or heard of. They were the first humans to walk on it, and thus they had to learn everything on their own. They, indeed, had a long, unknown, insecure, and difficult way to go. On their arrival, their confused, inexperienced brains had many extremely important and urgent questions that needed quick answers: "Where is the water?" "Where is the food?" "Where is the shelter?" "Where is the clothing?" Where is…?" "Where is…?" "Where is…?"

Their new environment was extremely harsh, compared to the blissful Garden they had to reluctantly and immediately evacuate. In this new environment, in fact, they needed not only to survive but also to prosper as a new creature among millions of other stronger and dangerous ones that preceded them to this new, harsh, mysterious place. They also needed to learn a good lesson from their extremely costly mistake. Most importantly, they needed to keep the fire of their faith constantly burning in their hearts, notwithstanding the violent winds that blew fiercely in all directions.

The test they failed in their first peaceful and comfortable home was easy—just to keep away from only one prohibited object. In their new home, nevertheless, their test was hard: They had to stay away from many forbidden things. Even worse, their wicked, vicious, relentless enemy was expelled to the earth with them, and his initial victory over them made him more experienced, more daring, more hopeful, and more confident to win the game.

That is a brief discussion of Adam and Eve's story in the Holy Qur'an. As we have seen, it has many precious lessons of taqwa that Allah teaches to people in a compassionate, effective manner. And between these lessons, He recurrently warns them that the Satan is their enemy and that they should deal with him accordingly.

Lessons of Taqwa from the Story of Prophet Yusuf

At the beginning of the surah of Yusuf, Allah addressed His Holy Messenger saying:

(... نَحْنُ نَقُصُّ عَلَيْكَ أَحْسَنَ الْقَصَصِ)

"We relate to you (Mohammad) the best of stories..."
(Qur'an 12:3)

Al-Qurtubi (2014) reported that scholars of the exegesis of the Holy Qur'an argued that the expression *"the best of stories"* in this ayah refers to the story of Prophet Yusuf. According to him, these scholars mentioned different reasons underlying this description of this story. Some of them, for example, argued that Allah describes it thus because it includes more lessons than any other story in the Holy Qur'an. Other scholars, however, stated that Allah has honoured this story with this description because of Prophet Yusuf's patience and easy forgiveness of his brothers (p. 80).[220] The following sheds a little light on some of the numerous, invaluable lessons of taqwa in this amazing story.

Chastity

Prophet Yusuf was unprecedentedly beautiful—perhaps he was the most beautiful human ever! The ladies' cutting of their own hands with the knives in reaction to his view helps us understand how exceptionally and astonishingly beautiful he was.[221] The comment they made on his incredible charm, in addition, represents further evidence of his extraordinary beauty. They said:

(... حَاشَ لِلَّهِ مَا هَذَا بَشَرًا إِنْ هَذَا إِلاَّ مَلَكٌ كَرِيمٌ)!

"...how perfect is Allah! No human is this! This is none other than a noble angel!"   *(Qur'an 12:31)*

---

[220] Al-Qurtubi and Al-Shawkani mentioned two more reasons regarding this issue, but it was decided not to include them here because they don't seem reasonable.
[221] You may refer to ayahs 30 and 31 for a better understanding of this incident.

This unbelievable beauty that Prophet Yusuf used to enjoy strongly infatuated the Egyptian governor's wife; thus, she lusted for sex with him. One day, she thought the atmosphere was in her favour—nobody was in, but Yusuf and her. She firmly locked all the doors, approached him, and said, (هَيْتَ لَكَ), meaning, "Come, Yusuf. I have prepared myself for you!" (Al-Shawkani, 2012, pp. 20–21). Being said by a woman in her position, such a statement can make millions of men easily collapse and fall in the bed of dirtiness, except those who are equipped with an exceptionally high level of taqwa. Yusuf confidently answered her saying, *"Allah forbid!"* In other words, "I seek refuge with Allah from what you want me to do," which reflects how badly he was alarmed and disturbed by her proposition.

Yusuf added another statement that reflects his high level of honesty and loyalty. In reference to her husband, he said, *"Truly, your husband is my lord! He made my sojourn agreeable!"* He also followed this statement with another one that proves his heart was full of eiman, taqwa, and wisdom. He said, *"Truly no good comes to those who do wrong."* The governor's wife approached him with her filthy desires, so he tried to treat her lustful heart with this Godly reminder. But he couldn't.

The fierce fire of her lust for sex with him destroyed her conscience and dignity—she couldn't see! She didn't give up; she even used force and pulled him from the back as he ran towards the door to exit the room. She also threatened to throw him in jail if he continued to resist, yet he refused to succumb. Here we learn that believers shouldn't give in to any pressure that threatens their Islamic principles and identity, no matter what the circumstances are or how awful the consequences might be.

This part of the surah, in fact, warns not only against unlawful sex but also against the development of any sexual desire towards anyone who isn't one's spouse. Believers' sexual desires should, therefore, be entirely under their control, not the other way around. Also those who are exceptionally attractive—women and men—need to be more careful; they should remember that their extraordinary charm is a test and that they are more vulnerable than others to fall in the Satan's trap of immoral sex.

A. Al-Ghazali (2004) narrated this amazing, inspirational story:

Suleiman ibn Yasar was exceptionally handsome. One day while he was sitting alone in his tent, a Bedouin woman saw him; she immediately went to his tent and entered. Then she removed her veil and revealed an extremely beautiful face and said, "*ahni'nī*."[222] Suleiman thought she needed food, so he hurried and brought her some. But the woman said, "I don't want this, but I want what a man does with his wife!" So Suleiman, who was, actually, on his way to Makkah to perform hajj, responded, "Has Iblis sent you to me?" Then he sat on the ground, hid his face between his knees, and started weeping. Seeing this, the woman left.

> When his friend, who went to buy food, returned, he noticed that Suleiman's eyes had swollen. He also noticed that Suleiman had been crying, so he asked him about the reason. Suleiman refused to tell him, but his friend insisted. When Suleiman told him his story with the Bedouin woman, his friend started to cry, too. Suleiman was astonished, so he asked his friend to explain to him why he cried. His friend replied, "I cry because if she had propositioned me, I would've slept with her."

> One day, after he arrived in Makkah, Suleiman slept by the Black Stone. In his sleep, he saw a tall, beautiful man, so he said to him, "May Allah have His mercy upon you, but who are you?" The man answered, "I am Yusuf." "Yusuf, the Honest [meaning Prophet Yusuf]!" Suleiman exclaimed. "Yes," said the man. Then Suleiman said to him, "Your story with the Egyptian governor's wife is amazing." Prophet Yusuf responded, "But your story with the Bedouin woman is more amazing." (p. 136)

Dependence on Allah

In reaction to the sexual harassment he experienced from the governor's wife and the distress she inflicted on him, Prophet Yusuf made an urgent call upon Allah to help him out. He declared to Him that if He didn't help him out, he would yield to the ladies' enticement. He said:

أهنئني [222]

(...رَبِّ السِّجْنُ أَحَبُّ إِلَيَّ مِمَّا يَدْعُونَنِي إِلَيْهِ وَإِلاَّ تَصْرِفْ عَنِّي كَيْدَهُنَّ أَصْبُ
إِلَيْهِنَّ وَأَكُن مِّنَ الْجَاهِلِينَ).

"...O my Lord! Prison is dearer to me than that to which
they invite me. Unless You turn away their plot from me, I
will feel inclined towards them and be one of the
ignorant."   *(Qur'an 12:33)*

In this context, the word "الجاهلين" is the equivalent of the English
phrase "the ignorant." According to Al-Saadi (2011), it refers to those
who prefer the limited pleasures in this life over the infinite,
indescribable ones in the Gardens of bliss (p. 347). It also means only
those who ignore or don't care that Allah will hold them accountable
for their evil deeds are capable of committing adultery. Nevertheless,
true believers, whose hearts are overwhelmed by the fear of Allah and
the realization of His Majesty, never involve themselves in such dirty
and disgraceful conduct.

Abu Hurairah reported that the Holy Prophet said:

"When someone commits adultery, he [she] does not
commit it while he [she] is still a believer."

". لا يزني الزّاني وَهُوَ مُؤْمِنٌ "

The underlying message of this hadith is that when a believer commits
adultery, he or she defects from eiman; that is, according to Ibn Al-
Uthaymeen, his heart becomes stripped of eiman [that moment].[223]
Based on this, believers may expose themselves to extreme danger if
they get involved in unlawful sexual relationships. In the light of this
hadith, therefore, imagine Muslims who die while they're committing
adultery, what identity will they have?

Thankfulness

Ideal believers always appreciate Allah's blessings that He bestows on
them. They don't attribute their success or gains to personal merits
and effort, but they attribute them to Allah only. So after the arrival of

---

[223] https://www.youtube.com/watch?v=bbp5pzR2l14

his parents in Egypt, Prophet Yusuf declared that all the fortune he was enjoying, including his assumption of the position of the governor of Egypt's, or even that of the king's,[224] was but a result of Allah's mercy and grace. He neither gave himself credit for the way he handled his prolonged hardship and sufferings, nor did he take pride in his relentless and continuous struggle against evil. Examine the following Qur'anic report that highlights his deep gratitude to Allah:

(وَرَفَعَ أَبَوَيْهِ عَلَى الْعَرْشِ وَخَرُّوا لَهُ سُجَّدًا ، وَقَالَ يَا أَبَتِ هَذَا تَأْوِيلُ رُؤْيَايَ مِنْ
قَبْلُ قَدْ جَعَلَهَا رَبِّي حَقًّا ، وَقَدْ أَحْسَنَ بِي إِذْ أَخْرَجَنِي مِنَ السِّجْنِ وَجَاءَ بِكُمْ
مِنَ الْبَدْوِ مِنْ بَعْدِ أَنْ نَزَغَ الشَّيْطَانُ بَيْنِي وَبَيْنَ إِخْوَتِي إِنَّ رَبِّي لَطِيفٌ لِمَا يَشَاءُ
إِنَّهُ هُوَ الْعَلِيمُ الْحَكِيمُ).

"And he raised his parents to the throne and they fell down before him prostrate. And he said: 'O my father! This is the interpretation of my dream aforetime! My Lord has made it come true! He was indeed good to me, when He took me out of the prison, and brought you (all here) out of the Bedouin life, after the Satan had sown enmity between me and my brothers. Certainly, my Lord is the Most Courteous and Kind to whom He wills. Truly, He! Only He is the All-Knowing, the Most Wise.'"

(Qur'an 12:100)

Focus on the Hereafter

In an ideal, outstanding supplication, Prophet Yusuf declared to Allah that he had taken him as a *Wali*[225] in this life and in the Hereafter. When believers take Allah as their "Wali," they completely submit to Him, perfectly trust in Him, and always depend on Him in all their affairs and without any exception, no matter how simple or easy such affairs might be. Prophet Yusuf had, of course, always taken Allah as his only Wali, but in this moment, where the story comes to its end, Allah stresses this important issue in Prophet Yusuf's ideal Islamic character.

---

[224] Al-Tabari, Al-Shawkani, and Al-Saadi
[225] *Wali* suggests the following meanings: protector, supporter, guardian, and helper.

Here, as the story reaches its end, the Holy Qur'an provides a wonderful, mental view, where all the story's characters disappear to let the surah's entire light shed and focus exclusively on Prophet Yusuf—the major character—making an ideal, historical prayer in which he mixes his deep appreciation of Allah, his eloquent praise for His kindness to him, and his own most precious wish. He said:

(رَبِّ قَدْ آتَيْتَنِي مِنَ الْمُلْكِ وَعَلَّمْتَنِي مِن تَأْوِيلِ الأَحَادِيثِ فَاطِرَ السَّمَـاوَاتِ وَالأَرْضِ أَنتَ وَلِيِّي فِي الدُّنْيَا وَالآخِرَةِ تَوَفَّنِي مُسْلِماً أَلْحِقْنِي بِالصَّالِحِينَ).

"My Lord! You have indeed bestowed on me of the sovereignty, and taught me something of the interpretation of dreams—the (only) Creator of the heavens and the earth! You are my Wali in this world and in the Hereafter..."   *(Qur'an 12:101)*

Obviously, this exceptional and historical supplication reflects that Prophet Yusuf's high position and great possessions, as a governor or king of Egypt, didn't distract him from Allah or from the reward He has prepared for the righteous in the Hereafter. So he prayed Allah to honour him with a good end and to link him with His previous righteous servants. He said:

(...تَوَفَّنِي مُسْلِمًا وَأَلْحِقْنِي بِالصَّالِحِينَ).

"...take my soul as a Muslim, and join me with the righteous."   *(Qur'an 12:101)*

Being deeply affected by the story of Prophet Yusuf, our Holy Prophet, Mohammad, made the last two sentences in this ayah part of his supplication to Allah in one of the most critical phases of his honourable work of the propagation of Islam. Specifically, he made this supplication after his army was badly defeated at the Battle of Uhud. He concluded it saying:

"O Allah! Take our souls as Muslims, bring us back to life
as Muslims, and join us with the righteous ones."

"اللهم توفنا مسلمين، وأحينا مسلمين، وألحقنا بالصالحين."

Hopefulness

Hope represents an essential ingredient of the Islamic faith. Believers should, therefore, keep the torch of hope constantly burning in their hearts that Allah will certainly be on their side as long as they observe and obey Him. The more sufferings that Prophets Yaqub and Yusuf incurred, the more firmly they held to the rope of hope that Allah would inevitably turn their relentless patience into a sweet drink of victory. Even when his sons came back from Egypt without Yusuf's youngest brother, Prophet Yaqub told them to go back and look for Yusuf and his brother with hope. He also advised them not to give up hope, for, according to him, only disbelievers are hopeless of Allah's mercy.

He, in fact, said to them words that were not only full of hope but were also capable of filling the most hopeless hearts with it. He told them:

(يَا بَنِيَّ اذْهَبُواْ فَتَحَسَّسُواْ مِن يُوسُفَ وَأَخِيهِ وَلاَ تَيْأَسُواْ مِن رَّوْحِ اللّهِ إِنَّهُ لاَ يَيْأَسُ مِن رَّوْحِ اللّهِ إِلاَّ الْقَوْمُ الْكَافِرُونَ).

"O my sons! Go and enquire about Yusuf and his brother, and never give up hope of Allah's Soothing mercy: truly no one despairs of Allah's Soothing mercy, except those who have no faith."

(Qur'an 12:87)

Further, through Yusuf's interpretation of the king's recurrent dream, Allah gave hope to the king of Egypt and his people—though they were disbelievers—that after those harsh years of drought, a year of abundant crops would finally arrive. Believers should, therefore, always remain hopeful that ease and victory will be theirs, no matter how badly or how long they have suffered. With regard to this, Allah says:

(ثُمَّ يَأْتِى مِن بَعْد ذلِكَ عَامٌ فِيهِ يُغَاثُ النَّاسُ وَفِيهِ يَعْصِرُون).

"Then thereafter will come a year in which people will have abundant rain and in which they will press (wine and oil)."
(Qur'an 12:49)

Forgiveness

After revealing his identity to his elder brothers, who caused him all the different types of distress he endured, Prophet Yusuf forgave them and prayed Allah to pardon them, too. He also treated them with honour, though he was able to make them pay the price, at least, twice as much. As mentioned earlier, this surah had a significant influence on the Holy Prophet's character and personality. The way he treated the disbelievers of Makkah when he opened it, for instance, sheds light on how deeply this surah affected him. With respect to this incident, as-Sibaa'ie wrote the following:

> [When] Quraysh surrendered and stood beneath his feet at the door of the Kabah, waiting for the ruling of the Messenger after they had resisted him for twenty-one years, he did nothing more than to say,

> "O Quraysh! What do you think I will do with you? They said, 'Good... (you're) a noble brother, son of a noble brother.' He said, 'Today I say to you what my brother Yusuf (Joseph) said before:

$$(\text{...}لَا تَثْرِيبَ عَلَيْكُمُ الْيَوْمَ يَغْفِرُ اللَّهُ لَكُمْ وَهُوَ أَرْحَمُ الرَّاحِمِينَ).$$

> *"No reproach on you this day; may Allah forgive you, and He is the Most Merciful of those who show mercy!"*
> *(Qur'an 12:92)*

> Go, for you are free ....'" (1999/2005, p. 149).

Notice the mental and even the linguistic effects of this surah on the Holy Prophet. Since these people rejected the Holy Qur'an and fought against it, perhaps the Holy Prophet wanted to show them the mercy it had for them. The underlying message of the Holy Prophet's statement above is that I forgive you because the Holy Qur'an, which you rejected, teaches me to do so.

Some Muslims argue that Yusuf and Mohammad are Messengers of Allah; thus, it is impossible to be like them. These people need to remember that the Holy Qur'an doesn't teach abstract idealism, but it teaches real and practical Islamic values so that believers can make them parts of their lives. In other words, Islam believes in humans' ability to think, choose, decide, and act in a way that improves the material and the moral aspects of their lives. Interestingly, the beginning of the story of Prophet Yusuf and the end of the whole surah have important messages pertinent to this issue.

Whereas the beginning of the story calls people's attention to the invaluable lessons in it, the end of the surah, as a whole, instructs them to apply these lessons in their lives. The story begins thus:

(نَحْنُ نَقُصُّ عَلَيْكَ أَحْسَنَ الْقَصَصِ بِمَا أَوْحَيْنَا إِلَيْكَ هَذَا الْقُرْآنَ وَإِن كُنتَ مِن قَبْلِهِ لَمِنَ الْغَافِلِينَ) .

"We relate unto you the best of stories through Our revelations unto you, of this Qur'an. And before this, you were among those who knew nothing about it."
(Qur'an 12: 3)

The surah concludes with this:

(لَقَدْ كَانَ فِي قَصَصِهِمْ عِبْرَةٌ لِأُوْلِي الأَلْبَابِ مَا كَانَ حَدِيثًا يُفْتَرَى وَلَكِن تَصْدِيقَ الَّذِي بَيْنَ يَدَيْهِ وَتَفْصِيلَ كُلِّ شَيْءٍ وَهُدًى وَرَحْمَةً لِقَوْمٍ يُؤْمِنُونَ) .

"Indeed in their stories, there is a lesson for men of understanding. It (the Qur'an) is not a forged statement but a confirmation of that which was before it and a detailed explanation of everything and a guide and a mercy for the people who believe."
(Qur'an 12:111)

The Prophet's companions were ordinary humans; nevertheless, they succeeded in the application of the Qur'anic teachings throughout their lives, even in the most difficult situations.[226] The Islamic history teems with wonderful stories in support of this, and the lives of Abu Bakr Al-Siddiq and Omar ibn Al-Khattab alone provides many.

---

[226] Sulh Al-Hudaibiyah (Treaty of Al-Hudaibiyah), which was previously discussed in "Chapter One," is one example of this.

For example, Mistah who was a poor relative of Abu Bakr used to receive regular economic assistance from the latter to help him make a living. Regrettably, Mistah involved himself in the *fitnah* of the *ifk*, an event in which the hypocrites, led by Abd Allah ibn Ubai ibn Salol, accused Ayishah (Abu Bakr's daughter and the Holy Prophet's wife) of adultery. Abu-Bakr, as a result, decided to stop his aid to Mistah, which is the least human reaction to such an extremely outrageous conduct. But the Holy Qur'an came down to tell Abu Bakr that he was wrong and that as a believer, his reaction in such a situation should have been better: to remain helpful to his relative and to forgive him. In this regard, Allah says:

$$\text{(وَلاَ يَأْتَلِ أُوْلُواْ الْفَضْلِ مِنكُمْ وَالسَّعَةِ أَن يُؤْتُواْ أُوْلِي الْقُرْبَى وَالْمَسَاكِينَ وَالْمُهَاجِرِينَ فِي سَبِيلِ اللَّهِ وَلْيَعْفُواْ وَلْيَصْفَحُواْ أَلاَ تُحِبُّونَ أَن يَغْفِرَ اللَّهُ لَكُمْ وَاللَّهُ غَفُورٌ رَّحِيمٌ).}$$

"And let not those among you who are blessed with graces and wealth swear not to give to their kinsmen, the poor, and those who left their homes for Allah's cause. Let them pardon and forgive. Do you not love that Allah should forgive you? And Allah is Oft-Forgiving, Most Merciful."
(Qur'an 24:22)

Abu-Bakr's reaction to the message in this ayah was amazing: According to Qutb (1992), he immediately reversed his attitude "and swore he would never stop helping him. He said, 'Surely, I would love to have Allah's forgiveness'" (p. 2505).

Also Omar ibn Al-Khattab's history includes many stories similar to that of Abu Bakr's with Mistah. This one, for example, proves that he had literally put himself in the hand of the Holy Qur'an to shape him the way Allah pleases. Ibn Kathir (2014), for instance, cited Imam Al-Bukhari to have reported Ibn Abbas saying:

Uyainah ibn Hissn asked his nephew Al-Hur ibn Qais,[227] who was honoured by Omar, to help him see the latter, who

---

[227] According to Al-Qurtubi (2014), Al-Hur ibn Qais was a member of Omar's counseling body, and he was one of the reciters who memorized the whole Holy Qur'an (p. 225).

was then the Head or Caliph of the Islamic State. Omar allowed Uyainah to enter. But as soon as he did, he verbally attacked Omar saying, "O Ibn Al-Khattab, I swear by Allah, you neither give us enough nor do you judge fairly among us!" Omar grew extremely angry in reaction to Uyainah's provocative statement, so he wanted to punish him. But Al-Hur quickly talked to Omar saying, "O Commander of the believers, Allah said to His Prophet:

$$\text{(خُذِ الْعَفْوَ وَأْمُرْ بِالْعُرْفِ وَأَعْرِضْ عَنِ الْجَاهِلِينَ).}$$

'Show forgiveness, enjoin what is good, and turn away from the ignorant.'"

(Qur'an 7:199)

He added, "This man is among the ignorant, so [please] forgive him." Hearing this, Omar—instantly and without hesitation—said, "I do." (pp. 259–260)

What Uyainah said to Omar was a shocking accusation. He meant Omar not only failed to carry out the mission that Allah had entrusted him with, but he also cheated the Muslim nation. Omar was such a powerful man whom, even before becoming the Caliph, no one would dare to upset. In reaction to this insult, therefore, he could have beaten Uyainah up with his own strong hands. And as a head of the most powerful state in the world then, he could have imprisoned or whipped him or both. But hearing the command of Allah in this ayah, he decided not to have another option.

These two stories prove how far in the world of excellent values and taqwa believers can reach when they follow the teachings of Allah and those of His Holy Messenger's. As Al-Hashimi expressed it:

The true Muslim who adheres to the teachings of his religion is tolerant and forgiving. Tolerance is a noble human characteristic, which is highly commanded in the Qur'an, where those who attain this virtue are viewed as the supreme example of piety in Islam and are included in the group of . . . doers of good who have succeeded in earning the love and pleasure of Allah. (2005, p. 215)

Propagation of Islam

The story of Prophet Yusuf teaches another fundamental aspect of taqwa: the propagation of Islam—dawah. While he was in the prison, Prophet Yusuf invited his two inmates to Islam using an effective approach. First, he called their attention to polytheism's nonsense; then he followed this with a question that required them to use critical thinking and to compare between believing in one God and believing in many. He addressed them saying:

(يَا صَاحِبَيِ السِّجْنِ أَأَرْبَابٌ مُتَفَرِّقُونَ خَيْرٌ أَمِ اللّهُ الْوَاحِدُ الْقَهَّارُ)؟

"O my two companions of the prison! Are many different lords (gods) better or Allah, the One, the Irresistible?"
(Qur'an 12:39)

Then he answered the question that he posed and told them that Allah is the only true God and that all the other so-called gods were false. He also informed them that Allah—the only true God—commands that people worship only Him. To do this, Prophet Yusuf chose the most effective time, which was the moment when they requested him to interpret their dreams for them. He realized their need for the interpretation of their dreams, so instead of beginning with the explanation of their dreams, he first brought their attention to their wrong faith; and then he told them about his faith. Finally, in a concise and precise manner, he interpreted their dreams. He said:

(مَا تَعْبُدُونَ مِن دُونِهِ إِلاَّ أَسْمَاءً سَمَّيْتُمُوهَا أَنتُمْ وَآبَاؤُكُم مَّا أَنزَلَ اللّهُ بِهَا مِن
سُلْطَانٍ إِنِ الْحُكْمُ إِلاَّ لِلّهِ أَمَرَ أَلاَّ تَعْبُدُواْ إِلاَّ إِيَّاهُ ذَلِكَ الدِّينُ الْقَيِّمُ وَلَكِنَّ أَكْثَرَ
النَّاسِ لاَ يَعْلَمُونَ . يَا صَاحِبَيِ السِّجْنِ أَمَّا أَحَدُكُمَا فَيَسْقِي رَبَّهُ خَمْرًا وَأَمَّا الآخَرُ
فَيُصْلَبُ فَتَأْكُلُ الطَّيْرُ مِن رَّأْسِهِ قُضِيَ الأَمْرُ الَّذِي فِيهِ تَسْتَفْتِيَانِ).

"You do not worship besides Him but only names which you have named (forged)—you and your fathers—for which Allah has sent down no authority. The command (or the judgment) is for none but Allah. He has commanded that you worship none but Him; that is the (true) straight religion, but most people know not. O two

*companions of the prison! As for one of you, he (as a
servant) will pour out wine for his lord to drink; and as
for the other, he will be crucified and birds will eat from
his head. Thus is the case judged concerning which you
both did inquire."*   *(Qur'an 12:40–41)*

Regrettably, the majority of Muslims today are either unaware of their
responsibility for the propagation of Islam or are indifferent to it.
Allah demands that His final message reach all people, wherever they
are and whenever they exist. The Holy Prophet's companions were
well aware of their heavy responsibility for the issue of dawah that
Allah had placed on their shoulders. They knew that, as trustees of
Allah's final Book to humankind, their mission was extremely
demanding and costly. They also understood that the universal role of
leadership (represented by *Khilafah*) [228] that they had to assume
wouldn't allow them to enjoy a safe, easy, and comfortable life.

Their brains, hearts, souls, tongues, and whole bodies, as a result,
became entirely engaged in the work of dawah. Nothing prevented
them from achieving this honourable yet difficult mission. They
overcame barriers of all kinds and of different nature—geographical,
geological, psychological, technical, financial, political, cultural, and
linguistic, to mention a few. In a considerably short period of time,
they spread Islam all over the world, and owing to their hard and
genuine work in the field of dawah, many of them were buried in
different lands, far away from their homes.

In surah Al-Baqarah, Allah shows Muslims their actual position in this
world as well as their responsibility for the propagation of Islam. He
says:

$$ \text{(وَكَذَٰلِكَ جَعَلْنَاكُمْ أُمَّةً وَسَطًا لِّتَكُونُواْ شُهَدَاءَ عَلَى النَّاسِ وَيَكُونَ الرَّسُولُ عَلَيْكُمْ} $$

$$ \text{شَهِيْداً...)} $$

*"Thus, have We made you a medium (just) nation, that you
might be witnesses over humankind and the Messenger a
witness over you..."*   *(Qur'an 2:143)*

---

228 Discussed previously in "Lessons of Taqwa from the Story of Adam and Eve.

This witness position that the Muslims have to assume all the time, as this ayah proclaims, signifies their responsibility for dawah. In reference to this ayah, Ibn Ashoor (1984) argued that the enjoyment of the honour of the witness position on the Day of Judgment requires Muslims to invite others to Islam (p. 21). Accordingly, if Muslims fail to deliver Allah's message to non-Muslims, they may not enjoy the honour of being witnesses over others on that day. On the contrary, non-Muslims may, unfortunately, become witnesses against them.

Being aware of his extremely huge responsibility for the delivery of Allah's message to humankind, the Holy Prophet, in his final sermon, wanted to verify that his contemporaries would acknowledge his delivery of Allah's message to them and that Allah would hear their acknowledgment. On that day, according to Imam Muslim, he addressed them saying:

> "You will be asked about me, so what will you say?" They answered, "We witness that you have delivered the message [of Allah] and advised the *ummah* [nation]." Then the Holy Prophet raised his arm and said, "O Allah! Be my witness."(Al-Odah, 1433, p. 364)

So with this in mind, we, Muslims of today, should ask ourselves the following important question: Would we dare to raise our hands and say—as the Holy Prophet did, "O Allah! We have informed the people of the world about Islam, so be our witness?"

Like all the other Qur'anic stories, the story of Prophet Yusuf plays a significant role in teaching invaluable lessons of taqwa. Our discussion, however, has shed light on only a few—chastity, dependence on Allah, His appreciation, focus on the Day of Judgment, hope, forgiveness, and propagation of Islam.

Lessons of Taqwa from Disbelievers' Ends

As a major element in the Qur'anic stories, the horrible, tragic ends of previous disbelieving communities teach invaluable lessons of taqwa. The punishment of each disbelieving community occurs frequently in the Holy Qur'an, but Allah projects it differently from surah to another. This, of course, allows the audience of the Holy Qur'an to look at each community's chastisement from different perspectives and, thus, experience different mental and psychological effects that are crucial to the creation of the ideal human response to the Qur'anic message.

This section looks at the question of taqwa in the light of the punishment of three disbelieving communities: the people of Prophet Noah, the people of Prophet Hud (Ad), and those of Prophet Salih (Thamud). The discussion of these communities' punishment is based on the information available about them in five surahs—Al-A'raf, Hud, Al-Qamar, Al-Ahqaf, and Al-Haqqah.

The People of Prophet Noah

In vain, Prophet Noah spent almost a thousand years trying to touch the too-far-to-reach, stony hearts of his people. The Holy Qur'an speaks about them in many surahs, but we will look at their end in the light of the first three ones mentioned above: Al-A'raf, Hud, and Al-Qamar.

In the Light of Surah Al-A'raf

The first time the story of these people occurs in the Holy Qur'an is in the surah of Al-A'raf. From the start, they prove to be arrogant and mean. They not only rejected Allah's message to them, but they also attacked His messenger, Noah, using defamatory slurs. Here is Prophet Noah brotherly and compassionately delivering Allah's message to them and expressing his genuine concerns about their destiny on the Day of Judgment. He says:

(... يَا قَوْمِ اعْبُدُواْ اللَّهَ مَا لَكُم مِّنْ إِلَهٍ غَيْرُهُ إِنِّي أَخَافُ عَلَيْكُمْ عَذَابَ يَوْمٍ عَظِيمٍ).

"...O my people! Worship Allah. You have no other god but Him. I fear for you the punishment of a dreadful day!"   *(Qur'an 7:59)*

But their stubborn mindset[229] prevented them from seeing the truth and the compassion in his merciful message, so in response to his kind advice, they rudely said to him:

---

[229] Surah Ibrahim casts light on an essential aspect of disbelievers' mindset, which is a strong, blind attachment to their fathers and ancestors' same faith. The following

(...إِنَّا لَنَرَاكَ فِي ضَلَالٍ مُّبِينٍ).

"...we see you are in plain error."   *(Qur'an 7:60)*

Then the surah explains that Allah drowned them. But how did He drown them? This surah doesn't provide any detail about this issue. Instead, it states the cause of this horrible effect; specifically, Allah punished them because they were blind, meaning "they failed to see the truth and follow the guidance of Allah" (Ibn Kathir, 2014, p. 21).

Allah concludes their brief story in this surah saying:

(فَكَذَّبُوهُ فَأَنجَيْنَاهُ وَالَّذِينَ مَعَهُ فِي الْفُلْكِ وَأَغْرَقْنَا الَّذِينَ كَذَّبُواْ بِآيَاتِنَا ، إِنَّهُمْ كَانُواْ قَوْماً عَمِينَ)!

"But they denied him, so We saved him, and those with him, in the Ark, and We drowned those who rejected Our signs. They were indeed a blind people!"

(Qur'an 7:64)

---

ayahs from this surah reflect this fact clearly:

(أَلَمْ يَأْتِكُمْ نَبَأُ الَّذِينَ مِن قَبْلِكُمْ قَوْمِ نُوحٍ وَعَادٍ وَثَمُودَ وَالَّذِينَ مِن بَعْدِهِمْ لاَ يَعْلَمُهُمْ إِلاَّ اللّهُ ، جَاءتْهُمْ رُسُلُهُم بِالْبَيِّنَاتِ فَرَدُّواْ أَيْدِيَهُمْ فِي أَفْوَاهِهِمْ وَقَالُواْ إِنَّا كَفَرْنَا بِمَا أُرْسِلْتُم بِهِ وَإِنَّا لَفِي شَكٍّ مِّمَّا تَدْعُونَنَا إِلَيْهِ مُرِيبٍ . قَالَتْ رُسُلُهُمْ أَفِي اللّهِ شَكٌّ فَاطِرِ السَّمَاوَاتِ وَالأَرْضِ ، يَدْعُوكُمْ لِيَغْفِرَ لَكُم مِّن ذُنُوبِكُمْ وَيُؤَخِّرَكُمْ إِلَى أَجَلٍ مُّسَمًّى قَالُواْ إِنْ أَنتُمْ إِلاَّ بَشَرٌ مِّثْلُنَا تُرِيدُونَ أَن تَصُدُّونَا عَمَّا كَانَ يَعْبُدُ آبَاؤُنَا فَأْتُونَا بِسُلْطَانٍ مُّبِينٍ).

"Has not the account reached you of those before you, of the people of Noah and Ad and Thamud, and those after them? None knows them but Allah. Their messengers came to them with clear arguments, but they thrust their hands into their mouths and said: 'Surely we deny that with which you are sent, and most surely we are in serious doubt as to that to which you invite us.' Their messengers said: 'Is there doubt about Allah, the Maker of the heavens and the earth? He invites you to forgive you your faults and to respite you till an appointed term.' They said: 'You are nothing but mortals like us; you wish to turn us away from what our fathers used to worship; bring us some clear authority."

(Qur'an 14:9–10)

In The Light of Surah Hud

The story of these people in the surah of Hud is longer, and it provides more details. The dialogue between them and Prophet Noah reveals important facts about their mental and psychological attributes. In particular, they were naive, arrogant, argumentative, and mean. First, they argued that it was impossible for Noah to be Allah's messenger because he was just a human—like them! Second, they looked down at both him and his followers. In fact, they considered the latter contemptible and the lowest of their community. Third, they claimed that Prophet Noah and his followers didn't have any special merits to qualify them for the assumption of the righteous' role because they believed that people's value stemmed from their material possessions, family roots, and history. Fourth, they ridiculed Prophet Noah as he was constructing the Ark,[230] which Allah commanded him to. They even accused him of lying.

Most of this reflects on the following part of their conversation with Prophet Noah:

(...مَا نَرَاكَ إِلاَّ بَشَرًا مِّثْلَنَا وَمَا نَرَاكَ اتَّبَعَكَ إِلاَّ الَّذِينَ هُـمْ أَرَاذِلُنَا بَادِيَ الرَّأْيِ وَمَا نَرَى لَكُـمْ مِن فَضْلٍ بَلْ نَظُنُّكُمْ كَاذِبِينَ).

"...we do not see in you anything but a mortal man like ourselves; and we do not see that any follow you save those who are quite obviously the most abject among us; and we do not see in you any merit above us; in fact, we think you are liars."   *(Qur'an 11:27)*

---

[230] It is narrated that while Prophet Noah was building the Ark, his people used to make fun of him because he was constructing it on the land, where there was no sea or even a river. They also used to ridicule him saying, "O Noah! Have you now become a carpenter, after being a prophet? (Al-Shawkani, 2012, p. 616) In reference to this, Allah says:

(وَيَصْنَعُ الْفُلْكَ وَكُلَّمَا مَرَّ عَلَيْهِ مَلأٌ مِّن قَوْمِهِ سَخِرُوا مِنْهُ...)

"So he began to build the Ark, and whenever leaders of his people passed by, they laughed at him..."   *(Qur'an 11:38)*

Also according to this surah, the people of Prophet Noah were, eventually, fed up with his continuous reminder, advice, and warning. As a result, they challenged him to bring the punishment against which he kept warning them. This, as Allah indicates in the previous surah, proves that they were blind. It also suggests that they wanted to prove that Prophet Noah was just a liar and wanted to put an end to his lying.

In a challenging impolite tone, they impatiently said to him:

(... يَا نُوحُ قَدْ جَادَلْتَنَا فَأَكْثَرْتَ جِدَالَنَا فَأْتِنَا بِمَا تَعِدُنَا إِن كُنتَ مِنَ الصَّادِقِينَ).

"...O Nuh (Noah)! You have disputed with us and much have you prolonged the dispute with us, now bring upon us what you threaten us with, if you are of the truthful."
(Qur'an 11:32)

Compared to surah Al-A'raf, this one throws enough light on the way Allah drowned them. In particular, the context in which Prophet Noah's Ark sailed suggests that the land was turned into a sea, the waves of which were as high as the mountains! In reference to it, Allah says:

(وَهِيَ تَجْرِي بِهِمْ فِي مَوْجٍ كَالْجِبَالِ...)!

"So it (the Ark) sailed with them amidst waves like mountains...!"
(Qur'an 11:42)

In the Light of Surah Al-Qamar

As previously mentioned, surah Al-Qamar, which provides a brief account of the stories of six messengers of Allah,[231] doesn't include dialogues between these messengers and their communities. It, nevertheless, projects the end of each community in a cause-and-effect format. With respect to the people of Prophet Noah, it shows that they not only rejected his message, but they also threatened to kill him! So, being in this situation, Prophet Noah turned to Allah and prayed Him to retaliate. Allah responded, and the punishment started.

---

[231] This surah includes short accounts of the disbelievers of Makkah and those of Prophets Noah, Hud, Salih, Lut, and Musa.

In only two ayahs, Allah provides a lively mental image of the extremely tragic manner in which He punished these people. The way He chose to punish them, in fact, makes the thoughtful audience of this surah wonder: What kind of people were they to be punished this mercilessly by the Most Gracious and the Most Merciful? The All-Mighty turned the sky into extremely wide gates that continuously poured water on them. He also turned the earth into countless springs that gushed water in extreme abundance under their feet. In this regard, He says:

$$\text{(فَفَتَحْنَا أَبْوَابَ السَّمَاءِ بِمَاءٍ مُنْهَمِرٍ . وَفَجَّرْنَا الْأَرْضَ عُيُونًا فَالْتَقَى الْمَاءُ عَلَى أَمْرٍ قَدْ قُدِرَ)!}$$

"So We opened the gates of heaven, with water pouring forth. And We caused the earth to gush forth with springs, so the waters (of the heaven and the earth) met for a matter predestined!"   (Qur'an 54:11—12)

Like corn beans between two grinding stones, the poor things were ruthlessly crushed under the mightiness of the two gigantic armies of Allah: the water of the sky and that of the earth. How wretched! Ibn Kathir (2014) cited Ibn Abbas to have said, "Neither before that day nor after it did the sky ever rain without clouds" (p. 331).

These are three surahs in which Allah shows His punishment of Prophet Noah's blind, rude, heedless community. Of course, their punishment was the same; nevertheless, each surah projects it from a different perspective that addresses the brain and the heart differently to create special mental and psychological effects necessary for the creation of the desired human response to the Qur'anic message.

The People of Ad

The discussion of the end of Ad, Prophet Hud's community, is based on their story in five surahs: Al-A'raf, Hud, Al-Qamar, Al-Ahqaf, and Al-Haqqah.

In the Light of Surah Al-A'raf

The dialogue in surah Al-A'raf reveals that the people of Ad accused

Prophet Hud of lying. They also accused him of lack of common sense—a man of *safahah*, according to them. This is clear in their dialogue with him in which they said:

$$(...إِنَّا لَنَرَاكَ فِي سَفَاهَةٍ وَإِنَّا لَنَظُنُّكَ مِنَ الْكَاذِبِينَ).$$

"...most surely, we see you in folly, and most surely we think you to be of the liars."   *(Qur'an 7:66)*

Further, this surah reveals a major aspect of their mentality; particularly, they were strongly and blindly attached to their ancestors and fathers' wrong, inherited faith. [232] So, like Prophet Noah's community who dared to challenge him to bring Allah's punishment, these people also challenged Prophet Hud to bring the punishment he threatened them with. In a disapproving, condescending, and challenging tone, they said him:

$$(...أَجِئْتَنَا لِنَعْبُدَ اللّٰهَ وَحْـدَهُ وَنَذَرَ مَا كَانَ يَعْبُدُ آبَاؤُنَا ، فَأْتِنَا بِمَا تَعِدُنَا إِنْ كُنْتَ مِنَ الصَّادِقِينَ).$$

"...Have you come to us that we should worship Allah alone and forsake that which our fathers used to worship? So bring us that wherewith you have threatened us if you are of the truthful.'"   *(Qur'an 7:70)*

Then briefly and without demonstrating how, Allah explains that he saved Prophet Hud, along with his followers, and that He entirely obliterated the disbelievers of his community and "left none of them [alive]" (Al-Qurtubi, 2014, p. 559). In this regard, Allah declares:

$$(فَأَنْجَيْنَاهُ وَالَّذِينَ مَعَهُ بِرَحْمَةٍ مِنَّا وَقَطَعْنَا دَابِرَ الَّذِينَ كَذَّبُوا بِآيَاتِنَا وَمَا كَانُوا مُؤْمِنِينَ).$$

"We saved him and those who were with him. By Our mercy, and We cut off the roots of those who rejected Our signs and did not believe."   *(Qur'an 7:72)*

---

[232]This way of thinking still influences most of the world's population, unfortunately.

In the Light of Surah Hud

The surah of Hud reveals the same previous mentality and attitude of Ad, represented in, again, blind allegiance to their fathers and ancestors' faith. It also shows that they confirmed to Prophet Hud that—no matter what—they would never believe him or follow his faith. Here is the surah shedding light on these people's nasty attitude and stubbornness:

(قَالُوا يَا هُودُ مَا جِئْتَنَا بِبَيِّنَةٍ وَمَا نَحْنُ بِتَارِكِي آلِهَتِنَا عَن قَوْلِكَ وَمَا نَحْنُ لَكَ بِمُؤْمِنِينَ).

"They said: O Hud! You have not brought to us any clear evidence, and we are not going to desert our gods for your word, and we are not believers in you."
(Qur'an 11:53)

This surah, in addition, reveals that their naivety led them to believe that some of their gods made Prophet Hud mentally sick, due to his negative attitude towards them. Addressing him with respect to this issue, they said:

(إِن نَّقُولُ إِلاَّ اعْتَرَاكَ بَعْضُ آلِهَتِنَا بِسُوءٍ...).

"All that we say is that some of our gods have seized you with evil (madness)..."   (Qur'an 11:54)

As He does in surah Al-A'raf, in this one, Allah explains that He saved Prophet Hud as well as his followers and that He severely punished the rest of Ad community. But how did He punish them? Allah, in this surah, doesn't provide any further details on this issue. Here is what He says about it:

(وَلَمَّا جَاءَ أَمْرُنَا نَجَّيْنَا هُودًا وَالَّذِينَ آمَنُوا مَعَهُ بِرَحْمَةٍ مِّنَّا وَنَجَّيْنَاهُم مِّنْ عَذَابٍ غَلِيظٍ).

"So when Our commandment came, We saved Hud and those who believed with him by a mercy from Us, and We saved them from a severe torment."
(Qur'an 11:58)

In the Light of Surah Al-Qamar

In his reflection on this surah, M. Al-Ghazali (2011) stated:

> After the people of Noah, there came Ad. It was an arrogant and
> insolent tribe that was given a lot of wealth and firm, huge
> physiques; . . . they were not ashamed to call their messenger a
> man of no common sense, though he invited them to believe in
> the oneness of Allah. (p.420)

In this surah, as mentioned earlier, the concise cause-and-effect
presentation concerning the different disbelieving communities that
Allah obliterated doesn't provide enough information helpful in the
understanding of these people's mentality or psychology. Again, it
mainly shows that each community didn't believe; then briefly, Allah
explains how He punished each of them.

So in this surah and with regard to the punishment of Ad, Allah says:

$$\text{(إِنَّا أَرْسَلْنَا عَلَيْهِمْ رِيحًا صَرْصَرًا فِي يَوْمِ نَحْسٍ مُسْتَمِرٍّ . تَنزِعُ النَّاسَ كَأَنَّهُمْ}$$
$$\text{أَعْجَازُ نَخْلٍ مُّنقَعِرٍ)!}$$

*"We sent against them a furious wind, on a day of violent
disaster, plucking out people as if they were roots of
palm-trees torn up (from the ground)!"*

(Qur'an 54:19—20)

These two ayahs provide a vivid account of this horrible human
tragedy. The extremely violent wind that the All-Mighty sent to punish
these people ruthlessly seized and threw them high in the sky and
struck them severely against the ground. Probably, this happened to
each of them countless times before and after he or she died. The
expression *tanziu,*[233] which means "seize with extreme violence and
humiliation," suggests the brutal, ruthless, and humiliating manner in
which the wind acted on them.

Further, the usage of this expression "tanziu" in connection with the

---

[233] تنزع

word *annas*,[234] meaning people, has a special message to convey and special psychological effects to create. The underlying message of this is that these humans—humans who were supposed to be honoured, if they honoured themselves—were treated in this ruthless, humiliating manner. In addition, the Arabic simile[235] *ka'anna*,[236] meaning "as if," in the second ayah, transforms the message in these two ayahs into a lively mental picture that perfectly reflects the terrifying scene of Ad's punishment during and after the event.

In this regard and in reference to the wind and the merciless way it treated these people, Allah says:

(تَنْزِعُ النَّاسَ كَأَنَّهُمْ أَعْجَازُ نَخْلٍ مُنْقَعِرٍ)!

"Plucking out men as if they were roots of palm-trees torn up (from the ground)!"   *(Qur'an 54:20)*

In the Light of Surah Al-Ahqaf

Al-Ahqaf, unlike surah Al-Qamar, reveals some information about these people's nasty attitude towards Prophet Hud and his message. Also, just like surah Al-A'raf, this one demonstrates that they openly challenged him to bring the punishment he had been threatening them with. This way, in fact, the people of Ad didn't challenge Prophet Hud; they, unfortunately, challenged the All-Mighty Himself!

In a challenging tone and in a rude, insolent manner, they said to Prophet Hud:

(... فَأْتِنَا بِمَا تَعِدُنَآ إِن كُنتَ مِنَ الصَّادِقِينَ).

"...then bring us what you threaten us with, if you are of the truthful ones."   *(Qur'an 46:22)*

Prophet Hud humbly told them that the issue of their punishment was entirely in Allah's Hands. He also informed them that his mission was to only deliver Allah's message to them. He said:

النَّاس [234]

[235] According to Arlov, "A comparison using 'like' or 'as' is called a simile" (2010, p. 90).

كَأَنَّ [236]

(...إِنَّمَا الْعِلْمُ عِندَ اللَّهِ وَأُبَلِّغُكُم مَّا أُرْسِلْتُ بِهِ وَلَكِنِّي أَرَاكُمْ قَوْماً تَجْهَلُونَ).

"...the knowledge (of that) is only with Allah. And I convey to you that wherewith I have been sent, but I see that you are a people given to ignorance."

(Qur'an 46:23)

At this moment, Prophet Hud's role was over, so Allah decided to act Himself. According to the scholars of the Qur'anic exegesis, that time the people of Ad were suffering from a prolonged drought. One day, they saw heavy clouds approaching their dry, desperate valleys; as a result, they became happy that finally they were going to have rain. For such a farming community, rain was extremely important; they needed it for their farms and for their livestock. They also needed water to drink.

Ironically, the clouds they saw didn't carry water to irrigate their dry farms and valleys, but they carried the torment they challenged Prophet Hud to bring! It was an extremely angry, dreadful, destructive wind that the All-Mighty sent to destroy them. With respect to this, He states:

(فَلَمَّا رَأَوْهُ عَارِضاً مُّسْتَقْبِلَ أَوْدِيَتِهِمْ قَالُوا هَذَا عَارِضٌ مُّمْطِرُنَا ، بَلْ هُوَ مَا اسْتَعْجَلْتُم بِهِ ، رِيحٌ فِيهَا عَذَابٌ أَلِيمٌ . تُدَمِّرُ كُلَّ شَيْءٍ بِأَمْرِ رَبِّهَا فَأَصْبَحُوا لاَ يُرَى إِلاَّ مَسَاكِنُهُمْ ، كَذَلِكَ نَجْزِي الْقَوْمَ الْمُجْرِمِينَ)!

"Then, when they saw it as a dense cloud approaching their valleys, they said: 'This is a cloud bringing us rain!' Nay, but it is that which you were asking to be hastened: a wind wherein is a painful torment, destroying everything by the command of its Lord! So they became such that nothing could be seen except their dwellings! Thus do We recompense those given to sins!"

(Qur'an 46:24–25)

The poor things were obliterated not only at the moment when they became hopeful but with the very thing that filled their hearts with hope! The exceptionally mighty wind entirely destroyed them and their villages; it left nothing, but the ruins of their dwellings. Here the

Qur'an paints a gloomy mental picture of this tragic event that portrays the All-Mighty's immeasurable power, represented by only one extremely mighty soldier of His—the wind. The following ayahs clearly and effectively communicate this horrible event to the human brain and heart. It says:

$$\text{(...رِيحٌ فِيهَا عَذَابٌ أَلِيمٌ . تُدَمِّرُ كُلَّ شَيْءٍ بِأَمْرِ رَبِّهَا فَأَصْبَحُواْ لاَ يُرَى إِلاَّ مساكنهم...)!}$$

"...a wind wherein is a painful torment! Destroying everything by the command of its Lord! So they became such that nothing could be seen except their dwellings...!"
(Qur'an 46:24–25)

The emptiness of the place in this woeful scene fills the listening heart with a deep sense of depression. This feeling, in fact, intensifies dramatically when one remembers that just a short while ago, Ad's villages were full of people, full of life, full of actions, and full of hope. In addition, the passive voice grammar that Allah employs in this context creates a special mental effect. It suggests that everything with an eye that saw Ad's obliterated homes had a chance to learn an important lesson from the extremely bad end of this community.

Again, focusing the Qur'anic light on Ad's tragedy, exemplified by their destroyed homes, Allah says:

$$\text{(...فَأَصْبَحُواْ لاَ يُرَى إِلاَّ مَسَاكِنَهُم...)!}$$

"...so they became such that nothing could be seen except their dwellings...!"

This surah, in addition, shows that Ad's homes were not totally destroyed. Perhaps their homes were partially preserved so that they would stand as a lesson for future generations. Further, in this context of anger, punishment, and destruction, Allah warns disbelievers of all times saying:

$$\text{(... كَذَلِكَ نَجْزِي الْقَوْمَ الْمُجْرِمِينَ).}$$

"...thus do We recompense those given to sins."

(Qur'an 46:25)

In the Light of Surah Al-Haqqah

Surah Al-Haqqah provides more information on the mighty wind that Allah employed in the obliteration of Ad. According to this surah, the wind continued its ruthless mission of punishment and destruction for seven successive nights and eight days. In reference to it, Al-Tabari (2010) cited Ibn Abbas to have said that Allah made that wind completely out of the angels' control (p 63).

This surah, in addition, projects the end of Ad from an angle different than that in surah Al-Ahqaf. To be exact, whereas their end in surah Al-Ahqaf focuses on their obliterated dwellings, their termination in this surah focuses on the scene of their gigantic, dead bodies scattered all over their villages. More precisely, the view of the people of Ad in this surah resembles the stems of significantly tall date-palm trees lying on the ground, as a result of being cut down from the very bottom of their roots.

This is how the All-Mighty projects these poor people's terrible scene after the wind had finished its merciless mission:

(وَأَمَّا عَادٌ فَأُهْلِكُوا بِرِيحٍ صَرْصَرٍ عَاتِيَةٍ. سَخَّرَهَا عَلَيْهِمْ سَبْعَ لَيَالٍ وَثَمَانِيَةَ أَيَّامٍ حُسُومًا فَتَرَى الْقَوْمَ فِيهَا صَرْعَى كَأَنَّهُمْ أَعْجَازُ نَخْلٍ خَاوِيَةٍ)!

"And as for Ad, they were destroyed by a furious violent wind. He (Allah) imposed on them for seven nights and eight days in succession: so that you could see the people lying overthrown, as they had been roots of hollow palm-trees tumbled down!"

(Qur'an 69:6–7)

Thus, the lesson to learn from their punishment in this surah springs from the view of their gigantic, dead bodies scattered throughout their villages, whereas the lesson to learn from their end in surah Al-Ahqaf stems from the depressing view of their demolished villages. With good reflection, each of these views addresses and touches the heart differently; thus, each of them creates special mental and psychological effects, capable of the generation of the required human attitude and behaviour.

Besides, Allah concludes Ad's tragedy in each of this surah and the surah of Al-Qamar with a question that carries a warning tone, invites critical thinking, and makes this community's lesson even more effective. In this surah, the question highlights the eradication of Ad from the surface of the earth, as a result of their nasty attitude. It says:

(فَهَل تَرَى لَهُم مِن بَاقِيةٍ)؟

"Do you see any of them left to survive?"

(Qur'an 69:8)

In surah of Al-Qamar, however, the rhetorical question stresses the mightiness of Allah's punishment. It warns:

(فَكَيْفَ كَانَ عَذَابِي وَنُذُر)؟

"Then see how (dreadful) was My punishment after My warnings?"   (Qur'an 54:21)

The People of Thamud

The discussion of the end of Thamud, Prophet Salih's community, is based on the information available about them in the surahs of Al-A'raf, Hud, and Al-Qamar.

In the Light of Surah Al-A'raf

Surah Al-A'raf shows that the people of Thamud were arrogant and stubborn. The dialogue that the leaders of this community had with the believers proves that the former were encumbered with closed-mindedness, which reflects on the following:

(قَالَ الْمَلَأُ الَّذِينَ اسْتَكْبَرُواْ مِن قَوْمِهِ لِلَّذِينَ اسْتُضْعِفُواْ لِمَنْ آمَنَ مِنْهُمْ أَتَعْلَمُونَ أَنَّ صَالِحًا مُّرْسَلٌ مِّن رَّبِّهِ قَالُواْ إِنَّا بِمَا أُرْسِلَ بِهِ مُؤْمِنُونَ . قَالَ الَّذِينَ اسْتَكْبَرُواْ إِنَّا بِالَّذِي آمَنتُم بِهِ كَافِرُونَ).

"The leaders of those who were arrogant among his people said to those who were considered weak among the believers: 'Do you know that Salih is sent by his Lord?' They said: 'Surely we believe in the message he is sent with.' The Arrogant party said: 'We, however, disbelieve in what you believe.'"

(Qur'an 7:75–76)

Even worse, Thamud's people not only disbelieved, but they also dared to kill Allah's she-camel that Prophet Salih warned them not to harm.[237] This crime, of course, reflects their nasty attitude towards both Prophet Salih and Allah Himself. They were, in fact, extremely reckless and apathetic, so after this hideous, unpardonable crime, they challenged Prophet Salih to bring the punishment he threatened them with. In His narration of this, Allah says:

(فَعَقَرُواْ النَّاقَةَ وَعَتَوْاْ عَنْ أَمْرِ رَبِّهِمْ وَقَالُواْ يَا صَالِحُ ائْتِنَا بِمَا تَعِدُنَا إِن كُنتَ مِنَ الْمُرْسَلِينَ).

"So they killed the she-camel and insolently defied the Commandment of their Lord, and said: 'O Salih! Bring about your threats if you are indeed one of the messengers (of Allah).'" *(Qur'an 7:77)*

Accordingly, Allah decreed their punishment, as the following ayah declares:

(فَأَخَذَتْهُمُ الرَّجْفَةُ فَأَصْبَحُوا فِي دَارِهِمْ جَاثِمِينَ)!

---

[237] Prophet Salih warned them of Allah's punishment if they harmed His she-camel. In this regard, Allah quotes Prophet Salih to have said to them:

(وَيَا قَوْمِ هَذِهِ نَاقَةُ اللّهِ لَكُمْ آيَةً فَذَرُوهَا تَأْكُلْ فِي أَرْضِ اللّهِ وَلاَ تَمَسُّوهَا بِسُوءٍ فَيَأْخُذَكُمْ عَذَابٌ قَرِيبٌ).

"And O my people! This she-camel of Allah is a sign to you, so leave her to feed (graze) on Allah's land, and touch her not with evil, lest a near torment should seize you." *(Qur'an 11:64)*

*"So the earthquake seized them, and they lay (dead),
prostrate in their homes!"*   *(Qur'an 7:78)*

This ayah provides a mental view of the people of Thamud after their punishment was over. More precisely, they remained "attached to the ground, lying on their knees and faces. In other words, they became motionless, as a result of the severity of the torment" (Al-Qurtubi, 2014, p. 158).

With regard to this issue, Ibn Kathir (2014) narrated the following:

> No one remained alive from Thamud . . . except Prophet Salih his followers, and a man who was at Al-Haram when the punishment took place. When he left [Al-Haram], however, he was struck dead by a stone that was sent to him from the sky. (p. 25)

In the Light of Surah Hud

Surah Hud sheds light on another aspect of Thamud's mentality. They were naive and blindly attached to their wrong, inherited faith. This reflects clearly on their discourse with Prophet Salih when—in an arrogant, disapproving air—they addressed him saying:

(...أَتَنْهَانَا أَن نَّعْبُدَ مَا يَعْبُدُ آبَاؤُنَا وَإِنَّنَا لَفِي شَكٍّ مِّمَّا تَدْعُونَا إِلَيْهِ مُرِيبٍ).

*"...do you forbid us from worshipping what our fathers
worshiped? We are really in grave doubt as to that to
which you invite us."*   *(Qur'an 11:62)*

Like Prophet Noah's and Prophet Hud's communities, Thamud lacked intellectual courage to question their ancestors' faith, which they inherited and accepted blindly and without questioning its credibility. In other words, the people of Thamud were hindered by intellectual cowardice, which, according to Paul and Edler refers to:

> Fear of [new] ideas that do not conform to one's own. If we lack intellectual courage, we are afraid of giving serious consideration to ideas, beliefs, or viewpoints that we perceive as dangerous. We feel personally threatened by some ideas when they conflict

significantly with our personal identity—when we feel that an attack on the ideas is an attack on us as a person. (2002, p. 24)

As it is the case in the surah of Al-A'raf, this one also explains that Thamud dared to kill Allah's she-camel, an issue that, unfortunately, expedited their doom. The following is the surah's brief account of the hideous crime they committed and the horrible punishment they received, as a result. Allah says:

(فَعَقَرُوهَا فَقَالَ تَمَتَّعُوا فِي دَارِكُمْ ثَلَاثَةَ أَيَّامٍ ذَلِكَ وَعْدٌ غَيْرُ مَكْذُوبٍ . فَلَمَّا جَاءَ أَمْرُنَا نَجَّيْنَا صَالِحًا وَالَّذِينَ آمَنُوا مَعَهُ بِرَحْمَةٍ مِنَّا وَمِنْ خِزْيِ يَوْمِئِذٍ إِنَّ رَبَّكَ هُوَ الْقَوِيُّ الْعَزِيزُ . وَأَخَذَ الَّذِينَ ظَلَمُوا الصَّيْحَةُ فَأَصْبَحُوا فِي دِيَارِهِمْ جَاثِمِينَ).

"But they killed her. So he (Salih) said: 'Enjoy yourselves in your homes for three days. This is a promise that will not be belied.' So when Our commandment came, We saved Salih and those who believed with him, by a Grace from Us, and from the disgrace of that Day. Verily, your Lord is the All-Strong, the All-Mighty. And the (mighty) Blast overtook the wrong-doers, and they lay (dead) prostrate in their homes." (Qur'an 11:65–67)

With respect to this incident, Ibn Kathir (2014) reported the following:

After they had killed the she-camel, Prophet Salih came to them . . . , and when he saw the she-camel, he cried. Then he said to them, "Enjoy yourselves for three days [which means, "you have a three-day respite before Allah's punishment starts"]. . . . Thamud killed the she-camel on Wednesday . . . , so on Thursday, the first day of the respite, their faces became yellow; on the second day of the reprieve, which was Friday, their faces became red; and on the third day, which was Saturday, their faces became black. On Sunday, they sat apprehensive and uncertain as what would happen to them or how they would be punished. At sunrise, a blast came down from the sky, and the earth started shaking. (p. 25)

In the above two ayahs, after showing how He punished Thamud people and the result of their obliteration, Allah begins the subsequent ayah with a sarcastic statement that adds darker shades to the above dreadful picture of this community's horrible end. He says:

!(كَأَن لَّمْ يَغْنَوْاْ فِيهَآ...)

"As if they had never dwelt and nourished there...!"
(Qur'an 11:68)

This statement, in addition, carries an underlying warning. Specifically, no matter how flourishing, prosperous, strong, or secure the enemies of Allah may seem today, He may erase them from the face of the earth at any time if they dare to challenge Him.

The rest of the ayah, in fact, has two sentences; each of them begins with the Arabic word *ala*.[238] According to Al-Ghalaini (2015), this word is "used to call the audience's attention to what comes after it; it also confirms the information it introduces" (p. 587). So when used at the beginning of a sentence, this word indicates the importance of the message it introduces; in this case, the addressee is expected to pay special attention to it. Its first usage in this ayah, therefore, highlights Thamud's most awful sin: their disbelief in Allah, which is, in fact, the worst sin a creature of Allah may commit. Its second usage, however, stresses the wretched destiny they brought to themselves. Precisely, they caused themselves to incur the wrath of Allah and all the misery associated with it—everlastingly!

With this in mind, you may now read these two statements that begin with the Arabic article "ala."

!(أَلَا إِنَّ ثَمُودَ كَفَرُواْ رَبَّهُمْ ، أَلَا بُعْدًا لِّثَمُودَ)

"Verily, Thamud disbelieved in their Lord. So away with Thamud!"   *(Qur'an 11:68)*

In the Light of Surah Al-Qamar

The surah of Al-Qamar, in addition, reveals that the people of Thamud were insolent. It also discloses the same previous negative

---

attributes that the surah of Al-A'raf highlights about them—arrogance and stubbornness. These attributes are, in fact, noticeable in the question form and the sarcastic, disapproving tone they used in addressing Prophet Salih. They said to him:

$$ \text{(...أَبَشَرًا مِّنَّا وَاحِدًا نَّتَّبِعُهُ إِنَّا إِذًا لَّفِي ضَلَالٍ وَسُعُرٍ . أَؤُلْقِيَ الذِّكْرُ عَلَيْهِ مِن بَيْنِنَا بَلْ هُوَ كَذَّابٌ أَشِرٌ).} $$

"...What! a single mortal from among us! Shall we follow him? We would surely be in error, or mad. Has the reminder been made to light upon him from among us? Nay! he is an insolent liar.'"   (Qur'an 54:24-25)

As a result of their rejection of Allah's message and their killing of His she-camel, which reflects their extremely nasty attitude, the people of Thamud incurred a tremendously dreadful end. In the light of the surah of Hud, the audience may not realize the merciless manner in which the All-Mighty punished these arrogant, argumentative people of Thamud. The audience may also think that their bodies remained intact. This surah, however, sheds more light on this issue and reveals new information about their horrible punishment.

Allah sent them an extremely mighty blast—a sudden, continuous, and exceptionally loud noise that came down from the sky. With respect to this, He says:

$$ \text{(إِنَّا أَرْسَلْنَا عَلَيْهِمْ صَيْحَةً وَاحِدَةً فَكَانُوا كَهَشِيمِ الْمُحْتَظِرِ)!} $$

"For We sent against them a single mighty blast, and they became like the dry stubble used by one who pens cattle!"   (Qur'an 54:31)

Hence, these wretched people suffered this much before they died. Imagine how the stubble and other plants used as food for livestock may look like in a stockade, where the animals eat, sleep, walk, run, and even fight. As a result of this incredibly powerful blast, the people of Thamud resembled the stubble under such a condition. Perhaps—as a result of this continuous, mighty blast—they continued shaking severely for a very long time until the body of each of them was cut into many small pieces!

If the addressees read or listen carefully, the way this ayah portrays
Ad's merciless punishment can touch their hearts more effectively
than if they had seen the actual view of this community's punishment,
for Allah uses special linguistic elements that depict this event in an
extraordinarily dramatic fashion.

First, reflect on the word *inna*,[239] meaning "We verily," which Allah
uses here to refer to Himself. Allah, of course, doesn't change,
whether He uses the first person singular pronoun, "I" or the first
person plural pronoun "We." But in His communication to the human
heart through the Holy Qur'an, He employs the Arabic language in a
way that helps this human organ to react to His messages in the best
positive manner ever. So here the use of "We"—the royal pronoun—
instead of "I," is supposed to help the brain sense, conceptualize, and
imagine the inexpressibly enormous power of the blast and thus aid
the heart to realize the mightiness of Allah and experience a high level
of awe, as a result.

Second, reflect on the Arabic word *wahidah(tan)*,[240] meaning "only one"
or "single," which suggests the extreme power of the blast and its
extended, uninterrupted continuation. Third, consider the simile that
Allah uses in this ayah to compare the view of these poor people (after
their obliteration) with *"the dry stubble used by one who pens cattle."*
Finally, the sound *"/rr/"* at the end of each ayah—from the start to
the end of the surah, without a single exception—has, of course, a
special role to play in the creation of the psychological impact that the
whole surah is intended to generate in the heart.

Obviously, Allah highlights the horrible ends of previous communities
of disbelievers to warn humans that they may subject themselves to
the same awful end and destiny if they choose to adopt a similar
attitude towards Him, His final message, and His final Messenger. If
the heart listens closely and carefully, this forceful Qur'anic way of
communication can have magnificent effects on people's lives today
and on their destiny in the Hereafter.

---

239 "إنَّا"

240 واحدة

In His closure of the surah of Yusuf—as mentioned before—Allah emphasizes the role of the Qur'anic stories in the guidance of humankind. He confirms:

(لَقَدْ كَانَ فِي قَصَصِهِمْ عِبْرَةٌ لِّأُوْلِي الْأَلْبَابِ ، مَا كَانَ حَدِيثًا يُفْتَرَى وَلَكِن تَصْدِيقَ الَّذِي بَيْنَ يَدَيْهِ وَتَفْصِيلَ كُلَّ شَيْءٍ وَهُدًى وَرَحْمَةً لَّقَوْمٍ يُؤْمِنُونَ).

"There is, in their stories, instruction for men endued with understanding. It is not a tale invented, but a confirmation of what went before it, and a detailed explanation of all things, and a guide and a mercy for people who believe." (Qur'an 12:111)

CONCLUSION

————— —— —————

In surah Al-Balad, Allah states that He has created humans in toil.[241] In other words, people's life on this planet entails inevitable, continuous sufferings of different nature and of various levels—from birth to death. But one fundamental aspect of these sufferings in true believers' lives springs from their concern and striving to remain continuously mindful of Allah and constantly obedient to Him. Accordingly, the acquisition of taqwa and the assurance of its prevalence throughout their lives constitute a major source of worry for them. Also owing to the demanding, complicated, stressful, and rapidly changing life today, true believers' level of challenge to observe taqwa is also always increasing.

Further, in the past, hajj was extremely difficult, even for people who lived only a few hundred miles away from Makkah. This was due to various reasons—lack of transportation, lack of water, lack of food, and harsh weather conditions. In surah Al-Baqarah and in the context of hajj, therefore, Allah advised pilgrims to take a provision[242] with them so that they wouldn't perish in the middle of the road to Makkah. But believers' journey to Allah is even longer, more challenging, and more difficult than their journey to hajj, for it is associated with many factors undermining to its successful completion.

As a result, Allah advises believers to equip themselves with taqwa because, according to Him, it is the best provision they need to have so that they may finish their journey to Him triumphantly. He says:

—————————————————————————

[241] (لقد خلقنا الإنسان في كبد)!

"Verily, We have created the human in toil!"　　(Qur'an 90:4)

[242]Al-Qurtubi 2014, p. 613

(الْحَجُّ أَشْهُرٌ مَعْلُومَاتٌ ، فَمَنْ فَرَضَ فِيهِنَّ الْحَجَّ فَلَا رَفَثَ وَلَا فُسُوقَ وَلَا جِدَالَ فِي الْحَجِّ وَمَا تَفْعَلُوا مِنْ خَيْرٍ يَعْلَمْهُ اللَّهُ ، وَتَزَوَّدُوا فَإِنَّ خَيْرَ الزَّادِ التَّقْوَىٰ ، وَاتَّقُونِ يَا أُولِي الْأَلْبَابِ).

"The Hajj (pilgrimage) takes place during the prescribed months. So whosoever intends to perform Hajj therein, then he should not have sexual relations (with his wife), nor commit sin, nor dispute unjustly during the Hajj. And whatever good you do, (be sure) Allah knows it. And take a provision (with you) for the journey, but the best provision is taqwa. So fear Me O men of understanding."
(Qur'an 2:197)

Also at the end of surah Al-Haqqah and in reference to the entire Holy Qur'an, Allah says:

(وَإِنَّهُ لَتَذْكِرَةٌ لِلْمُتَّقِينَ).

"And verily, this (Qur'an) is a Reminder for the muttaqeen (the pious)."   *(Qur'an 69:48)*

Finally, as mentioned earlier—in the discussion of the element of the question in surah Al-Qamar—Allah recurrently warns, challenges, and motivates everyone to seriously consider His Message in the Holy Qur'an. He says:

(وَلَقَدْ يَسَّرْنَا الْقُرْآنَ لِلذِّكْرِ فَهَلْ مِنْ مُدَّكِرٍ)؟

"And We have indeed made the Qur'an easy to understand and remember: then is there any that will receive admonition?"   *(Qur'an 54:17, 22, 32, 40)*

GLOSSARY

─── ── ───

Alhaq	الحق	The right thing or the truth
Aqeedah	عقيدة	Creed or doctrine
Ara'ik	أرائك	Couches
Ayah	آية	Qur'anic verse or a sign of the existence of Allah or a sign of His power
Badr	بدر	The name of the valley where the first battle in Islam took place. Originally, it means "moon."
Bilqis	بلقيس	The Queen of Sheba
Basiqah	باسقة	Considerably tall (feminine)
Birr	بر	Righteousness; good morals
Burooj	بروج	The signs of the zodiac
Dawah	دعوة	Informing people about Islam so that they may become Muslims; propagation of Islam
Duni	دنيا	This life. It literally means "of a lower level."
Eiman	إيمان	Belief or faith
Eimani	إيماني	The Arabic adjective of eiman; has to do with eiman
Fajr salah	صلاة الفجر	The Dawn Prayer. It is called thus because the earliest time to establish it is dawn, but it could be established any time before sunrise.
Fu'ad	فؤاد	Heart

283

Hadith	حديث	Whatever the Holy Prophet Mohammad said, did, or approved
Hajj	حج	Pilgrimage to Makkah
Hasrah	حسرة	The highest level of sorrow. It is called thus because a person who experiences it can't do anything to address its cause.
Hijab	حجاب	The Islamic dress code for Muslim women. It also means a cover.
Hiliah	حلية	An item worn for beautification, such as jewellery
Ibadah	عبادة	Worship
Ibrah	عبرة	A moral lesson to be learned from a bad experience, which is usually incurred by others
Ihsan	إحسان	Worshiping Allah as if one sees Him; doing things in the best manner possible
Ikhlass	إخلاص	Doing things, or not doing them, for the sake of Allah only
Inabah	إنابة	Devotion to Allah, love for Him, and complete submission to Him
Ishmi'zaz	إشمئزاز	Extreme dislike and aversion
Israf	إسراف	The state of being wasteful or extravagant or going beyond the limits
Istighfar	استغفار	Praying Allah for forgiveness
Istiqamah	استقامة	Continuous and firm commitment to the Islamic teachings; integrity
Jamal	جمال	Beauty

Juhood جحود — Ingratitude

Kawakib كواكب — Constellations

Khair خير — Goodness

Khubth خبث — Wickedness and internal dirtiness or evil

La'ib لعب — Activities that a person may be engaged in but without any significant benefits; playing

Laghw لغو — Idle talk. It also stands for all waste-of-time activities.

Lahw لهو — Whatever diverts from important matters

Maghfirah مغفرة — Forgiveness of Allah

Massabeeh مصابيح — Lamps

Mu'minoon مؤمنون — Believers (Masculine plural, in the subjective case)

Mu'mineen مؤمنين — Believers (Masculine plural, in the objective case)

Mutma'innah مطمئنة — Feeling safe and secure from any harm or threat (feminine)

Muttaqoon متّقون — Pious (Plural in the subjective case), people who have taqwa

Muttaqeen متّقين — Pious (Plural in the objective case)

Nadheed نضيد — Arranged in a well-organized manner

Nafs نفس — Soul

Nifaq نفاق — Hypocrisy

Niyyah نية — Intention

Qalb	قلب	Heart
Qunoot	قنوت	Persistent invocation and obedience to Allah
Qurratu ayun	قرة عين	Ultimate and perfect happiness
Rayn	رين	(Figurative) a thick cover that prevents the light of Allah's guidance from entering the heart
Sadr	صدر	Chest. It may be used to refer to the heart, too.
Safahah	سفاهة	Lack of common sense
Sakeenah		Tranquillity
Salah	صلاة	Prayer
Shahadah	شهادة	Bearing witness that there is no god but Allah and that Mohammad is His final Messenger
Shirk	شرك	Association of others with Allah
Sudoor	صدور	The plural form of sadr, which is chest
Tabsirah	تبصرة	Insight
Tafakkur	تفكر	Reflection on issues or things to understand them better
Tafsir	تفسير	Exegesis (explanation) of the Qur'an
Tahajjud	تهجد	Volunteer night prayer
Tahmeed	تحميد	Saying, "Thanks be to Allah."
Takbeer	تكبير	Saying, "*Allahu Akbar*," meaning Allah is the Greatest.
Tasbeeh	تسبيح	Glorification of Allah; saying "*Subhan* Allah!"

Tawheed	توحيد	Belief in the oneness of Allah; saying, "There is no god, but Allah" and believing in it.
Tawakkul	توكُّل	Believer's trust in Allah and full dependence on Him
Thabat	ثبات	Firmness of belief
Thikr	ذكر	Verbal and nonverbal remembrance and glorification of Allah
Thikra	ذكرى	Reminder
Tuhr	طهر	Internal and external purity
Tuma'neenah	طمأنينة	A very advanced level of security
Umrah	عمرة	It is also called the "lesser *hajj* (lesser pilgrimage)."
Wara'	ورع	Extreme level of caution; the state of being extremely cautious not to violate the rules of Allah, which results from a high level of taqwa
Zaygh	زيغ	Heedlessness and total deviation from the right path of Allah
Zayiannaha	زيَّاها	We beautified it
Zeenah	زينة	An item for beautification
Zoor	زور	Falsification or fabrication

Surahs' Numbers and Meanings of Their Names

Surah's/Chapter's Number	Surah's/Chapter's Name	Surah's/Chapter's Meaning
2	Al-Baqarah	The Cow
3	Al-Imran	The Family of Imran
4	Al-Nisa'	Women
5	Al-Ma'idah	The Feast (The Table Spread)
6	Al-An'am	Livestock
7	Al-A'raf	The Heights
8	Al-Anfal	The Spoils of War
9	Al-Tawbah	The Repentance
10	Yunus	Prophet Jonah
11	Hud	Prophet Hud
12	Yusuf	Prophet Joseph
13	Al-Ra'd	The Thunder
14	Ibrahim	Prophet Abraham
15	Al-Hijr	The Rocky Tract
16	Al-Nahl	The Bees
17	Al-Isra'	The Night Journey
18	Al-Kahf	The Cave
19	Mariam	Mary
20	Taha	Taha
22	Al-Hajj	The Pilgrimage
23	Al-Mu'minoon	The Believers
24	Al-Noor	The Light
25	Al-Furqan	The Differentiator
26	Al-Shu'ara'	The Poets
27	Al-Naml	The Ants
28	Al-Qassass	The Narration
29	Al-Ankabut	The Spider
31	Luqman	Luqman
32	Al-Sajdah	The Prostration
33	Al-Ahzab	The Confederates
34	Saba'	Sheba
35	Fatir	The Originator
36	Ya-Sin	"Ya" and "Seen," the 28th and the 12th Arabic letters
37	Al-Saffat	Those Ranged in Ranks
38	Sad	"Sad," the 14th Arabic Letter
39	Al-Zumar	The Groups
41	Fussilat	Made Distinct
42	Al-Shura	The Consultation
43	Al-Zukhruf	Ornaments of Gold
46	Al-Ahqaf	The Curved Sandhills
47	Mohammad	Prophet Mohammad
48	Al-Fath	The Victory
49	Al-Hujurat	The Chambers

Surah's/Chapter's Number	Surah's/Chapter' Name	Surah's/Chapter's Meaning
50	Qaf	*"Qaf,"* the 21st Arabic letter
52	Al-Tur	The Mount
54	Al-Qamar	The Moon
55	Al-Rahman	The Most Gracious
56	Al-Waqi'ah	The Inevitable Event
57	Al-Hadid	The Iron
59	Al-Hashr	The Gathering
64	Al-Taghabun	Mutual Loss and Gain
65	Al-Talaq	Divorce
66	Al-Tahreem	The Prohibition
67	Al-Mulk	The Dominion
69	Al-Haqqah	The Inevitable Hour
71	Nuh	Noah
73	Al-Muzzammil	The One Wrapped in Garments
75	Al-Qiyamah	The Resurrection
76	Al-Insan	The Human Being
77	Al-Mursalat	Those Sent Forth
78	Al-Naba'	The Great News
79	Al-Nazi'at	Those Who Pull Out
79	Al-Infitar	The Cleaving
83	Al-Mutaffifeen	The Dealers in Fraud
88	Al-Ghashiyah	The Overwhelming Event
95	Al-Teen	The Fig
98	Al-Baiyinah	The Clear Evidence
99	Al-Zalzalah	The Earthquake
104	Al-Humazah	The Slanderer

References

Abdel Haleem, M. (2008). *The Qur'an: A new translation*. Oxford: Oxford University Press.

Al-Asbahani, A. (1996). *Al-Musnad Al-Mustakhraj Min Sahih Al-Imam Muslim*. Beirut: Dar Al-Kutub Al-Ilmiyah.

Al-Baihaqi, A. (2003). *Shua'ab Al-Eiman* (1st ed.). Riyadh: Maktabat Al-Rushd.

Al-Basyuni, H. (2005). *Qasas Al-Qur'an*. Cairo: Dar Al-Hadith.

Al-Bukhari, I. (1422). *Sahih Al-Bukhari* (1st ed., Vol. 3). Beirut: Dar Tawq Al-Najah.

Al-Ghazali, A. (2004). *Ihya' Uloom Al-Din* (Vol. 1–5). Cairo: Dar Al-Hadith.

Al-Ghazali, A. (2006). *Mukashafat Al-Qulub*. Beirut: Al-Maktabah Al-Assryiah.

Al-Ghazali, M. (2006). *Al-Mahawir Al-Khamsah Lil Qur'an Al-Karim*. Cairo: Dar Al-Dhuroq.

Al-Ghazali, M. (2011). *Nahw Tafsir Mawdhui Lisuwar Al-Qur'an Al-Karim*. Cairo: Dar Al-Shuroq.

Al-Hashimi, M., Dr. (2005). *The ideal Muslim: The true Islamic personality of the Muslim as defined in the Qur'an and the*

Sunnah = Shakhṣīyat al-Muslim (4th ed.) (N. A., Trans.).

Riyadh: International Islamic Pub. House.

Al-Hilali, M., & Khan, M. (1417). *The Noble Qur'an in the English*

Languge. Madinah Munawwarah: King Fahd Complex For

The Printing of The Holy Qur'an.

Al-Jaza'iri, A. (2004). *Hatha Al-Habib Mohammad*. Cairo: Dar Al-

Hadith.

Al-Mubarakpuri, S. (2007). *Al-Rahiq Al-Makhtum*. Beirut: Al-

Maktabah Al-Assryiah.

Al-Mubarakpuri, S., & Mujahid, A. (2008). *The Sealed Nectar* (2nd

ed.). Riyadh: Dar Al-Salam.

Al-Nisaburi, M. (n.d.). *Al-Musnad Al-Sahih Al-Mukhtassar*. Beirut:

Dar Ihya' Al-Turath Al-Arabi.

Al-Odah, S. (1433). *Ishraqat Qur'aniah: Juz' Amma* (2nd ed.). R:

Mu'ssasat Al-Islam Alyawm Lilnashr.

Al-Qurtubi, M. (2014). *Al-Jami Li Ahkam Al-Qur'an*. Beirut: Al-

Maktabah Al-Assryiah.

Al-Rumi, F. (2011). *Dirasat Fi Ulum Al-Qur'an Al-Karim* (17th

ed.). Riyadh: Maktabah Al-Malik Fahad Al-Wataniyah.

Al-Saadi, A. (2011). *Taysir Al-Karim Al-Rahman Fi Tafsir Kalam Al-Mannan*. Beirut: Al-Maktabah Al-Assryiah.

Al-Samarraei, R. H., Dr. (1432). *Nitham Al-Falsafah Al-Akhlaqiyah* (1st ed.). Al-Riyadh.

Al-Samirraei, F. S. (2012). *Lamasat Bayanyiah Fee Nusoos Min Al-Tanzeel* (8th ed.). Amman, Jourdan: Dar Ammar Lil Nashr.

Al-Shawkani, M. (2012). *Fath Al-Qadir* (Vol. 1–2). Beirut: Al-Maktabah Al-Assryiah.

Al-Tabari, A. (2010). *Tafsir Al-tabari* (Vol. 1–12). Cairo: Dar Al-Hadith.

Al-Tafsir Al-Muyassar (2nd ed.). (2009). Madinah Munawwarah, K.S. A.: King Fahd Comlex.

Al-Tamimi, N. (2008). *Al-Madamin Al-Tarbawiyah Liwassaya Luqman* (1st ed.). Riyadh: Dar Taybah.

Al-Tirmithi. (1975). *Sunan Al-Tirmithi* (2nd ed.). Cairo: Maktabat was Mutbaat Mustafa Al-Babi Al-Halabi.

Ali, A. Y. (2008). *The Holy Qur'an: Text, translation and commentary*. Elmhurst, NY: Tahrike Tarsile Qur'an.

Ali, A. (2001). *Al-Qur'ān: A contemporary translation* (Rev. ed.). Princeton, N.J.: Princeton University Press.

Arlov, P. (2010). *A Guide to College Writing* (4th ed.). New Jersey: Person Education.

As-Sibaa'ie, M., Dr. (2005). *Civilization of Faitrh: Solidarity, Tolerance and Equality in a Nation Built on Shari'ah* (2nd ed.) (N. Al-Khattab, Trans.). Riyadh: International Islamic Publishing House.

Asad, M. (2012). *The message of the Qur'ān: The full account of the revealed Arabic text accompanied by parallel transliteration.* London: The Book Foundation.

Ashoor, I. (1984). *Al-Tahreer wa Al-Tanweer* (Vol. 1–30). Tunis.

Ba Jabir, M. A., & Ba Dahdah, A. O. (2012). *Al-Thaqafah Al-Islamiyah* (4th ed.). Jidda: Dar Hafith Lilnashr.

Being an Unforgivably Protracted Debunking of George Bernard Shaw's Views of Islam. (2008). Retrieved May 21, 2016, from https://idlethink.wordpress.com/2008/12/03/being-an-unforgivably-protracted-debunking-of-george-bernard-shaws-views-of-islam/

Dodd, C. (2004). *Managing Business and Professional Communication.* Boston: Person Education.

Fulwiler, T., & Hayakawa, A. (2002). *The college writer's reference*

(3rd ed.). Upper Saddle River, N.J.: Prentice Hall.

GainPeace. (n.d.). Retrieved May 23, 2016, from

http://www.gainpeace.com/index.php

Haleem, M. (2008). *The Qur'an: A new translation*. Oxford: Oxford

University Press.

Hart, M. H. (1992). *The100: A Ranking of the Most Influential*

Persons in History (2nd ed.). Carol Publishing Group.

Ibn Abi Shaibah, A. (1409). *Al-Musannaf Fial Ahadith wal Athar*.

Riyadh: Maktabat Al-Rushd.

Ibn Al-Qayim, S. (1988). *Al-Tafsir Al-Qayim*. Beirut: Dar Al-Fikr.

Ibn Al-Qayim, S. (1996). *Tahthib Madarij Al-Salikin*. Tanta: Dar

Al-Thaqafah wal Al-Ulum.

Ibn Al-Qayim, S. (2005). *Al-Fawa'id*. Beirut: Dar Al-Kitab Al-

Arabi.

Ibn Al-Qayim, S. (2012). *Zad Al-Maad* (Vol. 1–9). Beirut: Al-

Maktabah Al-Assryiah.

Ibn Al-Uthaimin, M. (1431). *Sharh Riyadh Al-Salihin* (Vol. 1–6).

Riyadh: Mu'assat Al-Amirah Al-Anud Bint Abd-al-Aziz

Bin Musa'd Bin Jalawi Al-Su-ud Al-Khayryiah.

Ibn Ashoor, A. (1984). *Al-Tahreer wa Al-Tanweer*. Tunis: Al-Dar

Al-Tunisiyah Lilnashr.

Ibn Kathir, A. (1994). *Tafsir Al-Qur'an Al-Athim*. Beirut: Dar Al-

Marifah.

Ibn Kathir, A. (2006). *Al-Bidayah Wa Al-Nihayah* (Vol. 1–7). Cairo:

Dar Al-Hadith.

Ibn Kathir, A. (2014). *Mukhtassar Tafsir Ibn Kathir* (Vol. 1–3).

Beirut: Al-Maktabah Al-Assryiah.

Ibn Manthur, A. (2008). *Lisan Al-Arab* (6th ed., Vol. 1–18). Beirut:

Dar Sadir.

Ibn Taymiyyah. (1978). *Al Kalim Al Tayib*. Riyadh: Maktabat Al

Ma'ari.

Ibn Taymiyyah. (2010). *Makarim Al-Akhlaq*. Beirut: Al-Maktabah

Al-Assryiah.

IbnHambal, I. (2001). *Musnad Al-Imam Ahmed Ibn Hambal* (1st

ed.). Mu'assasat Al-Risalah.

Ismail, F. (1993). *Al-Qur'an wa Al-Nnathar Al-Aqli*. Herndon: The

International Institute of Islamic Thought.

Khalidi, T. (2008). *The Qur'an* (Deluxe ed.). New York, New York:

Penguin Books.

Kolln, M., & Funk, R. (2002). *Understanding English Grammar*

Martha Kolln, Robert Funk. (6th ed.). New York: Longman.

Mayell, H. (n.d.). Oldest Human Fossils Identified. Retrieved March 28, 2016, from http://news.nationalgeographic.com/news/2005/02/0216_05 0216_omo.html

Muhammad - The Most Influential by Michael H. Hart (Muhammad No.1). (May). Retrieved May 21, 2016, from http://www.iupui.edu/~msaiupui/thetop100.html?id=61

Paul, R., & Elder, L. (2002). *Critical thinking: Tools for taking charge of your professional and personal life.* Upper Saddle River, NJ: Financial Times/Prentice Hall.

Pence, R., & Emery, D. (1963). *A grammar of Present-Day English* (2nd. ed.). New York [etc.: MacMillan.

Pickthall, M. (2009). *The glorious Qur'an: Translation* (5th ed.). Elmhurst, N.Y.: Tahrike Tarsile Qur'an.

Quirk, R., & Greenbaum, S. (1973). *A Concise Grammar of Contemporary English.* New York: Harcourt Brace Jovanovich.

Quran Tafsir Ibn Kathir. (n.d.). Retrieved April 21, 2016, from http://www.qtafsir.com/index.php?option=com_content

Qutb, S. (1992). *Fi Thilal Al-Qur'an* (17th ed., Vol. 1–6). Cairo: Dar Al-Dhurooq.

Sharh Asma' Allah Al-Husnah Fi Daw' Al-Kitab wa Al-Sunnah (12th ed.). (2010). Riyadh: Maktabah Al-Malik Fahad Al-Wataniyah.

The Holy Quran - القرآن الكريم - Koran Kareem. (n.d.). Retrieved July 23, 2015, from http://quran.muslim-web.com/

A. (n.d.). The Role of Socratic Questioning in Thinking, Teaching, and Learning. Retrieved May 16, 2016, from http://www.criticalthinking.org/pages/the-role-of-socratic-questioning-in-thinking-teaching-amp-learning/522

Notes

Notes

Notes

Notes

Printed in the United States
By Bookmasters